The McClay Library
College Park
Queen's University Belfast
www.qub.ac.uk/lib
tel: 028 9097 6135
email: library@qub.ac.uk

STANDARD

This item should be returned no
later than the due date but it may
be recalled earlier if in demand.

Fine rate: 10p per day
            50p per day if recalled

For due dates, renewals,
charges, loans and reservations
*see **My Account***

SPECIAL ISSUE
HUMAN RIGHTS: NEW
POSSIBILITIES/NEW PROBLEMS

STUDIES IN LAW, POLITICS, AND SOCIETY

Series Editor: Austin Sarat

Recent Volumes:

STUDIES IN LAW, POLITICS, AND SOCIETY   VOLUME 56

SPECIAL ISSUE HUMAN RIGHTS: NEW POSSIBILITIES/NEW PROBLEMS

EDITED BY

AUSTIN SARAT

*Department of Law, Jurisprudence & Social
Thought and Political Science,
Amherst College, USA*

United Kingdom – North America – Japan
India – Malaysia – China

Emerald Group Publishing Limited
Howard House, Wagon Lane, Bingley BD16 1WA, UK

First edition 2011

British Library Cataloguing in Publication Data
A catalogue record for this book is available from the British Library

ISBN: 978-1-78052-252-4
ISSN: 1059-4337 (Series)

CONTENTS

LIST OF CONTRIBUTORS

Robert C. Blitt	University of Tennessee College of Law, Knoxville, TN, USA
Elizabeth Heger Boyle	Sociology Department, University of Minnesota, Minneapolis, MN, USA
Laura A. Dickinson	Center for Law and Global Affairs, Arizona State University—Sandra Day O'Connor College of Law, Tempe, AZ, USA
Leila Kawar	Department of Political Science, Bowling Green State University, Bowling Green, OH, USA
Ethan MacAdam	Law, Jurisprudence, and Social Thought, Amherst College, Amherst, MA, USA
Hollie Nyseth	Sociology Department, University of Minnesota, Minneapolis, MN, USA
John R. Wallach	Political Science, Hunter College & The Graduate Center, The City University of New York, New York, NY, USA

EDITORIAL BOARD

SELF-OWNERSHIP AND SELF-ALIENATION: THREE CASE STUDIES

Ethan MacAdam

ABSTRACT

This chapter addresses the alienability or inalienability of the bodily self by looking at continuing legal, economic, and cultural issues surrounding three case studies: the growth of cell lines, live organ transfer, and the practices of "forced prostitution" as a contemporary form of slavery. The essay contends that it is, ironically, Locke and Hegel's shared hyperliberal notion of the self as inalienable property that sustains a potential basis, in law and in culture, for troubling cases of self-alienation which persist in the case studies offered.

While the state of knowledge across both the human and the natural sciences has done a great deal to disassemble the entrenched western doctrines of mind/body dualism, we still regularly resort, in law as in other endeavors, to the integrity of both entities: of a consciousness which is also the locus of intellectual/creative activity and psychological character on the one hand, and a physiologically discrete organism as the seat and instrument of that consciousness on the other. Yet, again, we no longer live (if we ever did) in a world where such dualism withstands scrutiny: as earnestly as

Special Issue: Human Rights: New Possibilities/New Problems
Studies in Law, Politics, and Society, Volume 56, 1–36
Copyright © 2011 by Emerald Group Publishing Limited
ISSN: 1059-4337/doi:10.1108/S1059-4337(2011)0000056004

Deleuze and Guattari (1977) asserted the psychological self to be far more diffuse than the physiological body of everyday life (which that self imagines in turn as similarly diffuse), so daily life reiterates to us that the body has far less integrity than a nominally unified psychological self may often need to suppose. Controversy over the collection of individuals' DNA from remnant biological materials, for example, reminds us that we daily slough off minute amounts of our physical selves; and even if we regard our alienation of bodily wastes as the return of ingested materials to the environment, there is, as at least one scholar has previously noted, a more genuine self-partition involved in men's alienation of reproductive material in sexual activity, or of a woman's giving birth to a child. More mundanely, we cut our hair and nails; we lose bodily matter when we are wounded; on occasion, we donate blood and even organs, and we may cause tissue to be excised in surgical procedures.

The converse of this phenomenon – that we daily incorporate outside matter *into* our bodies, most often via ingestion – is somehow more familiar to us, as is the varied integration of our environment and of beings around us into our physical and mental functioning. *Partition of or subtraction from* the self, however – the alienation of our body or any part of it – usually rubs against our intuitions as *un*natural and as deeply illiberal. Discomfited as we may be, for instance, with the pace of biotechnology that increasingly promises to add (even on a nominally voluntary basis) organic and inorganic components to our bodies in ways that may also offend our ideals of the bodily self's autonomy, our prohibitions against alienation of or from that self are far older and stronger; not only shall no individual be deprived of his or her physical liberty without just cause, but none shall similarly overcome that same individual's will and intentions for their own body, nor have a power of disposal over any part of that body.

So strident is this prohibition that liberalism finds its *limits* here as well: in most contemporary law codes, no person can willfully alienate their body or control of it to another in such a way as might be enforced by physical coercion, and no contractual agreement can create such an arrangement. This point is important: *physical alienation of the body (by others and/or by the self) is forbidden at the physical level.* Many other courses, after all, remain open to one who seeks to induce bodily acts in another, even to have disposal over another's body or its parts (via regimes of psychology, economy, etc.), and we may also conceive of an individual who succeeds in voluntarily "enslaving" himself to another's will by substituting his own self-discipline for the threat of violence (i.e., as outlined by Foucault, 1995, pp. 195–228), but these would not be cases of self-alienation in the physical-material sense so offensive to us (though they might certainly prove offensive in other jurisprudence). Self-alienation, marked by the surrender of some or all of the body, *matters most as a physical fact.*

This essay, then, examines the case for asserting, descriptively and/or normatively, the *in*alienability of the bodily self;[1] because the alienation thus denied does matter most in physical contexts, however, I want to frame this argument in terms of the question of the self as an inalienable *property*, rather than as the object of inalienable *rights* of ownership. This is an awkward distinction because property/ownership in the western legal tradition is of course a name for a constellation of rights (disposition, use extending to consumption, retention, abandonment, etc.),[2] and so we might readily say that we are always speaking of the latter in speaking of the former. I make no objection to this idea, but it remains that these rights always have an *object*, a *something*, in some aspect material and tangible,[3] to which they apply, and that we do not conceive of property without consciousness of both the abstract rights *and* this material substrate ("So inexorable is the movement from property to things (so inescapable the probability that property will be a thing)," says Best, 2004, p. 52, n. 43). When I speak (or wish to speak) in this essay about *inalienable* property, then, the issue becomes confused – as J. S. Mill pointed out, the idea of private property at least potentially presupposes alienability (see Radin, 1987, pp. 1888–1889), and to posit a kind of property which cannot be alienated seems in some sense to disqualify the material in question *as* property – *something that cannot be alienated cannot be owned.* But the discourse of our jurisprudence does not proceed along this path – instead, we usually cannot help but conceive of "inalienable" material as property owned by (or as) the individual from whom it cannot be alienated.

By contrast, inalienability is not a problem for our discourse of *rights*, which we do not regard ourselves as "owning" in this way; we "possess" rights certainly, but the semantic difference highlights the fact that rights are of course intangible and abstract in a way that the material substrates they may apply to never are. Some rights (like at least some property) are alienable ("waivable" in the language of rights) in themselves in a formal sense (e.g., the Fifth Amendment's right against self-incrimination); as for rights we may call *in*alienable (and it is to these that notions of inalienable *property* are usually linked), highly complex and in some cases metaphysical questions attend the idea of what would constitute alienation of such rights (if we do not exercise a right, do we still possess it in that declination? and if we are prevented from exercising it? by physical force, by other means?). This is true precisely because rights *are* largely intangible abstracts: we are all, as a rule, sure of when some property of ours has been alienated; we are often unsure as to whether a given right has been.[4] For all the inevitable crossings of these two discourses, then, I wish to examine the self as property most of all in its material, physical aspect, in the conviction that law touching the body naturally concretizes the issue of alienation in a way that may inform our more general ideas of both material property and the right to it. Thus it becomes possible to dispute, for example, Stephen Best's remark that "immateriality, evanescence, and lack of 'thingness' indicates [sic] inalienability from the person" (Best, 2004, p. 52, n. 43): this classical view of inalienability as what cannot be grasped is, after all, really almost purely descriptive – e.g., in the case of intellectual property (one among others which concerns Best), one simply *cannot* steal another's voice or ideas, for example, even if one can duplicate them with civil or fraudulent wrong; this view also ignores the fact that the physical body, in whole or in part, *can* be grasped and stolen in this way. If the more relevant concern is instead prescriptive, that the body *must not* be grasped thus, then surely also this assertion of *material* inalienability must be prior to any others which regard less tangible aspects of personhood, since "rights of property find their necessary anchor in persons" (Best, 2004, p. 52, n. 43). Thus, while the question of inalienable property *rights* is a matter for the law alone, that of inalienable *property itself* is here more broadly a matter for philosophy.

This argument, then, proceeds briefly from two foundational texts addressing the inalienability of the bodily self, John Locke's *Second Treatise of Government* and G. W. F. Hegel's *Philosophy of Right*. Disparate as their traditions are, Best classes both of these writings' property theories (along with Jeremy Bentham's) as liberal (Best, 2004, p. 52, n. 43) – if this is true, it is unsurprising to find inalienable property in the body famously defended in both. This coincidence is more troubled, however, if we agree with Margaret Radin that there is much, perhaps more, that is *il*liberal in Hegel, in whose writing the intensively autonomous individual becomes, so to speak, absorbed by its own historical development: "Hegel's theory of the state ... carries the seeds of destruction of all liberal rights attaching to individuals (because in the state particular arbitrary will passes over into willing the universal)" (Radin, 1982, p. 976, see also n. 69 to this passage). And yet if Best is correct in any register about Hegel's liberalism on this point of seminal self-property, then Hegel's larger approach in the *Philosophy of Right* becomes an instructive demonstration *of how the liberalism of private property tends to sabotage the liberalism of individual autonomy*; I argue the same about the definitively liberal Locke's ideas on self-property, and from there, attempt to demonstrate the same point in contemporary contexts. Since we continue to use both Hegel and Locke's thinking to consider questions surrounding bodily inalienability, I apply that thinking to three important case studies taken from such contexts, cases which might be seen as proceeding in order of severity of alienation: (i) tissue samples taken from individuals and used to create biotechnological commodities, (ii) transfer of human organs, and (iii) the practices of "forced prostitution" as a modern-day form of slavery. Along the way there will be opportunities for connection with other classical questions of self-alienability (again, e.g., those surrounding intellectual property), but I will mainly be concerned with using these cases to see how the Locke/Hegel heritage has positioned us in our approaches to allowing or prohibiting certain bodily alienations about which serious doubts are raised – culminating, again, with an example of contemporary slavery, which I account here as now universally rejected by all jurists (short, arguably, of penological considerations; see, e.g., Wacquant, 2002, for an oppositional characterization of this link). Between questions of description and prescription, voluntariness and involuntariness, I seek to learn why permission and prohibition in these areas, and their collisions with real, material circumstances, are so vexed, and whether Locke and Hegel's various accounts of the body as inalienable property help or hinder our efforts.

As for the notion of inalienability which I deploy here, I wish to speak of it largely (and sometimes oddly) in a physical sense with dual normative and descriptive aspects: (i) the ways in which the body perhaps *should* not be partitioned (from itself or from any larger context of being, e.g., from a mind–body unity), and (ii) the ways in which (again, perhaps) it *cannot* be. This conception will seem both broad, in a legal-philosophical context in which the idea of inalienability usually speaks only to the question of a formal (normative) "should," and narrow where that context usually encompasses a far broader range of *objects*, bodily and not, tangible and intangible (see, e.g., Radin, 1987, pp. 1852–1855). Again, my focus is on the inalienability of the body, and what the body's physicality (in relation to "self" and to other sectors of material reality) may tell us about these broader and narrower conceptions. The corresponding idea of *self-alienation* in this essay is thus either the violation of a principle of bodily inalienability (the alienation in fact of what should not be alienated by legal or other normative lights), or else the appearance or pretense of an alienation which cannot (in fact) be carried out. This dichotomy in turn gestures toward a third term, this time of agency, of whether it is oneself or another that performs (or purports to perform) the alienation of the (supposedly, rightly or really) inalienable body.[5] The distinction that seems to offer itself here – between (i) one's own volition or at least consent in alienating one's body, or in allowing this body to be alienated by another, and (ii) the unwilled and undesired alienation of one's body by another – is, as we shall see, at once deeply relevant and deeply unstable.

Lastly, I should emphasize what will already be evident, that I am treating the alienation of the body, in whole or in part, as potentially entailing the alienation of some larger selfhood which typically (dualistically understood) includes the mind (soul, spirit, etc.). In part, I am conflating body and mind in this context because, as I will argue, I believe that we cannot afford to regard them as separate – and no more in conscious thought and action altogether than in law specifically – but also because this conflation is eminently the thrust of Locke and Hegel's thinking: as a good empiricist, Locke regarded the mind as an elaborate emanation of bodily circum-stances,[6] and (rather the reverse) Hegel in some sense thought of nothing *but* the mind, regarding material reality as a concomitant of the dialectical evolution of spirit. Indeed, part of the insight of both thinkers on self-alienation is this very disregard for any significant idea of a mind–body divide; yet it is this unity of the self in their thinking which is so importantly threatened by their commitment to the juridical category of property.

LOCKE

Locke's famous labor theory of property (as we might call it by analogy with its more famous successor, Marx's labor theory of value) – that is, that the exertion of one's labor upon a material makes that material one's own, and that this material, "being by [an individual] removed from the common state Nature placed it in, it hath by this *labour* something annexed to it, that excludes the common right of other Men" (Locke, 1988, p. 288) – seems to rest, in good poststructuralist form, upon what is also a qualification of or an exception to that theory: "Though the Earth, and all inferior Creatures be common to all Men, yet every Man has a *Property* in his own *Person*. This no Body has any Right to but himself" (Locke, 1988, p. 287). An individual's body is alone excluded from nature's common, from the given pool of resources, or potential property, upon a part of which any individual may labor, thence possessing that part. And yet this exclusion makes good sense, since Locke makes clear that body-possession really amounts to the idea that "[t]he *Labour* of [one's] Body, and the *Work* of [one's] Hands, we may say, are properly [one's own]" (Locke, 1988, pp. 287–288) – that is, if one acquires property by investing common material with labor, that labor springs most directly, in Locke's primeval vision, from the (the material of) the body animated by that body's capabilities. One needs to labor in order to own, and one needs one's body in order to labor – thus the body must be a *given*, a starting point or a seed of capital, a property from or by which all other property is realized.

And yet Locke seems to conceive of the self-owning[7] individual as God's property as well, as the result of divine labor or "[w]orkmanship" (Locke, 1988, p. 271), and this idea is thus consistent with the labor theory of property, even as it displays theological commitments less related to a political economy of property rights, and even as it apparently confuses that theory's application with multiple ownership "claims." More importantly, however, God's ownership of the individual forms the basis for Locke's prohibition of self-alienation; suicide is perhaps the archetype for this prohibition ("Every one as he is *bound to preserve himself*, and not to quit his Station wilfully" [Locke, 1988, p. 71]), but the natural illegitimacy of slavery (if not of more limited indenture)[8] emerges from the same logic:

> For a man, not having the Power of his own Life, *cannot*, by Compact, or his own Consent, *enslave himself* to any one, nor put himself under the Absolute, Arbitrary Power of another, to take away his Life, when he pleases. No body can give more Power than he has himself; and he that cannot take away his own Life, cannot give another power over it. (Locke, 1988, p. 284)

From a juridical standpoint, it is interesting that there is an ambiguity here as to whether Locke is describing something which *may* not be done, or something which *cannot*; if someone does consent to their own slavery, is this (in Locke's natural-law sense) *il*legal, or a legal *fiction*? Slavery as a fact of life, of course, forms an important part of Locke's world picture, and he grants legitimacy to slavery resulting from a "just" (i.e., defensive)[9] war (Locke, 1988, pp. 322–323). And yet here, too, the move seems odd: if slaves, "being Captives taken in a just War, are by the Right of Nature subjected to the Absolute Dominion and Arbitrary Power of their Masters" (Locke, 1988, pp. 322–323), we might suggest that this state of affairs *potentially* implies that such captives *would* consent, or at least ought to consent – as beings conscious of the "Right of Nature" – to their just enslavement (perhaps in the same way that Locke's free individual tacitly consents to the rule of the government on whose road he walks [Locke, 1988, 347–348]); otherwise, we are left with the awkward thesis that a conqueror can legitimately *coerce* a condition to which his captive cannot legitimately *consent*.

Somewhere, here in this "fault" (to turn to a poststructuralist parlance) between these descriptive and normative readings, is the mystery of self-alienation, that it *does seem* to happen no matter how strong our convictions may be that it *cannot* (let alone *should* not) happen, that it is a material as well as a philosophical impossibility. In the case of Locke, I want to suggest that it is the very notion of the bodily self as property, whether God's or one's own, that allows for the reality and, behind that reality, the idea, of slavery and other modes of bodily self-alienation that Locke inconsistently attempts to reject.[10]

HEGEL

For Hegel in the *Philosophy of Right*, such discourse is famously descriptive only,[11] perhaps; in the case of property, too, it is not labor *per se* but will which invests material with ownership (Hegel, 1967, p. 41). Indeed, needless to say, a massive shift in general attends any analogy we might make between Hegel's and Locke's ideas on this heading: Hegelian property, for example, is not removed from a commons for more productive use (see Locke, 1988, pp. 294, 296–298), but rather given a philosophic end or "destiny" (Hegel, 1967, p. 41), in a self-reflexive and self-realizing mode, by the acquiring individual: "But I as free will am an object to myself in what I possess and thereby also for the first time am an actual will" (Hegel, 1967, p. 42).[12] And yet this mode of possession, *as* self-reflexive and self-determining, also begins, like Locke's account, with *self*-possession:

> I am alive in this bodily organism which is my external existence, ... the real pre-condition of every further determined mode of existence. But, all the same, as person, I possess my life and my body, like other things, only so far as my will is in them. (Hegel, 1967, p. 43)

> Therefore those goods, or rather substantive characteristics, which constitute my own private personality and the universal essence of my self-consciousness are inalienable and my right to them is imprescriptable. (Hegel, 1967, p. 53; see also the further Remark for this section)

While Hegel divides will from body and even from intellectual and emotional faculties, and insists that one must take possession of the others (Hegel, 1967, p. 43), in a way that might make little sense to Locke, the greater juridical significance of the Hegel's model emerges with the contention that "*from the point of view of others*, I am in essence a free entity in my body while my possession of it is still immediate" (Hegel, 1967,

p. 43, emphasis added). Thus, while self-possession's internal logic rejects an "unqualified[13] right to suicide" (Hegel, 1967, p. 242; see also pp. 57, 241–242), its external logic (i.e., the self's relation to others), while permitting temporary indenture (54), rejects slavery (a series of conclusions highly similar to Locke's): because "[t]he spirit is always one and single and should dwell in me" (Hegel, 1967, p. 241), because "I am entitled to the union of my potential and my actual being" (Hegel, 1967, p. 241) – that is, to my future self as well as my current one – "[i]t is in the nature of the case that a slave has an unqualified right to free himself" (Hegel, 1967, p. 241), and "[t]o adhere to man's absolute freedom ... is *eo ipso* to condemn slavery" (Hegel, 1967, p. 239).

Dialectically and counterintuitively, Hegel goes on to chastise the slave's own will, which he believes *allows itself* to be alienated, and here we can cross another bridge to Locke: while Locke forbids all voluntary enslavement and permits some involuntary (e.g., following just war), Hegel seems to suggest that even *in*voluntary slavery is voluntary in part: "Yet if a man is a slave, his own will is responsible for his slavery ... . Hence the wrong of slavery lies at the door not simply of enslavers or conquerors but of the slaves and the conquered themselves" (Hegel, 1967, p. 239). Taken in the wrong sense, Hegel's suggestion is abhorrent and unhistorical; but he intends this remark, entirely in the vein of his larger system, to point out that consciousness trumps material conditions as the engine of history and (along the way) of law or rights. This is to say that part of what is undeniably wrong, and justly prohibitable, about slavery is that it involves not only coercion but also, on *all* hands, a "species" consciousness of the self that is untenable. As with Locke, I wish to argue that this view results from Hegel's own formulation of the bodily self as a thing *possessed* at all, and it is here that Hegel's philosophical commitment to a purely descriptive regime encounters difficulty similar to Locke's, or rather its inverse: a philosophy of law like Hegel's, descriptive though it be, *describes what is itself necessarily normative* (i.e., law), and in a ubiquitous movement with which certain strands of Derridean poststructuralism have made us familiar, that description may be contaminated by its object; Hegel's system of law in its final form as the State is, after all, normative, decree as to what *should be*, but it is also a historical destiny, law as it will be or even as it already *is*.[14] I wish also to make out, then, that Locke and Hegel's notions of self-ownership also share this in common, that the normative prohibition against self-alienation rubs against the potential alienability which is always implied by their description of the self as property.

CASE ONE: MOORE V. REGENTS

In the mid-1980s, John Moore sued his doctor and the Regents of the University of California (among others) for causes including breach of fiduciary duty, lack of informed consent, and conversion liability in their use of his body tissue, which had been extracted in the course of his treatment for cancer and used to create a valuable cell line sold for research purposes. In the case that reached the state's Supreme Court, the majority sustained defendants' demurrers to the conversion claims, but (in the case of Moore's doctor) overruled those to fiduciary duty and lack of informed consent in an opinion which, together with concurrences and dissents, reflected not only the vexing new questions presented by the emerging biotechnology industry, but also a deeper confusion about whether human biological material of certain kinds should count as property, of what parties and according to what logic. Jane Gaines applies the Lockean paradigm, interpreting the majority opinion to mean that Moore

> failed to establish ownership of his own human tissue because, although he had produced it, he had not, as a subject, created anything new out of it. Although the producer of his cell line, he was not the "author" of it. In order to have made his tissue his own property, to establish his right to it, he would have had to mix it with his personal labor. The University of California medical research team had "worked" on his cell line, using its human labor to "invent" or "reproduce" it, thereby becoming the "authors" of Moore's cell line. Yet this case seems to fly in the face of common sense. How can another entity exploit parts of the very thing you thought you so indisputably owned – your own body? (Gaines, 1998, pp. 542–543)

In characterizing the opinion she criticizes, Gaines refers to Locke's formulation of the individual's acquisition of property through laboring upon material originally held in common; tellingly, this is also the standard that must be met in the relevant area of patent law, where "[i]n order to procure a patent on a biological, it must be shown that, through the 'process of their production', the 'natural' object has been transformed into an invention" (Lock, 2002, p. 74, quoting Cambrosio and Keating). And yet since, as we have seen, Locke does not actually apply his logic of property to the individual's special first property in his or her own self – since the body is *not* regarded as part of nature's common – Gaines' reading of the majority glosses over this very specialness of the category of *self*-ownership, that category which might allow us to describe others' peculiar appropriation of Moore "himself."

Indeed, that Locke's labor theory of property does not extend well to self-ownership is readily evident in the reasoning of Justice Broussard's partial dissent in the case, where he argues – against the majority's concerns for snowballing liability claims in biotech tort – that any legitimate conversion claim by Moore could reach only Moore's "contribution" (*Moore*, 1990, p. 168) of his bodily materials themselves, and not the cell line derived from those materials through the work of researchers:

> If, as the majority suggests, the great bulk of the value of a cell line patent and derivative products is attributable to the efforts of medical researchers and drug companies, rather than to the "raw materials" taken from a patient (maj. opn., *ante*, pp. 141–142), the patient's damages will be correspondingly limited ... (*Moore*, 1990, p. 159)

That is, the researchers' labor on Moore's tissue provides them with the Lockean entitlement to their labor's transformed fruits, and to those fruits' commercial value; Moore, who has not so labored, can thus recover from that value only to the extent of his own body tissue's *original* value, but not to that of the commercial products derived from them (also assuming, of course, that this tissue was misappropriated, e.g., via breach of fiduciary duty or lack of informed consent). And yet Broussard's picture of appropriate liability raises a clear question: it would be, relatively speaking, simple for a court to place a value on the developed commercial products as a whole, to date and in some likely future, and to award that entire value to a defendant like Moore, were this the proper course of action. In Broussard's opinion, though, it is not, and so we are left with a more challenging problem: how might a court valuate the property for which Moore *is* entitled to damages – the original tissues from his own body – as some fraction of the commercial value of the cell line derived from those tissues?

This would be easy to do in a case involving a more conventional type of property; where, for example, a steel manufacturer's wrongly appropriated metal has been used by another company in the development of a profitable new alloy – the manufacturer could simply be awarded damages on the basis of the ill-gotten steel's market value, and the remainder of the much greater value of the alloy itself would be left to its now-chastised developers. And yet of course it is not clear what such a case would involve, precisely because, by analogy with *Moore*, we need to imagine some sort of misappropriation which involves a *civil* liability (not, e.g., theft), just as Moore attempted to hold his doctor civilly liable for breach of fiduciary duty and lack of consent on the basis of his claim that he had not been not told that his cells would be used in the way that they were, much less consented to this use (i.e., Moore did not attempt to characterize his cells as having been stolen). In our example of the steel manufacturer, such liability is difficult to imagine because steel has a readily establishable market value, and any one who manufactures it has the full expectation that those to whom he or she willingly sells it will put it to any number of uses which may, precisely because of the further labor the purchasers expend upon it, increase that value – indeed, it is through the manufacturer's *own* labor in producing the steel as raw material for such use/labor that the *original* market value of that material has been determined (and the same is true of the value of the iron ore which a mining company extracted and sold to that manufacturer). This is to say that Lockean labor is seen *by all parties* to determine value *at every stage* in such a case, that knowledge of and consent to this fact are implied in the very acts of manufacture and sale, and that consequently, there can be no such thing as steel which is misappropriated in *Moore*'s sense – the steel manufacturer transferring this material to any buyer cannot but do so in the full knowledge of its possible future use, including use resulting in increased commercial value, whereas Moore's complaint alleged that the commercial destiny of his cells was *concealed* from him by his doctor (*Moore*, 1990, p. 126) – the further implication being that, unlike the steel manufacturer, Moore had no expectation that his body tissues might be used, and their value augmented, in such a way, indeed that they had any "value" (in this market sense) at all! As Justice Mosk points out in his dissenting opinion (*Moore*, 1990, p. 161), the relative newness of biotechnological endeavor is at issue in part, and on this basis it might be possible to characterize Moore, as a defendant of his time, as having had no *knowledge* that his tissues even *could* be used in such a way (let alone an expectation that they *would* be, and without his consent) – as having not been made aware, in accordance with his physicians' fiduciary duties, of the fact that his body tissue could be labored on at all in a way which conferred value.[15] No such ignorance or oversight afflicts the steel manufacturer, who knows the market value of his or her raw product; conversely, such problems are central for Moore, who does not even conceive of his tissues as *having* a market value.

The larger problem looming here, of course, is that of the way or ways in which the body may be unlike other material, of whether bodily material is given to a community in common – thence of whether it can be labored upon, thence of whether it is or is not property in Locke's sense. Locke is ready to backstop the chain of labor-created property *at* nature's common (even if, with Genesis, Locke perhaps supposed that God had labored to create the common land which humans appropriate as raw material, even if perhaps God himself used no raw material to do so, creating *ab nihilo*) – that is, our bodies, lying outside that common,[16] are our property, but evidently not because we labor upon them. We cannot even say that we "earn" our body by laboring to improve it, since Locke would certainly regard a child as just as entitled to his or her body as an adult athlete – unless we mean by such labor a trivial *fait accompli*, for example, the daily activities of moving, eating, and simply maturing. The real issue here, again, is that the body for Locke is a given – given by God (and, as Locke implies, doubtless incorporating his labor upon biblical clay). But if we do not labor upon our bodies – and if we do not presume to valuate God's infinite and inscrutable labor – how do we determine their value? Locke might say that the body has no such value in the sense we mean, that is, a potentially commercial one. But even Broussard in *Moore* accepts that it does, and that Moore ought to be compensated to that extent.[17]

Gaines' response to these questions in *Moore*, again, is that "this case seems to fly in the face of common sense. How can another entity exploit parts of the very thing you thought you so indisputably owned – your own body?" However, this summing remark seems to miss the ever-present threat of Locke's proto-capitalist logic – that the body *is* property (alienable or not), and so will always be at risk from the temptation to treat it as property of other kinds is treated; the body is indeed "indisputably owned" for Locke, but "indisputably" does not necessarily imply "inalienably," and indeed "owned" itself implies *potential* alienability – the idea of inalienability must therefore be separately supplied, as it is by Locke and Hegel both, as a sort of snow fence rather high up on the hill down which the logic of capital snowballs, a fence which will protect the bodily self, if nothing more, from that logic. Commenting on copyright questions in *Gross v. Seligman*, Gaines marvels that "the author can lose his right because he has that right," that his property right to what he has intellectually/emotionally produced can be sold on (Gaines, 1998, p. 543); the analogy with physical, bodily property like Moore's is precisely parallel: as long as the law regards us as owning our body, there is always at least the bare, logical potential for us to alienate some or even all of that body, for another to own the alienated portion via transfer.[18] Gaines considers her copyright reversibility fascinatingly "absurd" (p. 545), but this characterization obscures the simple truths, firstly, of the continual possibility of transferral inherent in the idea of ownership (an idea that supposes other persons, though not alienability [since we can imagine a world of completely static ownership], from the start), and secondly, of the deep roots which such a logic has in liberal thought, thought which perhaps is not entirely, or not always, compatible with our ideals of human rights. In this sense, it is the liberal Locke who writes of labor making property, and the Locke of human (*qua* "natural") rights who prohibits slavery without reference to property; his notion of the inalienable self lies somewhere in between, a Derridean "hymen"[19] which tests and sabotages his political usefulness as a thinker caught between the rights of commerce and self-integrity.

CASE TWO: TRANSFER OF ORGANS

Conversion liability aside, there is of course a simple aspect in which the cells originally alienated from Moore's body, if done so in breach of trust and/or consent – even if deemed criminally *stolen* – can only be so severe as an offense. In the obvious sense, Moore can and will grow more cells to replace those taken; the rare and valuable cancerous cells which were removed may not reappear, of course, and should not – the point of any medical treatment like Moore's (see notes 16 and 17) – but the extraction of cancerous cells impugns the integrity of his body no more than would that of healthy ones. Biologically, of course, this is because tissue taken in such "sample" quantities is renewable, in the same way as blood taken in amounts typical of donation (Lock, 2002, p. 69). This is not a reason to excuse or even mitigate the wrongs committed by those who, with civil or criminal fault, alienate these tissues, but it does give a free pass in practical terms to those who may seek to prevent any (even consensual) act of bodily alienation itself – if it happens in this case, there is, in the immediate sense of bodily integrity, "no harm done."

Interestingly, moving to the more extreme case of bodily alienation constituted by organ transfer,[20] the same seems to be true to some extent: for example, the medical fact that one can typically donate a kidney and depend on the remaining kidney to take on the original function of both (though such donation is certainly not without short- and long-term risk and debility; see, e.g., Cohen, 2002, p. 20). And yet, entering into all the various indistinct contexts of organ donation and sale (voluntary or not), it is interesting to note cases like that of poor female donors in Madras for whom the proceeds from one kidney may not be enough, and who express a wish for organs to be quite as easily renewable as blood and sampled tissue: "If only there were three kidneys, with two to spare, things might be better" (Scheper-Hughes, 2002, p. 38).

But though live, lawful organ donation *might* be no more harmful to the donor than removal of body tissue in sample amounts, the alienation is clearly different in kind and degree; Margaret Lock notes two sides of an anxiety associated with organ transplantation, namely that donors may feel that they "liv[e] on" in recipients, and that recipients may share this feeling (with good or bad implications depending on their view of the donor; Lock, 2002, p. 72). While it is certainly possible, especially in the nascent era of cloning, to conceive of similar individual feeling regarding a cell line or other product based on one's tissue, just as a donor to a sperm bank might see himself as extended or perpetuated in an unknown offspring, organ donation/reception clearly intuitively prompts another level of thought and feeling about the integrity of our bodies; one kidney may do the work of two, but the first kidney does not (like blood, sperm or other tissue) replace itself. It is biologically a truer loss to the body, and – as reflected in these sorts of donor/recipient feelings – it can also be felt as a loss to the self more fully, or rather *a transfer of the self elsewhere* (the donor "lives" "in" the recipient); indeed, we might even discern here that the conviction that an organ *cannot be* separated from a donor's body in the way we suppose, or rather that the donor "comes along with" the alienated organ. In any case, it seems significant that these feelings can reside with those receiving an organ in a way which would likely be less true of those receiving a mere blood transfusion; in the same way as the steel merchant above operates in a context where all understand and accept the fungibility of his wares, the less than perfectly fungible nature of organs here likewise seems reflected on all sides.

The law seems to reflect these anxieties in part: thus the illegality in the United States of the outright sale of organs in interstate commerce (Radin, 1987, p. 1855, n. 23)[21] and, under international agreements such as the GATT TRIPs of 1994, a denial of inherent property or commercial rights of organ donors (Lock, 2002, p. 65). And yet these anxieties betray themselves, as we can see by looking at two issues: briefly, (i) the well-known anthropological/philosophical question of the nature of donation or the "gift" in general; and at greater length, (ii) the preference for *intrafamilial* donation (and thus fundamentally for family "ownership") of organs.

In the case of live organ transplants in the United States, again, there seems to be a cultural and legal preference in favor of making a *gift* of one's organs to a recipient; this is in part because the *sale* of organs raises with unusual intensity the familiar problem of judging the presence of consent (e.g., Bales, 2005, pp. 53–54, where coercion can be disguised, and where the exploitation or even the simple existence of various social inequalities may enervate the category of volition, as with Scheper-Hughes' Madras women – to adapt Marx once more, many individuals in many societies may "have nothing to sell but their organs"). And even imagining organs donated free of such pressures, scholarship in the field draws our attention to the powerful social pressure that can be exerted within families, to the residual sense of entitlement that donors sometimes exert on recipients. Issues such as these put into question, not so much whether an organ is a gift or not, but in what senses gifts are really gifts at all – the discourse of the gift promises to expand the question of inalienability beyond Marxist-framed debates over whether the body can be commodified, or rather it asks in what sense commodification is always tacitly *re-* or *pre*introduced via sub-capitalist regimes of exchange. In this context, Lock summarizes Marcel Mauss' classic articulation of the gift in pre-exchange societies:

> Mauss' thesis was that the gifts that are central to so many non-capitalist economies are not themselves of overriding importance, but that the bonds of reciprocity established between the involved persons, donors and recipients, are primary. In effect, individuals give away a modicum of their "essence" with gifts, which must, therefore, be returned in kind .... (Lock, 2002, p. 69)

Thus, on such an understanding, the gift in general might even best be conceived of as something ultimately transferred to the apparent giver.[22] Why then, especially in a case of deep self-alienation like live organ transfer, should donation be a more acceptable regime than sale, when donation can still smack of pre-capitalist modes of exchange, when it fails even to appear as a clearly defined category – indeed, when it makes itself a potential tool for the justification of coercion, as Stephen Best points out in using Mauss' gift-thinking to read Justice Taney's opinion in *Dred Scott* as an apology for legal slavery (Best, 2004, pp. 82–84)?

Another form which attempts to speak to the nonfungible regimes attached to organs betrays a logic no less ideologically contaminated than that of the gift. Nancy Scheper-Hughes recounts the experiences of a Rosemary Sitsheshe in a South African township, who went to the police to claim the body of her son who had been killed in gang war crossfire (Scheper-Hughes, 2002, p. 38). On finding that, with police collusion, her son's eyes had been posthumously removed and transferred to a local hospital as transplant organs, Sitsheshe asked "[I]s it good that [my son's] flesh is here, there and everywhere, and that parts of his body are still floating around? Must we Africans be stripped of every comfort?" (Scheper-Hughes, 2002, p. 39). Not even the remains of her son's eyes were returned to her. As a case of posthumous organ removal (let alone of theft), her story is easily comprehensible as a horrible account of how one niche of organ transplant practices sabotages the broadly human tradition of a family claiming its dead: Sitsheshe was not able to recover the complete body of her son, since her familial claim to the body ended up competing sublegally with police and hospitals' (doubtless financially lucrative) claims on that body's organs. Yet it is important to realize that this competition would have persisted if, for example, Sitsheshe had been legally offered the option of *selling* her son's eyes – only in this example, the competition would have been transferred within Sitsheshe herself, that is, would she serve her family's spiritual interests or its financial ones?

This hypothetical point is important because organs tend to join the limited ranks of those possessions often considered inalienable precisely on a *family* basis. Commenting on the work of Annette Weiner, Lock remarks that

> [i]nalienable possessions, whether in the form of land, property or valued objects, signify social difference, and such possessions tend to attract other kinds of wealth (symbolic capital in Bourdieu's terms). Inalienable possessions are powerful, and more often than not are associated with genealogies, the ancestors and reproductive continuity. (2002, p. 70)

In other words, such possessions are family property, and if circulated at all, should be so only within family groups – a model of inheritance. Of such properties, land is surely the anthropologically and historically fundamental example, but it is interesting to note that children follow a close second: this is because children in pre-industrial societies were almost as precious a resource, as they promised to either work or steward a family's land as that land supported them – they were family property that helped to preserve other family property beyond a single generation. (This is why the "provenance" of children, the concern for their legitimacy, was often crucial; if a child did not fully "belong" to a family – that is, if its father was someone from outside the marriage – then traditionally that child was in some measure "disowned," in the sense of dis-acknowledged and thus disinherited, thus dis-possessed, *disowned so that they themselves could not own*, a model of God's punishment of the propertyless vagabond Cain, on whom God's mark simultaneously shows owning – Cain is God's property who cannot be murdered, reminiscent of Locke – and disowning.) In latter-day settings, bodily organs can traditionally fall under the same restrictions, as seen in the preference for intrafamilial donation;[23] in Cuba, for example (thin though the pretext may be), "medical tourists" taking advantage of the country's easy transplant regulations must arrive in the country "with a living donor, who is assumed to be a blood relation" (Scheper-Hughes, 2002, p. 46). All of these materials, then, can fit within the "inalienable" category of "objects that people never trade, or do so only when reduced to dire straits" (Lock, 2002, p. 70): it is only the ruined noble house that sells its land, it is usually the poor family that sends its children (at best) into foster families and/or apprenticeships or (at worst) into begging or prostitution, and it is the same family that may feel compelled to sell an organ to strange parties for money (in contrast to donating to a blood relation in need). Intrafamilial limitations on alienability decipher Rosemary Sitsheshe's story insofar as her attempt to collect her son's body in its greatest possible integrity is part of the same system of inalienable property circulation – the physical being of the dead and their organs (like that of children or of land) is "owed" *within* the family that originally produced that being (in Sitsheshe's case, a tragic reversal of the inheritance model). And yet intrafamilial transfer, whether of deceased bodies or living organs, is transfer nonetheless, an alienation which mimes inalienability because it is "kept within the family," but which is ultimately betrayed *as* alienation by its likeness to other claims from the outside world. A more mundane example of this movement can found in U.S. tax law: to a certain amount, assets can be "gifted" to others, including family members,[24] to avoid tax liability, a provision which can thus be used to retain wealth within a family unit; however, assets passed on within a family as a result of the asset holder's death are famously and controversially taxed. In some sense, these rather contrary bits of tax code are not really part of any doctrinal battle over whether intrafamilial wealth has an exceptional nature – family and state simply constitute rival claims to social wealth. Indeed, we might even say that this very scheme *creates* the supposedly exceptional categories of gift and patrimony, not as sacred or external to the category of property, but as marking that category's pervasiveness [this is more or less the thesis advanced by Roberto Unger (1986, pp. 57–90)]. As long as we "deed" land, "donate" organs and "claim" bodies, the category of the family offers our dearest property no durable or fundamental protection from alienability.

From a policy perspective, this is surely not to say that families should not transmit property between generations, provide loved ones with a needed organ, or claim the bodies of those who have died; indeed, perhaps these few examples of the problems raised by organ transfer prove only that alienability is so fundamental to the consciousness of human societies that inalienable property of the bodily kind (or any other) is only a mirage sustainable by absolute legal fictions – fictions which, as we have seen so far in the cases of tissue and organs, do not exist in U.S. law; the very notion of Lockean property in the body continues to provide for all kinds of potential alienations which Locke seems, with many of us in different times and contexts, to seek to forefend.

By contrast, the position of international law on slavery *does* constitute an absolute legal prohibition (Bales, 2005, p. 42), or appears to, and one aspect of this exceptional category will be the focus for the final part of this essay: the phenomenon often referred to as "forced prostitution" is widely held to be a form of modern-day slavery, and will offer some new perspectives on the peculiar mystery of bodily self-alienation. Prostitution, of course, is a charged category in this regard, and for present purposes, I wish to bypass here, as with organ transfer, the conventional questions of the quality or even reality of consent to such activity,[25] and most of all the traditional questions of whether "sex work" alienates the individual body and/or its capacities to an extent which transgresses the boundaries of labor generally, in a way which is unacceptably dangerous, tortious, morally or otherwise philosophically troubling, etc. – indeed, if there is a significant self-alienation involved in the intimate bodily aspects of prostitution, it is perhaps that movement that prepares the way for the further alienation of slavery, just as Siddharth Kara points out that sexual slavery combines an unusually lucrative activity with the even more profitable regime of slavery itself (Kara, 2009, pp. 16–23, 33–34). Slavery as an underlying category is fundamentally my interest here because, like tissue and organ transfer, it explicitly involves another's coercive jurisdiction over the body (or part of it) and also a physical deprivation of that body (or part of it) – though it is precisely the point that slavery makes this jurisdiction and deprivation not partial but entire, giving way to a strange antinomy that, for Hegel, seems to promise redemption even as it functions.

CASE THREE: FORCED PROSTITUTION

As Locke's labor theory of property provides an apt initial framework for discussing what others may ultimately *do with* our body (i.e., with its tissue in smaller or larger amounts), Hegel's more abstract understanding of self-ownership seems to comes to the fore in the context of slavery (i) because the enslaved person's *will* appears to be uniquely involved *past* the initial moment of alienation, and (ii) because that will at the same time seems precisely *usurped* in a way which appears not to apply to those who surrender tissue/organs. This is to say that the patient or donor of our first two case studies (absent issues of deception, exploitation and/as sublegal coercion) consents to the alienation of his or her tissue or organs to others, *after* which point the alienated material is subject to the will and claims of at least one other party (and perhaps multiple parties – even if this material may still also be subject to the will and/or claims of the donor him or herself, e.g., as it seems Moore would have had it). But the alienated material itself, to state the obvious, exerts no "will" of its own (unless perhaps at the nonconscious level of cellular reproduction); this point is worth stating only because in the case of slavery, the alienated material *is* the bodily self of the "donor" altogether, and this self somehow brings along with it the individual's will – and yet, again in an obvious sense, that same will is co-opted as the individual comes under the control of another. As we have noted of the example of the singer's "intangible" voice in intellectual property, the slave's eminently tangible body also displays this curious property of remaining both "here" and "there"[26] – "there" in another's possession, of course, in the sense of its locus and its lacking liberty, but "here" with its original owner, in a unified configuration of self which is also somehow, by virtue of enslavement, less unified than it was; the alienator remains with, indeed remains, what he or she has alienated. There is therefore, in Locke's sense, no real *labor* that an enslaver can easily be said to perform on the body of the slave (unless in the weak senses of acquisition, restraint, instruction, etc.) – thus the traditional paradigm of the enslaver's "*theft* of the *another* person's labor" (Gates, 2009, p. xxx). Instead, Hegel attempts to attack directly this paradox of the will that seems to attend slavery's wholesale bodily alienation, in which the will of the alienated self plays a more lasting, yet also co-opted, role.

But first, what is slavery in contemporary concrete fact – in our case, slavery of the kind practiced in forced prostitution? Kevin Bales suggests a definition with three parts: the loss of one's labor to another (the Lockean concern), this other's complete disposal over one's bodily freedom, and the threat of violence (Bales, 2005, p. 68). This is, of course, largely what the phenomenon often labeled "forced prostitution" of trafficked women today entails: such women are lured from their homes with various promises of gainful employment and perhaps marriage in more prosperous regions or countries, and begin by giving up their freedom of movement to traffickers who manage their transportation to the promised destination (or sometimes to a different one); once arrived, a variety of tactics (most importantly including violence or the threat of it) are used, first, to prevent these women from retaining the income generated by the sexual activities in which they engage, and second, to prevent them escaping from the situation in which they are thus exploited. For these reasons, Bales accurately characterizes forced prostitution as slavery (Bales, 2005, p. 64; the account of circumstances given here is fairly standard, see Bales, 2005, pp. 128–153); and yet, interestingly, Bales makes a terminological distinction between that phenomenon and circumstances of "sexual slavery," where the women in question are simply confined and sexually assaulted without any economic rationale. The distinction is clear enough for practical purposes, and yet Bales admits that "since the slave is forced to provide a service that has economic value, this act might be seen to represent the theft of the labor power of the enslaved; but it is better conceptualized as an accepted form of rape" (Bales, 2005, p. 65). In other words, we might look at sexual slavery as the maximally exploitative form of forced prostitution, in which the woman is simply not paid for her activities by parties who cannot be obliged to pay – that is, in which the prostitute is "robbed." The reason that this distinction is not purely academic is that the logic bound up even in the etymology of "rape" (from L. *rapere*) betrays the ancient and persistent ethic that this act is more a form of *theft* than of simple assault – a reminder of the anthropological commonplace that rape in earlier societies mattered far more as one male's "stealing" of a bloodline from another male than as tortious violence against a woman. The point here is that Bales' category of sexual slavery, just as much (if not as explicitly) as that of forced prostitution, continues fundamentally to be grounded in the idea of a woman's body as property.

Where this idea inheres in the circumstances of forced prostitution, then, it is clear that Bales' criteria for slavery are found as easily here as in, for example, the European colonial or antebellum U.S. regimes of legally sanctioned slavery. So when Mack (actually arguing *for* the alienability of rights against such treatment) points out that to be "treat[ed] ... like a slave" way is to be "order[ed] ... around," with the "enforc[ment of] those orders with physical threats, physical[] manipulat[ion]" of the person in question, "and so on" (Mack, 1999, p. 164), his simile of being treated "like a slave" reminds us that slavery is now as much a *de facto* phenomenon as it once was a legal category. Mack adds, as we would expect, that such treatment "is almost always non-consensual" (Mack, 1999, p. 164), and in one sense, this is *sometimes* the distinction to be made with regard to plain coercion/ birth into slavery versus different sorts of conceivably consensual and fair indenture (even if we feel that, in one or more cases, such consent exists only in theory – and it would be nonsensical, as well as morally horrible, to argue some sort of Lockean tacit consent in the case of coercion/birth). Yet Mack's ideas on consent highlight something obvious and important about Locke's and Hegel's prohibition of self-alienation, that this prohibition (or its violation) makes sense only in the context of voluntariness; in their sense, the individual born into slavery is (legally) free but under (illegal) coercion. In a way, Mack seems to wish to argue *back* from the fact that slavery is an "initially impermissible but perfectly *possible* treatment" to the somewhat Nozickian conclusion that "such treatment might be rendered legally permissible (whether or not morally permissible) by the consent of its subject" (Mack, 1999, p. 164, emphasis added). Despite the larger argument Mack deploys, here he almost seems to want to argue from *is* to *ought*, that since slavery may be a "fact of life," it should be a potential object of consent, as if in amelioration of the evil consented to.

To a highly pragmatic mind, Mack's approach makes some sense if we take into account the pervasiveness of slavery-like conditions in many contexts. Considering, for example, the "direct and indirect discrimination in the provision of food, medical treatment, education, and above all physical and sexual violence" (Kara, 2009, p. 31) which afflict married women in many parts of the developing world as part of the reigning social and domestic milieu, we might view the move to forced prostitution (posited as an escape by many of Kara's interviewees [Kara, 2009, p. 32]) as a *voluntary* self-alienation following upon an *involuntary* one, or upon another's violent attempt to induce or mimic such an alienation, the attempt of the husband to become or at least to imitate the enslaver (the converse of the *in*alienability-mimicry of family organ donors noted in the previous section). And indeed, if the consequences for personal safety and autonomy of *not* marrying are at least as grave (Kara, 2009, p. 7), then forced prostitution of adult women in these contexts is perhaps simply the exchange of one or more types of practically inevitable social slavery for another. In this case, then, someone like Mack would presumably argue that the permitting of self-alienation simply acknowledges realities of this type, and perhaps promises to remove the notorious legal and social stigmas of choosing one kind (prostitution) over another (traditional marriage) (a solution, perhaps, to the traditional problem of abused women engaged in prostitution who do not dare to approach the police [see, e.g., Murray, 1998, p. 54]).

And yet we will lose any interest in Mack's consent-based pragmatism if enslavement itself is something more intangible than a relatively complete co-opting of an individual body, coming as this body does with an individual will *against* which, in some or potentially all cases, we might presume the slave her-"self" acts. There is a slightly metaphysical question here which jurisprudence bypasses easily, that is, whether acting under compulsion, against our will in Hegel's purely voluntaristic sense, comprises a sort of derivative will of its own, for example, is there any sense in which an enslaved person may be said to labor as a voluntary effort to avoid punishment? This is perhaps a question for cognitive psychology or neurology, but for the law, no residue of will remains posterior to genuine coercion. Yet the question is more relevant than it seems, and Hegel knew it – this is why the *Philosophy of Right* (again, in a way that has traditionally threatened to put Hegel's liberal reputation at risk) places the will of the enslaved person at the center of the juridical wrong. There is, fundamentally, something *wrong* with the enslaved *will*, which continues to give the slave a fundamental or immediate jurisdiction over his or her own body, and yet is simultaneously negated (in dialectical terms that Hegel would surely have acknowledged) under the influence of actual or threatened coercion from others. The first of these dissonant aspects of individual volition can find some measure of unity with the second, I want to argue, precisely because of its innocent consciousness of the self, *it*self, as property – the very doctrine Hegel spells out in the *Philosophy of Right*, and the very doctrine that he uses to prohibit *others'* ownership of the self. This decay of the idea of self-property into the property of others allows Hegel's juridical prohibition against voluntary enslavement – a point which at first appears largely academic – to encompass (explain and forbid) *in*voluntary enslavement as well (i.e., enslavement as it often appears in the actual material world, under legal regimes in Hegel's time and in forms such as forced prostitution in ours); this move makes irrelevant the moral/legal/ philosophical question of sanctioning some *actual* slavery that Locke (at least in the *Second Treatise*) had to ignore. This is also where Hegel's anti-slavery argument is fundamentally different from Locke's, which can be read basically as an argument about consent (again, even unto the tacit); the difference makes Hegel's thinking germane to our contemporary concerns about the initial consent that sometimes seems to attend trafficked women's progress into forced prostitution (Bales, 2005, pp. 126, 130f), but is later made decisively invalid by the enforcement of slavery-like conditions. Hegel's argument concerns not *ought* but *is*, not consent but consciousness – not the illegality of voluntary slavery, but the simple historical-philosophical untenability of the slave's state of mind.

What is this state of mind like, and how can we tell? In a way, the story begins once again with the physical, though in forced prostitution, no part of the body is actually partitioned or taken away (as with organs or tissue) – rather the *whole* body seems somehow separated from its putatively indwelling autonomy, and yet of course the curious effect is that this body's integrity is uninterrupted (in a way that the integrity of the tissue/organ donor is not). Physically, the enslaved person's body remains whole, and so perhaps it is only the *potential* for violence to the whole person, even to death, that continues the common thread of corporeal threat in bodily self-alienation. Yet this aspect seems to concern neither Locke nor, importantly in this case, Hegel. In what other mode relevant to Hegel's thought, then, does this slavery-alienation take place? In part, forced prostitution often proceeds by alienation of the "legal self": Bales notes traffickers' regular practice of confiscating identifying documents from the women under their control, pointing out that "[t]o be without documents while in transit is to be placed immediately in the control of the trafficker" (Bales, 2005, p. 145). The surrender of documents is a legal figuration of self-alienation, and simultaneously the subtraction of legality from the process. The confiscation of these documents most centrally hampers independent movement on the part of the trafficked women, but birth certificates, passports and other such certifications – in some sense "deeds" to the self, the documents of self-ownership and not simply of identification – also provide a mock legality to the enslavement which defies legality, a mimicry which lays bare the extent to which the regime of property, like that of the more complex mode of capitalism, extends beyond any legal regime which attempts to contain it: illegally held property is, apparently, property nonetheless. Confiscation of documents transfers personhood more than it depletes it – it is a figure of a tactic often used with Nigerian women, whereby traffickers create a sachet of confiscated hair, blood and fingernails (Bales, 2005, p. 131) which for these women constitutes a sort of hostage alienation, via bodily personhood, of their spiritual selves (a telling concretization of the ethos of Nigeria's Edo women, for whom the swearing of repayment alone is enough to bind them [Kara, 2009, p. 16]).

The same is true of the use of debt bondage, which often follows these tactics. There may be, after all, nothing contractually legal or otherwise legitimate about the debt which many women trafficked a new destination are told they must now repay via prostitution, let alone about the imaginary schedule of compensation and repayment which tends to make the indebtedness perpetual, and backed up by violence (Bales, 2005, pp. 59–62; Kara, 2009, pp. 5–15).[27] While this is simply fraudulent betrayal of a contract which is illegal to begin with, Bales notes an even more telling version of debt bondage in which "the labor power (and indeed the very lives of the debtor and his or her family) becomes collateral for the debt. ... Since all the labor power of the debtor is the collateral property of the lender until the debt is repaid, the debtor is unable to ever earn enough to repay the debt by their own labor" (Bales, 2005, p. 59; see generally pp. 59–62). The physical violence and/or threat of it, which compels adherence to this arrangement (and creates a parodic sort of imprisonment for debt) reminds us again, of course, that bodily alienation matters most at the physical level: no fiction of slavery – the confiscation of documents or symbolic bodily matter, the pretense of a legitimate arrangement of debt and repayment – determines the slavery-like condition without the reinforcement of physical violence. And yet these fictions persist, less as effective instruments of enslavers than as artifacts, firstly, of the slave's consciousness, and secondly, of human consciousness of the body in general – species of an enslavement which becomes "mental" (Bales, 2005, p. 147). The body is ready to be understood as property, and thus as collateral for the transport offered by traffickers, thus as something to be bought "back" again. Similarly, when indices of identity (e.g., passports) become easily alienated titles of ownership, identity becomes commodity. It is at this point that Hegel depends on the *Phenomenology of Spirit*'s master-slave dialectic to advance the self-objectification of human consciousness to the point at which "servitude... . will really turn into the opposite if what it is immediately; as a consciousness forced back into itself, it will withdraw into itself and be transformed into a truly independent consciousness" (Hegel, 1996, p. 34)[28] – the same point at which, we might suppose, the identity-related tactics of enslavement could not possibly retain their force, where the wrongful held "property" would realize its status beyond property, or as its own property, where violence would be the sole, ineffective stay of continued subjection. The law, however (our law as opposed to Hegel's), does not wait for such a process – nor should it, I have tried to argue, as long as Hegel *begins* the self's emancipation from a discussion of the self as property, as long as Locke promises liberal autonomy via the same strategy. Here in the context of enslavement, though – here at the top of the scale of self-alienation – there is hope (indeed, dialectical hope) for an alternative understanding of the self, one which may trouble the regimes of modern-day slavery such as forced prostitution, while offering guidance in more ambiguous practices such as organ transfer and the growth of cell lines.

CONCLUSIONS, SOLUTIONS

Scheper-Hughes records the words of a fourteen-year-old girl working as a prostitute in Brazil: "[T]he first time I was paid to 'put out,' I knew what it meant to be a person and to be the *owner (dona) of* myself" (2002, p. 51). It is difficult to contemplate the circumstances in which this lesson is learned, to realize that perhaps we do not conceive or ourselves as "owning" ourselves until we try to "sell" ourselves; that property presupposes alienability, that it must in fact *begin* from alienation, and that the category of property therefore cannot be dependably used to establish, preserve, recover, or even articulate what is *in*alienable. *What is there* before property, *who are we* before we are property, and why do we seem to have so much trouble perceiving it? The response of some economists or neurologists, that our species' brains are perhaps hard-wired for structures of exchange, even for markets, may well be true, but it does little to solve the moral and legal problems raised by the alienations of organ and tissue transfer – and it certainly does not speak to these problems as they are posed by the alienation of the whole self into conditions of slavery.

And even if the problem here is indeed some strong, *a priori* sense of our bodily selves as partially or even wholly fungible, another problem may underlie it. After all, the odd paradox (maybe) here is that the very faculties which enable us to perceive our own body as commoditizable, as a potential material substrate of property, as an object of property rights, are our capacity to see, touch, and hear that body – and yet, of course, these very sensory capacities find their origin *in that same body* (just as Locke found his fundamental laboring capacity there). In voluntarily or involuntarily alienating ourselves, then – whether our parts or ourselves wholesale – we transfer to another, not only ourselves as property, but as parcel of that physical self, the faculties or means by which we make *sense* of ourselves as property, again returning us to the idea that physical self-alienation brings to the fore, importantly and recursively, the phenomena of physical life.[29] This conception might be imagined as explaining (if only in part) the anxiety of the apprentice of earlier times who indentures himself and then gazes at his own hands, seeing anew, as another's, that which his sight (also now sold) first allowed him to conceive as his (see Toombs, 1999, p. 75); the hands are somehow "at once subject and object" to him (Toombs, 1999, p. 82). (The comparatively insignificant, because far less total, anxiety experienced by the singer of today who hears on an album her purchased voice, from which she has sold only the exclusive right to *profit*, nevertheless resonates with this dilemma.) This anxiety, of course, only exists where the apprentice's mind "thinks legally," indeed metaphysically; because of the strange double consciousness which we have noted attends enslavement generally – because of the self which is kept whole even as it is wholly usurped – we may also imagine the indentured individual instead casting off this feeling and reasserting his original self-ownership by throwing down his tools and standing idle, by exercising his still somehow *un*alienated will, to recover what has seemed to him (and to his master) his *alienable* body, and by regarding any subsequent consequences as external and illegitimate (and the individual who has been born into slavery, rather than later indentured or coerced – a person who has *never* seemed to own what his sensory intuitions have always told him he does – may do the same).

But we are not, of course, creatures of our immediate will only; we are both metaphysical and practical, and thence juridical, in our thinking and feeling. As Hegel has shown, this fact of consciousness more than any other makes a phenomenon like slavery what it is; and as I have stressed in turn, our very consciousness of ourselves as our own property opens the "fault" which reveals slavery always as the ultimate horizon. If we are not confident in our ability to hold back the logic of this fault, through different varieties of intellectual property and tissue/organ transfer to wholesale enslavement, then this fact of consciousness itself must be attacked. Locke and Hegel's paradigms of self-property must be discarded in favor of others, recognized as an overreaching extension of their (our) concept of property in general. Could we, in fact, do this? Could we cease to regard the body as fungible and therefore commoditizable – even as integral to the mental "self" rather than instrumental to it? Could the body be its *own* self, its own Archimedean starting point?

One tool for initiating such a project might be the conception of an individual's moral relation to his or her body advanced by Immanuel Kant. Thomas Powers has already used this conception in an evaluation of the morality of donating or selling organs: concluding that, while post-mortem donation would be thus acceptable (1999, p. 224), live donation would not be (pp. 222f) unless via a "barter" system (pp. 227–228), Powers' argument focuses on Kant's enstatement of the will as the great title to personhood: "One of the supervenient characteristics of life is will, so to will the destruction of the very body on which life is conditioned is to will to negate the will. In this Kant finds a self-contradiction" (Powers, 1999, p. 216). In this fundamental prohibition of suicide (mirroring Locke and Hegel's), Powers discerns the rationale of self-contradiction famously forbidden by Kant's categorical imperative, and it will be clear from our earlier discussion that Hegel, also reserving the will as the essential kernel of personhood, must have borrowed sympathetically on this idea. Yet the Kantian body remains instrumental to the morally teleological will (Powers, 1999, pp. 212, 217, 219), and therefore not entirely integrated with it; it is this fact that prevents that body from being a dispositive concern in itself. The injunction to self-preservation, for example, prohibits bodily self-alienation (Powers, 1999, p. 219), from enslavement to suicide, but this provision can be overridden if the morally purposive will and intellect which guide the body are threatened – Kant gives the example of the soldier who self-murders in order to satisfy moral requirement of honor (Powers, 1999, p. 217), and neither Locke nor even Hegel go quite so far. But this instance involves no alienation to other parties; in these cases, Powers is clear that cases "Kant's doctrine of the humanity of the person insists that the body is not at the disposal of the person, since the body is not a mere thing" (Powers, 1999, p. 219, see also p. 220);[30] this is fundamentally a prohibition of the commodification of the body by self *or* others, of its treatment as property, which begins with an external thing; any non-thing (or anything non-external, rather)[31] is to be considered a rational creature to be treated as an end. This is why, while Kant does treat the will as *instrumentalizing* the body, he does not (Powers points out) wish the body to be therefore considered *incidental* in the Cartesian mode (Powers, 1999, pp. 211–212; see Scheper-Hughes, 2002, p. 51, and Toombs, 1999, p. 85, for the likely consequences of such a view for the idea of organ transfer). In this, of course, his view of volition departs from Hegel's, for whom the individual will actualizes itself in property beginning with the body; for Kant, the will is sufficiently *prior* that it can define property without first being defined *by/as* property, and this liberates the body from the Lockean/Hegelian configurations of personhood and ownership; in the meanwhile, Kant is no less capable than Locke and Hegel of reproducing the latters' cherished liberal positions, for example, limitation on indenture and a broad rejection of slavery (Kant, 1796, pp. 120, 193–194).[32]

And yet it is easily said that Locke and even Hegel, with their paradigms of bodily self-ownership, have a more secure place in the history of our jurisprudence than does Kant; with scholars such as Gaines, we may readily speak of Locke in discussing the issues of *Moore*, but Kant's likely conception of Moore himself as an end (who therefore errs in his wish to profit by his tissues' alienation) goes unheard by comparison; Radin may use Hegel to discuss what we cannot alienate, but Kant appears almost a Marxist by comparison (i.e., as one of Radin's pure "anti-commodifiers" [Radin, 1987, pp. 1871ff]). There are at stake here accidents of legal history, as well as comparisons of Kantian philosophy with other traditions, but in our immediate context, Kant's relatively radical stand against bodily alienation counts for little precisely because it is insufficiently linked to his views on property, or is only negatively so. And yet, as far as coherently prohibiting the conditions of slavery, this is precisely its strength, that Kant does not even introduce selfhood into the category of property. In doing so, he actually makes some progress in closing the Cartesian gap, in restoring the Sartrean intuition that "I *am* my hand" (quoted in Fabré, 2006, p. 101, and in Toombs, 1999, p. 80; emphasis in Fabré, who wishes to stop short of this formulation), that the body is, if instrumental, part of a unity; this is "the phenomenological account of the lived body" which "provides the insight that the relation between person and body is a relation of *existing* (and not 'having'). ... *I AM* my body ..." (Toombs, 1999, p. 87; although, in the same argument, Toombs herself symptomatically revives the property relation, calling the body "that which is most intimately *me* and *mine* (the body which *I AM*) ..." [1999, p. 89]).

Again, it certainly remains an open question to what extent (let alone whether) we would want to prohibit organ and tissue donation – and as Powers and others demonstrate, a Kantian jurisprudence certainly moves in that direction – but the fact remains that the logics driving those practices of bodily alienation, adding property to fungibility to authorize commoditization, ultimately make potential, retroactive sense of the bodily enslavement of others. As long as our own protections for individual autonomy begin from liberal principles, and as long as liberalism begins from property, we must be continually on guard against the implications of the bodily alienations for slavery-like destinies and the depletion of personhood; but is equally correct that "'[t]he person,'" says John Frow, "is at once the opposite of the commodity form and the condition of its existence" (quoted in Gaines, 1998, p. 546, n. 43). Until we are ready to recognize the truth of this formulation, of the Kantian insight that personhood must be entirely prior to property in order to have a jurisprudential being of its own, the irresolvable specter of slaveries, past and present, will linger.

NOTES

1. I would like, above all, to thank Austin Sarat for the opportunity to develop this piece, and for his help and encouragement in doing so; I would also like to express my gratitude to *Law, Politics & Society*'s anonymous reviewer.

2. J. S. Mill offers some of the classic formulations of this idea (see Radin, 1987, p. 1889); see also Best, 2004, p. 52, n. 43. I am indebted to *Law, Politics & Society*'s reviewer for pointing out that the category of disposal does not exhaust the "bundle" of rights entailed in ownership, and that the majority in *Moore v. Regents of University of California* (see below) makes this mistake, contra Justice Mosk's dissent in that case.

3. Some types of property, of course, traditionally offer resistance to this characterization, for example, the purchase of rights in intellectual property or in the market (e.g., options); while neither example is my topic here, I would suggest that the rights supposedly alienated in transactions involving these kinds of "intangible" property (though this intangibility is sometimes held to indicate certain amounts of inalienability!, see Best, 2004, p. 52, n. 43) usually devolve importantly to a physical/material basis. Indeed, the current confusion of rights and property intervenes here too: the intangibility of these commodities makes us more ready than usual to speak of the equally intangible *right* to them (we buy an automobile, but it is an almost metaphorical stretch to say that we "buy" a singer's voice – instead, we more readily

say that we buy the commercial rights to that voice); but the substrate of the actual property persists and asserts itself, beneath the right, indeed conditioning our idea of what that right is. The singer's voice to which a record company purchases a title, then, is such an intangible substrate, and unlike its tangible cousins, that voice (like an image or an idea) presents the peculiar mystery of remaining with the seller as well as with the buyer, of being both here and there – nor is it the rights to very determined *instances* of that voice that have been purchased (who knows what shape promised performances or recording sessions will take?); what is most in play is what the record company and the singer somehow both "own," the singer's voice, and thence, more tangibly, the singer's body as the source or perhaps substance of that voice. (The purchase of rights to the voice of a deceased singer provides a far simpler demonstration, as such a sale will ultimately revolve around a catalogue of transcribed or recorded music ...)

4. See notes 10 and 18 below for further discussions of this difference.

5. It is this question of agency which, in our time, is often ignored by treating inalienability only normatively, as a matter of right; this treatment understands rights of inalienability (and indeed rights in general) as comprehensible only as "claim-rights" against others (Mack, 1999, pp. 147f), thus sidestepping the question of what one may or may not do to oneself – this question, I hope to show, can be eminently worth considering without inviting the theological rationales which Eric Mack seeks to sidestep in Locke (Mack, 1999, pp. 147–152).

6. See note 7 below.

7. Again, where the empiricist Locke speaks of the *body*, he is referring also to the individual as a whole (including mental faculties, etc.), a mindset preserved in the disjunct English pronouns of his time ("no body," "any body," etc.). We shall see that the issue may not always be so simple (though perhaps it *should* be) in cases of slavery.

8. Locke makes an exception for indentured servitude as being temporary and without the master's power of life and death (1988, p. 285), though again, slavery in general will not always turn on these factors.

9. Interestingly, Locke seems to take for granted the just/unjust distinction on which he relies so continually in the *Second Treatise*'s chapter on conquest; the inference that just war is defensive war (and that unjust war is characterized by "initial" aggression) seems supported throughout (e.g., 1988, p. 385).

10. Mack notes that "[l]ike all of us, ... Locke was sometimes unwilling to accept the implications of his own theory" (1999, p. 151); "Locke ... is commonly thought *both* to have endorsed the inalienability of natural rights over one's person, life, and liberty, and to have articulated a conception of natural rights that does not permit those rights to be inalienable" (Mack, 1999, p. 144). This complaint, on the basis of which Mack discounts Locke's commitment to inalienable rights, takes a route concerned with voluntarism (right-as-choice) versus paternalism (right-as-duty to self); my argument also embraces the ambiguity indicated by Mack's remark, but from the standpoint of voluntarism (slavery as self-alienation) versus coercion (slavery as forcible alienation by another).

Mack's understanding is also opportune, however, in its concern that inalienable rights cannot be inalienable if one is paternalistically obliged to exercise them, that (again) such an obligation makes a right-as-choice into a right-as-duty (Mack, 1999,

p. 148); as George Khushf correctly points out, though, inalienability in a right does imply unlimited jurisdiction in the rightsholder (1999, p. 189). This kind of debate highlights the reason that I seek here, again, to discuss the body and any greater self as inalienable property (rather than as the subject of an inalienable right of ownership): the choice/duty debate over rights involves us in thorny issues, for example, of whether choosing *not* to exercise an inalienable right constitutes (i) a legitimate *exercise* of that right-as-choice, (ii) a paradoxical *alienation* of the right-as-choice itself (as Mack seems to feel, 1999, pp. 144–145), or (iii) a (perhaps more illegal than paradoxical) sort of *defiance* of what is in fact a right-as-duty. These questions are far from unimportant, but in discussing property and what it means to alienate it, the nature of property will seem comparatively more settled (if only because more concrete) than that of rights, and it will be correspondingly easier (though not in itself simple) to decide what constitutes alienation. This is not to say, of course, that the two discourses do not frequently cross paths in this discussion, but rather that law touching the body gives the issue of alienation a special corporeality that may inform our ideas of both property and the right to it.

11. See the Preface: "When philosophy paints its grey in grey, then has a shape of life grown old. By philosophy's grey in grey it cannot be rejuvenated but only understood" (Hegel, 1967, p. 13).

12. For a discussion of Hegelian self-realization through property, see Margaret Radin, "Property and Personhood" (1982, pp. 971–978). On the subject of self-ownership within Hegel's framework, Radin comments that "[i]f property in one's body is not too close to personhood to be considered property at all, then it is the clearest case of property for personhood," that is, of the category of property Radin considers most closely related to the constitution of individual personality (p. 978); this is a category in which she also includes other objects invested with sentimental value, including personal dwellings (Radin, 1982, pp. 959–961). My own ultimate contention in this essay is that one's body is indeed too close to personhood to be considered property – Radin reaches this conclusion in *some* cases, though for different reasons, in her essay "Market-Inalienability" (1987).

13. For qualification, see his intriguing reference to what may be a question of assisted suicide (Hegel, 1967, p. 57).

14. As commentators have pointed out, Hegel perhaps perceived the Prussia of his own day as already fulfilling this ideal.

15. Mosk notes that damages for breach of fiduciary duty do not actually protect Moore since, in order to reach this finding, it must be shown that the plaintiff would have made a different decision had he been properly informed, and it is virtually impossible to imagine that Moore would have refused the life-saving splenectomy that gave the defendants access to his tissues (*Moore*, 1990, p. 180). Interestingly, then, while this threshold would be easy to meet in many suits for, say, medical malpractice, Moore's suit for a sort of "medical exploitation" sidelines fiduciary duty, since the risk of medical "loss" (i.e., worse illness or death) outweighs the possibility of financial gain (i.e., from the cell line); thus Moore can comprehensibly have sued for a share of the profits from his exploited cells via a conversion action, but not via fiduciary breach, since he presumably would never have argued that he would have undergone likely or certain death to avoid the exploitation in the first

place. (Interestingly germane here, too, is S. Kay Toombs' observation that "*malfunctioning* organs" – or diseased cells, in this instance – "are experienced as other-than-me in the sense that they 'have me in their grips,' and are essentially beyond 'my' control" [1999, p. 86]; perhaps this observation helps explain Moore's implicit readiness to have alienated the diseased/profitable portion of his body under the right commercial circumstances. Indeed, Toombs posits the same of healthy organs to which we do not have sensory access [such as kidneys; see 1999, pp. 83 (quoting E. W. Straus), 86].)

16. There are ways that we might restore the Lockean body to the commons. For example, some bodily aspects reproduce themselves, allowing a certain excess to pass into the pool of common resources: for example, think of present-day techniques used to extract energy from human feces (and without the producing bodies' consent; see "The Seat of Power," 2010); of a producer of intellectual property who can alienate and then reproduce his or her body/mind's less tangible mental products (*with* his or her consent); and of Moore's diseased cells, which can (and must) be extracted as a *harmful* excess, and the healthy functioning of which his healed body will replace with new cells (the issue of consent here being confused).

It is interesting to note that, when considered at the cellular level (as at the excretory!), the individual body and the individual person as a whole tend to lose their stamp of uniqueness. As Broussard points out, the uniqueness of property is irrelevant to the question of its protection in *Moore*:

> [A]lthough the question whether plaintiff's cells are "unique" may well affect the amount of damages plaintiff will be able to recover in a conversion action, the question of uniqueness has no proper bearing on plaintiff's basic right to maintain a conversion action; ordinary property, as well as unique property, is, of course, protected against conversion. (*Moore*, 1990, p. 157)

But the majority's debate on uniqueness is not without relevance to the question of whether such cells *are* property in the first place. In Moore's case, his cells' uniqueness is at issue (the majority writes of them as having, "unlike a name or a face, ... the same molecular structure in every human being," and the related "genetic material ... which defendants use to manufacture [the cell line] in the laboratory" as "also the same in every person; it is no more unique to Moore than the number of vertebrae in the spine or the chemical formula of hemoglobin" [*Moore*, 1990, pp. 138–139]; by contrast, Mosk insists on "the patient's contribution of cells with unique attributes" [*Moore*, 1990, p. 175]). But any uniqueness Moore's tissue *may* have had affects not merely the amount of his potential damage claim for wrongful deprivation of his property, but also the extent to which we might want to call that tissue property at all. Ordinary external property, of course, is occasionally accounted unique on purely natural grounds, without the involvement of some human causation – for example, the world's largest known diamond, or a chemical element which alone displays a particular reactivity; but the existence of such unique property does not preclude the possibility that a still larger diamond, or a similarly reactive element, may be discovered, *arrivistes* who would usurp (the new diamond) or dilute to rarity (the new element) the uniqueness of their predecessors. It is otherwise with uniqueness tied to persons – no matter how many more oil paintings our species produces in the future, the singularity of Van Gogh's *Starry Night* will remain unthreatened, protected by our sense of *absolute* and *timeless* uniqueness attributed to individuals (i.e., the sense that gives strength to the laws of intellectual property). Genetics wanders between these two types of uniqueness, rediscovering absolute human individuality by positing a unique DNA sequence for each individual (barring the fascinating exception of identical twins [DNA fingerprinting, 2011]), and yet acknowledging a vast amount of shared sequencing – and an entirely shared pool of constituent elements – that suggests at least the possibility of duplication (potentially by natural forces, but more readily in the notion of cloning). For a geneticist who attempts to take a biologically determinist view of human beings, the latter conception feeds the former – that is, Van Gogh was naturally (genetically) unique, and this fact occasioned the *absolute* uniqueness of *Starry Night*. Moore's cells wander here too: if their uniqueness is merely natural (perhaps another patient has or will produce the same special cells), then they may yet be readily comprehensible as property; if they are part of "who he is" in an absolute sense, they still may be so (as it seems Moore would have wished), but at the same time they will belong to a different category which, as we can see in this case of biological "property" (and as we do in cases of intellectual "property"), consistently blurs property and personhood in a way that other types of property do not.

17. Another side of the same problem is highlighted by Drake Danforth, who claims that others' enrichment through a patient's body at the patient's expense is unquantifiably wrong, and then goes on to speak of the "dignity and sanctity" of body and mind – and yet apparently this sanctity is restored, and the patient's tissues are once again quantifiable, if he or she is properly brought in on the business of biotechnological tissue research (quoted in *Moore*, 1990, p. 174). To the extent that the only "sanctity" at stake here seems to be that of a truly free and open market, Danforth seems to lose himself between a wish for such a market and a wish that one's body be entirely unquantifiable in any commercial sense.

18. The mind/body analogy (which really expresses a unity) also highlights the fact that inalienable properties, like inalienable rights (to property and other things), always seem (again, as Best remarks) to be more fundamental than their alienable cousins. And yet in a liberal context, we are even *more* apt to speak of the alienability of property, in the crude physical sense at least, than to speak of alienable rights, though such of course may exist, for example, the right against self-incrimination in U.S. constitutional law; at the ulterior limit, libertarian fantasy of the Nozickian type tends to capitalize on the notion of "having" rights by simply treating rights *as* property, and perhaps without an inalienable "bottom" in sight.

19. See Derrida (1981, pp. 175–226).

20. I am using the term "transfer" generally to cover donation, sale, and confiscation of organs on both a living and post-mortem basis, as well as in acknowledgement of the traditional difficulties with which the categories of consent (at the legal level) and donation (at the anthropological-philosophical level) are fraught (see further on in this section). My discussion, of course, will concern just a tiny sample of this spectrum: a brief examination of gifts by living donors, and a case of confiscation after death. (Lesley Sharp also opts for the term "organ transfer," though with different force [2006, p. 3].)

21. Although, for example, California permits limited sales by patients (Radin, 1987, p. 1924, n. 261).

22. Best also bases this analysis on Mauss' gift-thinking (2004, pp. 82–83).

23. Though we should note that bodily tissue of the reproductive kind must of course be alienated exclusively external to the family to avoid incest taboos and genetic difficulties; yet even here, we might note aristocratic practices of marrying and reproducing within a given social stratum (which indeed produced inbreeding), and most fundamentally the fact that reproductive material returns to family in the sense of Annette Weiner's "keep[ing]-while-giving" (quoted in Lock, 2002, p. 70) – in the form of heirs (for the husband's family) and of allies (for the wife's), with all the various wealth transfers these relations imply.

24. I am indebted to *Law, Politics & Society*'s anonymous reviewer for clarification of this point.

25. See, for example, Kara (2009, pp. 40–41) versus Murray (1998, pp. 51–64), and Doezema (1998, pp. 43–44); Bales (2005), briefly surveys the controversy, pp. 62–63.

26. See note 3 above.

27. That such fraudulent debt rationales are used seems undisputed, though many researchers make the point that sometimes the satisfaction of debt is possible, and repayment can lead to later economic empowerment (e.g., Murray, 1998, p. 57) – even if, we might suppose, otherwise slavery-like conditions still inhere in the interim, made temporary by the different circumstances. My concern, of course, is with the unreality of more durable debt.

28. Bales notes in parallel his observation that "those who have been enslaved from a very early age often show an acceptance of slavery and a willingness to define themselves in relation to their masters" (2005, p. 56), a sociological description of that initial consciousness which Hegel sees as ultimately self-reflected.

29. Giorgio Agamben's development of the *bios–zoe* dichotomy would be relevant here as well; see Lawrence Cohen's use of this distinction in the context of kidney transplants (2002, pp. 22–26).

30. Conversely, Powers finds the consequences of violating this principle in Kant's remark that, "[i]f the agent uses himself as a thing, others are entitled to use him as a thing, since 'he has made a thing of himself, and, having discarded his humanity, he cannot expect that others should respect humanity in him'" (Powers, 1999, p. 220, quoting Kant; cf. Mack, 1999, p. 152). Khushf reads a similar fear of a loss of rational humanity into Locke's prohibitions of self-alienation (1999, pp. 198, 200), though on the basis of the theological prohibition we have already noted, rather than on that of any self-guaranteeing notion of personhood. Indeed, the particular strength of Kant's prohibition of self-alienation may result from that notion's nature *as* self-authorizing (though it might be better to describe it, in Kant's terms, as noetic, *a priori*, unauthorizably given).

31. See Kant's explanation of the concept of externality (1796, p. 62).

32. Interestingly, Kant does depart from Locke on the question of prisoners of war, whose enslavement he rejects because it would be punitive in nature (1796, p. 222), where punishment between nations is nonsensical outside of any juridical context (p. 219; correspondingly, he permits virtual enslavement of some criminals [p. 198]).

REFERENCES

Bales, K. (2005). *Understanding global slavery: A reader*. Berkeley, CA: University of California Press.

Best, S. (2004). *The fugitive's properties: Law and the poetics of possession*. Chicago, IL: University of Chicago Press.

Cohen, L. (2002). The other kidney. In: N. Scheper-Hughes & L. Wacquant (Eds.), *Commodifying bodies* (pp. 9–29). London: Sage Publications.

Deleuze, G., & Guattari, F. (1977). *Anti-Oedipus: Capitalism and schizophrenia* (R. Hurley, M. Seem & H. R. LANE Trans.). New York, NY: Viking-Seaver.

Derrida, J. (1981). *Dissemination* (B. Johnson, Trans.). Chicago, IL: University of Chicago Press.

DNA fingerprinting. (2011). In Encyclopædia Britannica. Retrieved from http://www.britannica.com/EBchecked/topic/167155/DNA-fingerprinting

Doezema, J. (1998). Forced to choose: Beyond the voluntary v. forced prostitution dichotomy. In: K. Kempadoo & J. Doezema (Eds.), *Global sex workers: Rights, resistance, and redefinition* (pp. 34–50). New York, NY: Routledge.

Fabré, C. (2006). *Whose body is it anyway? Justice and the integrity of the person*. Oxford: Oxford University Press.

Foucault, M. (1995). *Discipline and punish: The birth of the prison*. Westminster, MD: Vintage.

Gaines, J. (1998). The absurdity of property in the person. *Yale Journal of Law & the Humanities*, *10*, 537–548.

Gates, H. (2009). Abraham Lincoln on race and slavery. In A. Lincoln, H. Gates (Ed.), D. Yacovone (Coed.), *Lincoln on race and slavery* (pp. vii–lxvii). Princeton. NJ: Princeton University Press.

Hegel, G. W. F. (1996). Lordship and bondage [from *Phenomenology of Spirit*, 1807] In J. O'Neill (Ed.), *Hegel's dialectic of desire and recognition: Texts and commentary* (pp. 29–36). Albany, NY: State University of New York Press.

Hegel, G. W. F. (1967). *Hegel's philosophy of right* (T. M. Knox, Trans.). London: Oxford University Press (Original work published 1821).

Kara, S. (2009). *Sex trafficking: Inside the business of modern slavery*. New York, NY: Columbia University Press.

Khushf, G. (1999). Inalienable rights in the moral and political philosophy of John Locke: A reappraisal. In: M. Cherry (Ed.), *Persons and their bodies: Rights, responsibilities, relationships* (pp. 177–206). Hingham, MA: Kluwer Academic Publishers.

Lock, M. (2002). The alienation of body tissue. In: N. Scheper-Hughes & L. Wacquant (Eds.), *Commodifying bodies* (pp. 63–91). London: Sage Publications.

Locke, J. (1988). An essay concerning the true original, extent, and end of civil government. In J. Locke (Author) & P. Laslett (Ed.), *John Locke: Two treatises of government* (pp. 265–428). Cambridge: Cambridge University Press (Original published 1690).

Mack, E. (1999). The alienability of Lockean natural rights. In: M. Cherry (Ed.), *Persons and their bodies: Rights, responsibilities, relationships* (pp. 143–176). Hingham, MA: Kluwer Academic Publishers.

Moore v. Regents of University of California. (1990). 51 Cal.3d 120.

Murray, A. (1998). Debt bondage and trafficking: Don't believe the hype. In: K. Kempadoo & J. Doezema (Eds.), *Global sex workers: Rights, resistance, and redefinition* (pp. 51–64). New York, NY: Routledge.

Powers, T. (1999). The integrity of the body: Kantian moral constraints on the physical self. In: M. J. Cherry (Ed.), *Persons and their bodies: Rights, responsibilities, relationships* (pp. 209–232). Hingham, MA: Kluwer Academic Publishers.

Radin, M. (1982). Property and personhood. *Stanford Law Review, 34*, 957–1015.

Radin, M. (1987). Market-inalienability. *Harvard Law Review, 100*, 1849–1937.

Scheper-Hughes, N. (2002). Commodity fetishism in organs trafficking. In: N. Scheper-Hughes & L. Wacquant (Eds.), *Commodifying bodies* (pp. 31–62). London: Sage Publications.

Sharp, L. (2006). *Strange harvest: Organ transplants, denatured bodies, and the transformed self.* Berkeley, CA: University of California Press.

The seat of power. (2009). *The Economist*, December 30. Retrieved from http://www.economist.com/node/15172621

Toombs, S. (1999). What does it mean to be some*body*? Phenomenological reflections and ethical quandaries. In: M. J. Cherry (Ed.), *Persons and their bodies: Rights, responsibilities, relationships* (pp. 73–94). Hingham, MA: Kluwer Academic Publishers.

Unger, R. (1986). *The critical legal studies movement.* Cambridge, MA: Harvard University Press.

Wacquant, L. (2002). Deadly symbiosis: Rethinking race and imprisonment in twenty-first-century America. *Boston Review, 27*. Retrieved from http://bostonreview.net/BR27.2/wacquant.html

CONSTITUTIVE PARADOXES OF HUMAN RIGHTS: AN INTERPRETATION IN HISTORY AND POLITICAL THEORY

John R. Wallach

ABSTRACT

Two paradoxes constitute the discourse of human rights. One concerns the relationship between "the human" and "the political"; the other invokes the opposition between the universalist moral character of human rights and the practical, particular context in which they become manifest. This chapter argues how and why these paradoxes will not go away – a good thing, too – over and against classical and contemporary writers who have argued for the priority of one or the other. After elucidating the powerful and enduring character of these paradoxes in history and political theory, I argue that human rights discourse only makes sense in terms of the arguably more primary discourses of democracy, political virtue, and justice if it is to avoid being a deceptive, rhetorical cover for dubious political practices.

Special Issue: Human Rights: New Possibilities/New Problems
Studies in Law, Politics, and Society, Volume 56, 37–65
ISSN: 1059-4337/doi:10.1108/S1059-4337(2011)0000056005

INTRODUCTION

Humans have not always had rights; nor have they always wanted them. Rights are creations of moral philosophy and political power. Sometimes they are asserted; sometimes they are fought for; sometimes they are taken for granted. The practical association of rights with humanity (or human beings generically understood) is a creation of the tumultuous seventeenth and eighteenth centuries of Europe, when Hobbes, Locke, and Rousseau identified "natural rights" as the foundation for the political rights of legitimate governments.[1] Of more political significance for the idea of human rights was its enunciation in three later historical moments, moments that also signaled fundamental crises of political legitimation. The first was France's 1789 *Declaration of the Rights of Man and Citizen*, in which human rights were understood as the rights of the civilized (male) citizens of France. Yet the potential of this moment fulfilled the pretensions of its name as a practical injunction designed to better the condition of *all* human beings only in the second moment, when the United Nations General Assembly unanimously passed (48-0, with eight abstentions) the *Universal Declaration of Human Rights (UDHR)* in December 1948.[2] This event was certainly in gestation for centuries, but it was catalyzed by the desire for a new ethical discourse in a world transformed by the horrific killings of millions of persons during the First and particularly the Second World War. This universalized political idea finally gained political traction after the end of the Cold War, when the ideological politics and interpretive divides that separated NATO and Warsaw Pact conceptions of human rights lost their moorings. From its checkered, historical evolution, the idea of human rights is evidently a historically and highly contingent, as well as politically contested, idea.[3]

Yet many view "human rights" – as articulated by the French National Assembly, Franklin Roosevelt,[4] or the United Nations General Assembly, or elaborated in subsequent official, international documents – as a substantive entity, a *thing* captured in discourse to be honored or violated, a universal code for moral and political conduct or mask for Western imperialists and capitalists.[5] But the prevailing presumption is that human rights are neither contingent nor contested. If we are good moral and political beings, we should do our level best to "realize" human rights (Balfour & Cadava, 2004; Habermas, 2010; Power & Allison, 2000).[6] We should take human rights discourse, as it were, "off the shelf" and use it as a moral guide and template for political practice – in the words of the Samantha Power (journalist, human rights policy-maker, and political consultant) – an "inspiration" for "impact."[7]

That said, the range of human rights to be realized surely will differ depending upon whom one consults. They may include civil and political rights alone, or they may include economic, social, and cultural rights, not to mention the rights encoded in various international conventions – such as the right to be protected from torture, racial discrimination, discrimination against women, unjust treatment as a refugee or member of an indigenous people, or, the most popular of human rights, the rights of the child, and so on. My simple point here is that "human rights" are typically regarded as good, whatever "they" are, and the political setting for their realization is taken to be bad – as it were, on the wrong side of morality. Practice is incorrigible or backward and needs enlightening and improving by the idea and practice of human rights – whether the tools for implementation are persuasion or ammunition.

But two basic problems belong to this formulation, each of which generates an ineluctable or "constitutive" paradox of human rights. One is *substantive* and directly *political*; it concerns the relation between "the human" and "the political" and belongs to the domain of political ethics in general. The other is *epistemological* and *moral*; it addresses the issue of how one relates ideas and actualities, or moral universality and cultural relativity. Each stems from the fact that human rights cobbles together two kinds of concepts and practical relations that are not innately friendly and treats them as one, failing to recognize the potential lack of complementarity of their relationship. In other words, the discourse of human rights synthesizes and occludes basic features of the origins, history, and character of human rights as an idea and practice. The notion of human rights immediately implies constitutive paradoxes – making it far from self-evident as a conceptual "thing" or a guide to moral and political practice.

Paradox has marked the invocation of human rights from their first articulation, and since that time the initial paradoxes have not been solved so much as layered by new iterations of them. Joining them together is the overarching paradox that human rights stitches together normative, universal, and moral notions of the human or humanity that would transcend politics, power, and cultural differentiation with a notion of rights which, by its very nature, is a political term of power and contestation whose exercise displaces the social order. The fluid semantics of human rights might suggest that any theoretical analysis designed to advance a general understanding of the concept amounts to a fool's errand: leave it for use by metaphysicians, rhetoricians, activists, or ethnographers.[8] To do so, however, leaves a significant realm of public discourse to detached observations or the instrumental deployment of practical actors.[9] While such projects often affect and benefit our understanding of human rights in political discourse, they do not exhaust its meaning. Moreover, if paradoxes constitute human rights, they suggest that it is not entirely either good or bad and need not be wholly contradictory or self-defeating. And despite the radically contestable, diverse usages, and questionable cogency of the notion of human rights, the term retains primacy as the principal currency for the realm of international political ethics; indeed, it has major potential as a lever for improving the human condition.[10] The discourse of human rights will be with us for the foreseeable future. Philosophical analysis cannot argue it away, and yet the troubling instabilities that belong to human rights also will remain – even trumping the consternation caused by "essentially contestable concepts" (see Gallie, 1955–1956; cf. Connolly, 1974/1983).[11]

Political theorists who address the fundamentally international or transnational character of contemporary political ethics, therefore, cannot ignore the pivotal, albeit fungible and paradoxical, character of "human rights." Indeed, human rights discourse warrants the kind of critical analysis that academics not contractually bound to the official exercise of political power are positioned to provide. We need to understand the constitutive paradoxes of human rights if we are to benefit from their discursive use. Understanding the constitutive paradoxes of human rights enables us to appreciate more than we may have the complex context in which its meaning gets used. Moreover, the two constitutive paradoxes I adumbrate below – one substantive and political; the other epistemological and moral – reveal conceptual openings and political opportunities. But they can only do so if we acknowledge their nature and power.

Many of these paradoxes have been noted by others, including myself.[12] My effort here to move the debate forward is designed to achieve three objects: *describe how* two paradoxical elements *unavoidably constitute* human rights theory and practice, and have done so from the beginning of their usage in political discourse; *note that* the *effect* of these paradoxes tends to marginalize human rights ideals in political practice, and *argue that* if we do not fully appreciate these paradoxes, the ethical and political well-being signified by various projects currently and potentially associated with human rights will not fare well in the world. After so doing, I shall offer some preliminary suggestions about what should be thought and done about human rights in light of its constitutive paradoxes. Ultimately, human rights should be understood *not* as a first-order philosophical or moral concern but a second-order political construction which, in order to function effectively, must be understood in terms of related discursive, ethical, and practical realities that form the context of its operation – in fact, a plurality of democratic virtues.

DELINEATING THE PARADOXES

The *first* paradox stems directly from the diverging, substantive parts of human rights, namely *"the human"* as a fact, value, norm, or ideal and *"rights,"* which belong to subjectively asserted and objectively protected domains of political ethics. At first glance, the couple of the human and the political looks fairly glamorous. The "human" is a relative constant across historical time, providing a link between our past, present, and future.[13] Across the centuries and in every language, the number of genes belonging to *Homo sapiens* have remained constant, and we continue to make many of the same mistakes we always have. By contrast, the "rights" of humans are seen to signify a progressively better and wider set of goods for human beings. First articulated in Roman times to *differentiate* status (and coordinated with another oxymoronic Roman neologism, "natural law"), they subsequently became associated with *natural* human traits that transcended status and rank (though not gender in theory, and certainly not wealth in practice) – particularly in seventeenth century Europe, even as they marked an egalitarian *achievement* of status and rank for many citizens.[14] This democratization of the idea of human dignity could be said to reformulate the rhetorical democratization of political virtue that marked that establishment of Athenian democracy.[15]

When this occurred, the political rights of citizens of various states – particularly those of England, the United States, and France – began to be seen as ipso facto human or "natural" to human beings, in the form of *natural* rights. However, these clearly justified rights of citizens in particular states – necessarily shy of universally human rights. So the next step in a progressively understood march of history was to dispense with the political identity that guaranteed rights and simply refer to *human rights* possessed by *human beings* regardless of their political affiliation – or lack thereof. The problematic political character of the human as a subject of "human rights" was mostly ignored. Now, the challenge simply became that of *realizing* human rights, over and potentially against the states that enabled and would guarantee human rights. The institutionalization of the United Nations and the rhetorical force of the *UDHR* were to overcome the particularistic ideas and practices of human rights of the past so as to enact their genuine promise in the future. But here, too, the tension between the human and the political is denied, and the need for potentially cooperative rather than necessarily hierarchical relations between the idea of human rights and social practices is ignored. Indeed, recent attempts (in Kosovo and Libya) to couple the human and the political in the form of "humanitarian intervention," with dubious regard for the harm or good for its purported beneficiaries caused by its enactment, have used the peaceable idea of human rights as an instrument of military violence.[16]

This first paradox ineluctably leads to the *second*, namely that the justification of human rights has to be universal while their "realization" has to be relative and particular – which is another way of saying that human rights are necessarily *both* universal and monological *as well as* particular and relative – even as logically it cannot have all of these characteristics at once (unless human rights descend from the sky commanded by good gods or universal reason into the hands of the right persons). In other words, human rights are supposed to be *both* universal *and* particular – even as the secular logic that supposedly informs human rights says that they cannot be. In recent anthropological literature, the universalism–relativism debate has been transcended as a problem for human rights practice, by recognizing (1) the multivocality of culture, not to mention its reflections and disjunctures of power, and (2) the effects of globalization.[17] But human rights is then shorn of its substantive content and viewed as a tool, while the paradoxical tension between the *idea* and the *practice* of human rights – remains typically denied or ignored.

THE TWO PARADOXES AT THE ORIGINS OF HUMAN RIGHTS AS A POLITICAL DISCOURSE

In an article published 10 years ago, the cultural historian Lynn Hunt noted what she called "the paradoxical origins of human rights" (2000). By this she refers to the oft-noted paradox that accompanied the dramatic invocation of human rights in political discourse in the late eighteenth century – namely its use in justifying the democratic overcoming of privilege and illegitimate authority, in the United States and France. She combines features of my two "constitutive" paradoxes when she states that universality was invoked as "self-evident" in order to overcome a recalcitrant opposition born of imperial or feudal regimes. In my terms, the so-called *universal* and *political* morality of *the human* was realized as a *particular practical* intervention in singular states. These political efforts were surely warranted and typically justified through the language of the Enlightenment. Reformist or even revolutionary politics marked the exercise of human reason, human reason was good, and its practical exercise would yield historical progress. Immanuel Kant felt able to claim in the wake of the French Revolution that historical progress would result from the mere instantiation of law – even in a "nation of devils" (1980, p. 112). Good ideas deserved imminent enactment – aspiration, impact.

But the notion of self-evidence in political documents is partly ironic – a feature whose seriousness Hunt only lightly acknowledges. For the invocation of "self-evidence" in political discourse iterates either the need for persuasion – otherwise, why make the point – or more than a touch of intolerance – insofar as it forecloses debate. On behalf of human rights, political opposition was killed, banished, or subordinated in revolutionary upheavals. In other words, the political invocation of self-evidence not only undermines the universality implicit in its claim but transforms a fact of nature into a value on the march, such that theory aspires to rule or emancipate practice. Meanwhile, the new political language of human rights obscures the damage produced by the resulting domination. Interestingly, in her more recent, award-winning book, Lynn Hunt does not emphasize the paradoxical character of the origins of human rights but simply invokes their "self-evidence" (Hunt, 2008). She regards them as a natural efflorescence of Western culture in the second half of the eighteenth century, echoing previous claims made by the Argentinian jurist Eduardo Rabossi and the American pragmatist Richard Rorty that human rights are best regarded not as a philosophy or moral theory but as a Western cultural practice that ought to be extended by engaging the sympathies of others.[18] Yet one has to wonder about the inherent beneficence of Western culture if it can be deployed on behalf of genocide and the destruction of planet earth. Which is not to say that Western culture per se caused these phenomena or uniquely enacts them, but it hasn't protected us from them either.

The elision of the implicit conflict between the human and the political as domains of experience was first enunciated by Aristotle when he identified "man" (*ho anthropos*) as a political animal (*politike zoon*) – that is, an individual whose potential only could be fully realized in the life of a *polis*.[19] Modernity, as influentially articulated in the political theory of Thomas Hobbes, disintegrated the *telos* of Aristotle's conception of the natural character of political man. In so doing, he eliminated the natural differentiation of status that belonged to Aristotle's metaphysical teleology. But insofar as the notion of a natural, human, and political *telos* enabled Aristotle to conceptualize notions of the common good that elided the potential for enduring conflict between the human and the political, Hobbes's critique of that notion and its complementary egalitarianism produced a radical critique of the notion of the common good as a challenge to the power exercised in a political community. The political emergence of the discourse of rights in the liberal revolutions of the late eighteenth century regenerated the Aristotelian elision on the bases of Hobbesian metaphysics, endowing the modern notion of human rights with its first distinctive paradox.

In the United States, for example, subsequent to the enunciation of the unalienable [human] rights of life, liberty, and the pursuit of happiness, a Constitution was written only on the condition that citizens possessed certain civil rights that would protect them from the government which they had just authorized. Similarly, the first version of the new French republic relied on a Declaration of the Rights of Man and Citizen – recognizing the difference between the human and the political but denying the prospect of conflict between them. Man, or more ecumenically, human beings, were natural creatures marked by differences but also equal moral faculties. These human characteristics would be fulfilled in their rights as citizens. Thus, republican rights *were* human rights, and republican France *ipso facto* promoted the interests of humanity. But here, the danger of not acknowledging the constitutive gap between theory and practice that belongs to human rights clearly emerged. Robespierre and Napoleon believed they understood this, but perhaps all too well in their projects of republican virtue as terror and civilization as imperial rule. In so doing, they paved the way for many features of the nineteenth century's era of moralistic politics. If conducted by states, such as the United States, the United Kingdom, and France, guns were often its agents. If conducted by groups seeking membership in the cherished circle of citizens, it occurred through protests against slavery, the subordination of women as second-class citizens, imperialism, and the domination of wealth in legal determinations of citizenship. Eventually, these protests achieved success. Sometimes they employed the vernacular of human rights; sometimes, civil rights; sometimes, human dignity or equality. In each case, a universal claim was invoked as part of a particular political struggle. No international covenants or institutions sanctioned these struggles, but progress on behalf of "human rights" seemed to be on the march.[20] For many, it often was wise to get of its way.

THE TWO PARADOXES AMID THE MODERN, FORMAL UNIVERSALIZATION OF HUMAN RIGHTS

Need it be said, all of the above occurred prior to the official invocation of human rights as a binding norm on all states, authorized by the *Universal Declaration of Human Rights*. One might think that the global scope of this declaration could, in theory, if not immediately in practice, in aspiration if not in impact, eliminate the two original ("constitutive") paradoxes of the human and the political, on the one hand, and the universal or moral and the particular or cultural, on the other, by establishing international norms that applied to all nations and peoples. As the opening words of the Preamble in the *UDHR* states, this document champions "the inherent dignity of the equal and inalienable rights of all members of the human family [as] the foundation of freedom, justice, and peace in the world."[21] The first paradox would be overcome insofar as the norms were to apply to all states equally – which masked differences in political power; the second also would be because the *UDHR* eliminates the distinction between human beings and citizenship – indeed, between universal human rights and the particularity of democracy. The document's failure to account for the constitutive paradoxes of human rights – viz., the disjuncture between its claim as a virtuous human norm and power-driven mechanisms for its enforcement, as well as the differences between universal moral standards and the differentiated cultures in which they would become real – must be fully recognized lest there be serious harm done – again, not in order to sabotage human rights but to acknowledge its inherent instability and encourage greater critical and political notice of its pretensions.

The modern version of the first paradox of human rights was initially noted by Hannah Arendt. She described the manner in which the political discourse of human rights became fully revealed only when human beings had been stripped of their dignity, becoming bare, or barely human, during the period of the Minority Treaties and the Holocaust. Only when *human* beings could act and be effectively heard within discrete *political* communities that differentiate them from other human beings could their human rights become something more than signs of the dispossessed. And, indeed, the discourse of human rights has gained the most traction when it is cited as a radical loss of humanity – through the torture, arbitrary imprisonment, or genocidal attack on individuals and peoples. But this entails a peculiar result: that which should be most cherished by us becomes an effective part of politics only when it has been lost. And so Arendt claimed that human rights must amount to, in what has now become a poster-phrase in much academic discourse, "the right to have rights."[22]

But this phrase doesn't solve *her* paradox. Nor does it solve Arendt's modernization of the two paradoxes of human rights – because the previous question about where is the human whose rights will be protected simply becomes another: who or what enforces "the right to have rights"? What does its substance consist of? One could say that the *UDHR* and attending covenants amount to its basic substance and mechanisms of enforcement. But, as mentioned previously, those covenants are enforced fitfully – according to morally arbitrary criteria, even if the effects may be beneficent. After all, the *UDHR* was an aspirational document, not a legally binding document, and subsequent human rights conventions still are not enforced (although this is marginally changing with the creation and slow strengthening of the International Criminal Court). And as previously noted, these rights are enforced by governments – one of the many agents of power that jeopardize, if not abuse, the norms and practices associated with human rights. The assumption is that the moral standard of human rights, adhered to by signatories of the *UDHR*, will be smoothly, albeit imperfectly, politically enforced by the states which that standard would bind – aka "the international community" a term that signifies a putative consensus among the Western economic and military powers. Useful, critical standards for this hypothetical entity have been spelled out recently by Charles Beitz (and will be discussed below).[23] But they do not dissolve the paradoxes.

We ignore these paradoxes, if not contradictions, because there often seems to be no better alternative. For no one wants a world state, nor we do want to allow the absolute sovereignty of states over their citizens and residents. Some would solve this paradox by redefining human rights as democracy and democracy in terms of human rights. But that begs the question we have raised in the first paradox, namely the relationship between the human and the political, of which democracy is a constitutive part.[24] So what's a global citizen to do?

REFORMING THE FIRST PARADOX: PROTECTING HUMAN RIGHTS VIA LIBERALISM

One response to the potentially overreaching significance of human rights discourse has been to shrink the practical content of the *UDHR* to the security rights of individuals that are commonly understood and protected by judicial institutions and considerations of state security. That is, human rights amount to liberal rights. This has been the tack taken by liberal champions of human rights, such as Isaiah Berlin, Maurice Cranston, John Rawls, Michael Ignatieff, and Amartya Sen, each of whom emphasizes the priority of rights or capacities of individuals in the general articulation of ethical political discourse. In so doing, they marginalize the significance of political power in the conception and constitution of human rights – a discursive move that characterizes the liberal tradition of political thought.[25] I shall discuss the approaches of Rawls and Sen, along with the related approaches of Charles Beitz and Martha Nussbaum, because of their highly intelligent and percipient character and because their aporiai can be understood in terms of the constitutive paradoxes of human rights.

In *The Law of Peoples*, Rawls frankly states that his conceptualization of this law is not itself a theory of global justice but rather a theory "which extends the idea of a social contract to a Society of Peoples" – thereby making the world peaceful and safe for liberal democracies.[26] Indeed, Rawls states explicitly that in his "Law of Peoples ... we work out the ideals and principles of the *foreign policy* of a reasonably just *liberal* people" (Rawls's italics).[27] Human rights play a relatively minimal role in the theory as a whole, even as Rawls also designed the theory to protect and promote "basic human rights" across the globe.[28] He primarily regards human rights as restrictions on state sovereignty that protect the state's citizens, particularly the restrictions that have gained international acceptance since World War II. They apply to non-liberal, as well as liberal, states. But not all states observe them – in particular, states that fall under his category of "outlaw states" (the leaders of which *do not* observe obligations to their citizens or other states) and "burdened societies" (states which *cannot* observe obligations to their citizens or other states). However, "benevolent absolutist" (i.e., antidemocratic) states that are not "decent" or "well-ordered" are regarded as observers of "human rights."[29] The so-called well-ordered societies of liberal and decent peoples (i.e., nondemocratic, potentially theocratic, but consultative societies) have a "duty to assist" burdened states, but how to exercise that duty is a matter of political statesmanship rather than legal obligation – what Kant called "imperfect obligations."

Rawls associates his definition of human rights with those identified in Articles 3-18 of the *UDHR*. He also defines their political role as follows: Its practice (1) is necessary but not sufficient for the social conditions of decent peoples; (2) prohibits intervention in societies that uphold human rights; and (3) limits the pluralism of peoples – that is, nonviolently establishes a floor upon which acceptable cultural diversity could develop.[30] As a result, economic, social, and cultural rights are, as they have been in the past, subordinated to the civil rights and some of the political rights guaranteed in the *UDHR*. In addition, democracy is not understood as a basic human right. For Rawls, this is the price one has to pay for generating a useful and coherent political theory, which he calls a "realistic utopia" – something that he does not associate with the *UDHR*. But it also interestingly reveals how a Rawlsian theory of human rights that could inform American foreign policy ultimately regards human rights as different from democracy and not requiring democracy – even as the United States articulates "human rights and democracy" as conjoint ideals of American foreign policy. Indeed, Rawls's political theory of human rights suggests that conceptions of human rights informed by his theory that function as guideposts of public policy may do so at the expense of democracy, systematic attempts to redress economic inequality on a global scale, or other forms of injustice (Brown, 2004). The influence of this, Rawls's last book, is considerable.[31]

More recently, Charles Beitz has analyzed international relations from a Rawlsian perspective in order to elaborate Rawls's insufficiently spelled out conception of human rights. Rather than defining it from the normative position of Rawls's liberalism-inspired "realistic utopia" of The Law of Peoples, Beitz offers an analytical examination of "the idea of human rights" as an "emergent ... normative ... practice." He believes it helps to view human rights through the lens of a theory of justice or comprehensive moral value (Beitz, 2009, pp. 7–12).[32] And yet Beitz regards human rights primarily as practices to be protected by states. While recognizing the state-centric paradigm through which human rights functions as a practice, Beitz does not acknowledge the extent to which this framework may privilege institutionalized, rather than aspirational and agency-based, conceptions or practices of human rights.[33] Ironically, "the idea of human rights" is understood primarily in legitimating, rather than critical, terms. To put it another way, the ethical and political paradoxes of human rights (namely, the tension between the facticity of being human and the socially constructed nature of the individual as a rights-bearing creature) and the practical paradox of the UDHR (in which the institutionalization of rights as protection against states is carried out by states) are handled by accepting the normativity of "human rights" while making its primary interpretation the responsibility of states. Like Rawls, Beitz does not believe that human rights (as a practice) should be a tool of states, but the only constraint on states stems from a Skinnerian discursive medium – such as that invoked by The New York Times when it mentions the views of "the international community." Insofar as human rights merely function as protections for individuals against states, human rights as a practice in our international system can only amount to a weak, defensive mechanism – typically invoked after the fact in an ad hoc manner to protect individuals whom the major political powers have little to worry about. In other words, the paradoxes that have bedeviled the discourse of human rights have been suppressed. Beitz's analytical explanation of "the idea of human rights" surely has clarified the discursive and critical terrain of human rights as a practice, but its political effect may simply reinforce prevailing conceptions of human rights.

The least thoughtful adaptation of liberal conceptions of human rights to contemporary issues occurs in the work of Michael Ignatieff and other "liberal hawks" (such as Thomas Friedman, Peter Beinart, and Paul Berman). Ignatieff linked human rights and the use of military force to justify NATO's effort to protect threatened Albanians in Kosovo from the potential of ethnic violence (which violated international law) and, later, the American government's invasions of Afghanistan and Iraq as responses to terrorism. Ignatieff only allows human rights to signify the non-derogable security rights – rights that states have been uniquely created to protect (see Ignatieff, 2000, 2004).[34] More boldly than Rawls, who wants his "Law of Peoples" to constrain the power politics of states, Ignatieff only assigns "negative rights" (a term popularized by his mentor, Isaiah Berlin) the mark of genuine human rights. And since such rights require the protection by states for their existence, the definition of the ground rules for protection and the nature of what is to be protected ("values") are determined principally by states and their national interests. Constraints upon states that stem from the political agency of ordinary citizens or democracy more generally disappear in what amounts to a neo-Hobbesian conception of human rights.[35]

But even liberal theorists who are more critical of state power and the status quo view human rights through the lenses of their liberal theories rather than propose distinctively new ethical and political standards for human rights. This is the case with the work of Amartya Sen. To begin with, Sen's effort to chart a theory of human rights is slightly ironic. After all, his contribution to political theory principally involves showing how the affirmation of "rights" is insufficient for the protection and promotion of human freedom/s. One should rather think in terms of the language of "human capabilities." Indeed, in the manner of the *UDHR*, Martha Nussbaum (who has worked with Sen on these issues) has developed a list of human capacities whose development ensures the fullest expression of human freedom (though Sen disagrees with the strategy of constructing lists).[36] But the capabilities approach does not stray from rights-based liberalism. The protection of many individual "rights" are crucial for the development of the central human capabilities, and an increase in capacities to exercise rights and obtain primary goods is measured by an increase in the "opportunities" to develop them rather than their actual achievement (Sen, 2009). In addition, as with the *UDHR*, the capabilities approach identifies political aspirations without a political mechanism to develop them. As a result, Sen's theory of human rights, like Rawls's, operates primarily as a moral minimum for the global development of justice (Sen, 2004). We are to think of human development without a developer and without recognizing the implicit connection between any strategy of development and political goals (Sen, 1999).[37] To be sure, Sen's focus on capabilities justifies an emphasis on economic and social rights that Rawls and Beitz tend not to highlight. However, he mostly relabels their subordinate status, under the Kantian category of "imperfect obligations" – that is, obligations that are not legally enforceable – bolstering them only by insisting that such obligations warrant wide-ranging public discussion as part of a theory of human rights.[38]

Ultimately, Sen states contentedly, "there is ... no great deficit in the balance of trade between theory and practice" with in his conception of human rights (Sen, 2004, p. 356). But I have my doubts. Amartya Sen wants us to focus on building human capacities as a way of protecting human rights, but he also finds no inherent conflict between capacities and rights or between public reasoning and political power. Failing to respect this tension has bedeviled important strands in Western political thought. Recall Marx's famous vision at the end of the first part of "On the Jewish Question," where he declares:

> Human emancipation will only be complete when the real, individual man has absorbed into himself the abstract citizen; when, as an individual man, in his everyday life, in his work, and in his relationships, he has become a species-being; and when he has recognized and organized his own powers (*forces propres*) as social powers so that he no longer separates this social power from himself as *political* power (1978, p. 46).

Like Marx, Sen waves away the first constitutive paradox of the human and the political.[39] And in the case of efforts to implement Marx's ultimate practical agenda, the results have been decidedly mixed. As for Sen, development is a social and economic process that does not produce serious political conflict. In this respect, both he and Nussbaum reflect their intellectual debt to Aristotle (as well as Smith, Wollstonecraft, and Kant). For they have modernized and liberalized the Aristotelian process that "naturally" and smoothly (in theory if not in practice) between potentiality and actuality. Sen and Nussbaum make this move in order to avoid the limitations connoted by human rights conceived in the liberal tradition represented by John Rawls, which seeks to identify a human rights norm against which injustice and outliers may be judged. Sen seeks to overcome these limitations by more fulsomely integrating cultural diversity into the notion of human rights. But this effort mostly splits the difference between "rights" and "virtues," stipulating how the former can be shorn of its narrow individualism and the latter can lose its potential for corrosive collectivism, promoting cultural diversity without sanctioning unjust inequalities.[40]

Sen's confidence in his theory of human rights stems from his consideration of them solely from concern with the logical coherence of his definition. Attention to the practical coherence of instantiating it does not concern him – or only concerns him through the process of "public reasoning." Structural limitations that impede the development of public reasoning are relegated to the level of practical resistance to his theory. Similarly, when he conceptualizes democracy as "a universal value," a political order that can develop from any of the world's cultural traditions, he primarily considers democracy as a form of ethics rather than a form of power.[41] Thus, as examples of his conception of democracy as a universal value and government by discussion [*sic*], Sen invokes John Stuart Mill – a radical in the domestic politics of his own country, to be sure, but also a good civil servant for the British East India Company and its colonial ventures. Moreover, two of the examples Sen cites to demonstrate the central value of "government by discussion" as the key to both democracy and human rights – those of the Bengali famine and the Great Leap Forward – surely occurred in countries where the government did not operate through public discussion. But that avoids a prior question: Why did they have governments that avoided public discussion? Fulsome, diverse public debates certainly can improve public policy. But their energy and success depend on collective conditions of ethics and power which foster mutual respect, economic well-being for the many, and political equality for all – none of which immediately arise from public reasoning.

Tough political questions about the manner in which one is to relate ethics and power in particular collectivities are precisely those which Sen's capabilities approach avoids because its *telos* is freedom understood as self and social development rather than the exercise of collective power by the most ordinary human beings in society – that is, by a contemporary version of the *demos*. Sen translates his capabilities into actualities, like Rawls translates his rights into realities, by means of procedural reasoning that does not address the constitutive role played by politics in the determination of human goods. Ironically, while Sen and Nussbaum found historical and philosophical roots for their theory of capabilities in Aristotle, both minimize the manner in which human capacity for Aristotle was measured against the bar of exercising *both* political power *and* political ethics.

Anyone unable to participate practically in actually and effectively determining the political good for society had only partially achieved the development of his (*sic*) virtue and freedom. There were no human rights, per se, in ancient Greece (Burnyeat, 1994). One must attend to the means for achieving human virtues as the preconditions for achieving human rights. In practical terms, this must involve contestation, not just protection. In this vein, Sen's theory of human rights, like that of all liberals, highlights the rights or virtues of individuals in words but practically defaults to the power and authority of the state in deeds.[42]

The drafters of the *UDHR*, operating as an arm of the United Nations, never imagined that they actually were drafting a constitution of global ethics. But they hoped it would motivate states to move in the directions sanctioned by that document. They believed that it could generate a language for political legitimation on a global scale. It has generated attention to human rights as such a language, but its significations remain unclear and its productivity unsure. Among the various reasons that might account for this state of affairs is the manner in which human rights discourse has been shaped by the liberal ideologies of large and powerful nation-states. But the problem is not unique to liberalism or nation-states. For the constitutive paradoxes that belong to "human rights" tend to marginalize *both* the "human" in relation to the rights of their citizens (see Arendt) *and* the active exercise of the rights of their citizens in relation to the power of their states (see realist critiques of rights). As for those who continue to champion human rights as an international practice or as vindicated by the *UDHR* as a whole, one can only marvel at the extent to which they regard human rights as transpolitical phenomena – thereby sublimating the paradoxes that constitute the heart of modern conceptions of human rights.

REFORMING THE SECOND PARADOX: GOVERNING HUMANITY

This quandary generates the modernization of the second constitutive paradox – the effort to supplement the ethical deficiencies of governments that fail to honor human rights declarations and conventions by establishing and operating human rights or humanitarian nongovernmental organizations. Exasperated by the failure of states to live up to their commitments to the *UDHR* or attending covenants, humanitarian agencies and nongovernmental organizations have stepped into the breach – either identifying and potentially saving individuals suffering at the hands of their governments or naming and shaming those engaged in human rights abuses of various kinds. These organizations – such as Doctors Without Borders, Amnesty International, Human Rights Watch, not to mention the thousands of other NGOs in the global east, west, north, and south – surely have good intentions, seek to alter the behavior of governments for the better, and often do so. They have been constructive agents of change, often moving governments to end their most abusive ways and respect international human rights. They contribute mightily in making human rights a major concern of the United Nations.[43] They aid those who experience extreme suffering, generally as a result of forces beyond their control, and by and large do good deeds. At the same time, the principal modus operandi of NGOs typically takes the form of intervention – which tends to manifest itself as paternalism, depoliticization, and *either* indirect support for regimes that have instigated the suffering they would alleviate *or* the delegitimation of regimes they would like to enhance.

In the last decade, the unintended consequences of such interventionism have been notably exposed. Thus, policy analysts Marina Ottaway and Thomas Carothers, of the Washington, DC-based Carnegie Endowment for International Peace became skeptical of efforts by NGOs to democratize civil society in authoritarian or post-authoritarian societies. They were radically limited by their narrow political basis and dependence on funding from foreign sources (Ottaway & Carothers, 2000). For them, "nation-building" as an international enterprise of promoting "democracy" and "human rights" does not receive "two thumbs up." Correlatively, the journalist David Rieff offers a bitter critique of humanitarianism after having noted that, in Serbia, humanitarian relief efforts unintentionally propped up or protected agents of violent regimes (Rieff, 2002). The Harvard Law School professor David Kennedy, also noted the inherently political and contextual character of humanitarian relief efforts. For him, following international law on the ground may well have unwanted, unintentional consequences; a more pragmatic and political approach is needed (Kennedy, 2004).

Humanitarian organizations and other human rights NGOs presuppose, often rightly, that the citizens of various countries are unwilling or unable to care for themselves. Need it be said, that often is the case. Jews could have used more than a little outside help in dealing with the Nazis during the 1930s. The residents of Darfur need outside help, as do the people of Bahrain, Congo, North Korea, Saudi Arabia, and Haiti (even though the latter may be said to have received too much outside help).[44] So do the citizens of Iran, Iraq, and Afghanistan – not to mention the stateless Palestinians. But are NGOs – businesses of good samaritans and the flag-bearers of human rights acting in the context of a weak United Nations or powerful and self-interested, if not overtly terrible, states – the place where our energies and money ought to flow?

Perhaps social movements should become the locus of our human rights energies. But if they succeed, they, too, become institutionalized and face many of the political problems they previously bracketed (Stammers, 2009). In that case, the first constitutive paradox of human rights reasserts itself, insofar as the *human* has become institutionalized as a form of *political* power. One must wonder whether these organizations and movements are side-stepping, and not addressing, the sources of hegemonic *power* and *injustice* that ravage the lives of millions of human beings – phenomena that inevitably involve interactions of individuals and institutions and making judgments about them. But doing so is difficult for a human rights or humanitarian organization, insofar as they maintain their status in the United States, for example, by being (relatively speaking) "nonpolitical." The problem is further evidenced by the fact that the boundaries between human rights law, which are supposed to apply prior to the outbreak of war, are merging with those of humanitarian law, which apply during or immediately after war (e.g., see Chandler, 2001). The boundaries between the political and nonpolitical, war and peace, are becoming more difficult to discern. This new merger is reflected in the efforts of the group associated with the phrase "Responsibility to Protect" (R2P), a policy adopted by the United Nations in 2005 which attempts to codify terms that justify internationally-based military intervention in order to prevent humanitarian suffering and protect human rights.[45] But will this prevent or instigate unnecessary violence?[46]

Perhaps the problems human rights and humanitarian organizations address are most clearly and cogently understood when their more traditional definitions remain in place – when human rights count as the preconditions or guideposts for, rather than the principled expression of, justice, and humanitarianism is regarded not as an activist project but as a remedy for suffering caused by political agents.[47] Indeed, how does one use the discourse of human rights to identify and comparatively evaluate the injustices experienced by Iranians under an authoritarian regime; Iraqis suffering from the aftermath of the regime of Saddam Hussein and the invasion of the Americans; Afghans who have to choose between a corrupt government, a zealously militant, religious, and patriarchal guerrilla network, and an army of Westerners that would benefit them even as they bomb them – not to mention the experiences of the Palestinians as people under Israeli occupation, ruled by manipulating politicians, and abandoned by their neighboring Arab states? Is the problem to be understood in terms of whether their experience of abuse can or cannot be found under the articles of human rights law *or* whether there can be agents for the amelioration of their indignant conditions? I do not mean to suggest that these questions have easy answers, but *not* asking or addressing them assures unnecessary harm and destruction in light of which assertions of human rights function merely as rhetorical cover.

CONCLUSION

The notion of human rights nonetheless retains moral and political appeal, for millions of human beings as well as thousands of academics. Is there a way to make it more politically effective for the individuals on whose behalf the *UDHR* was designed? I think there is, and in a manner that draws on, even as it departs from, the *UDHR* and human rights as a practice. The *first* step in doing so is to recognize that the constitutive paradoxes of the *UDHR* characterize any version of human rights that would aspire to be a beacon for international or global political ethics. The *second* is to recollect the motivation of the *UDHR* as a restraint on the power of states. But rather than immediately identifying states as the primary agents for defining the extent of such restraint, determine the manner in which "the many" in different societies have reason to demand better behavior from states. Even so, and *third*, one must appreciate how the power of humanity is still principally actualized through the power of states, so that the realization of human rights depends on ongoing activities of political membership. Insofar as such rights amount to claims that such activities are goods for states, they amount to political calls for *political virtues* as much as human rights – unrealized virtues that need to complement politically calls for rights that human beings are not currently able to exercise. *Fourth*, a working conception of human rights that protect and promote human well-being must recognize that they only will flourish in democratic political orders – just as the *UDHR* asserts. But such democracies will only enhance and effect human rights if the power they exercise in sustaining their political order primarily derives from the many rather than the few. Insofar as such human power cannot plausibly be exercised in a unified, global manner, it has to be rooted in a plurality of *demoi* asserting a plurality of virtues more than from those few whose official roles are to protect the law, order, and Gross Domestic Product of nation-states. This mandate may seem overly optimistic, particularly because these states depend upon receipts from capitalist economies. But the state is more than a business enterprise, and, despite practical efforts to the contrary, fellow citizens treat one another as more and better than consumers. One might substantively associate the political agenda of such *demoi* at least with the protection of the environment and decreasing the gap between rich and poor.[48]

These conditions for generating greater coherence for a contemporary conception of human rights are surely steep. They indicate that it must not be understood primarily as the civil and political rights officially upheld by liberal democratic states – important as they are to protect. Nor must it rely on definitions of human rights that derive from normative, institutionalized practice. Instead, it ought to define the human beings whose well-being would be safeguarded in the *UDHR* primarily as citizens who authoritatively constitute the power of the state in which they are members – democracy understood as political direction by the *demos* rather than as consensual deference to elites. And it must recognize that the rights to which human beings are to aspire cannot be limited to the security rights fitfully protected by the institutions of state power. Instead, it must recognize that the only way to harness the power of the state for good rather than ill is to understand "human rights" as functional and ethical virtues that require manifold material and cultural conditions for their achievement.

Because of these two paradoxes, and despite the supportive armor of international human rights law – not to mention the attractive character of human rights as a principal banner for myriad political actors – human rights function mostly as a dependent, rather than independent, concept in political ethics. As a result, if human rights are to occupy a unique and valuable position in a political discourse that promotes the well-being of most human persons, if not humanity, then it ought *not* to be understood primarily in the grandiose terms offered by official documents and authorized agents of political legitimation or philosophical justification – via, for example, the dominant discourses of liberal rights or human capacities. Despite the pretensions of much human rights discourse to define what human beings universally ought to have as their protected, normal condition, I argue that it is best rendered as a form of politically engaged ethical criticism that operates on the margin of public realms and the agendas of established political actors.

In this role, it can fulfill its potential as a variegated standard of virtue for transnational political ethics in a world whose codeword for political legitimacy is democracy. Human rights have served as a principal locus for significant political debates about democracy and political virtue in the post-1948 world of international politics and transnational cultures. It is an ethical and political concept whose usage contributes to local, national, and global practices; as such, it warrants critical analysis and theoretical exposition. But whether its conception warrants practical support depends on the appreciation of its paradoxical character and a savvy, practical appreciation of how it might be productively employed. In this way, my argument seeks to deconstruct the popular, policy-driven, state-sponsored linkage of democracy and human rights that occurs frequently in the discourse of governmental officials and to reconstruct it in a way that strengthens its utility for ethical criticism rather than legitimation – while noting the myriad ways in which human rights functions as signs of pluralized global virtue in the discourses of contemporary political democracies.[49]

These conditions do not forecast an easy path for practically articulating or actualizing the promise of human rights. But at least they preserve human rights as a critical tool that benefits ordinary human beings rather than an ideological tool that legitimizes the power of hegemonic discourses and dominant states. They define human rights as a paradoxical, political concern, in which a productive linkage between human rights as words and deeds stems from, rather than constrains, rule by the people. If human rights depend upon and express these critical virtues they can begin to accommodate the political boundaries and moral horizons – the civil, political, economic, social, nondiscriminatory, egalitarian, and cultural dimensions – of the human rights that inform them as "the highest aspiration of the common people."[50]

NOTES

1. To be sure, interpreters find the idea of human right, if not human rights, in the work of Thomas Aquinas (see Finnis, 1998, pp. 135–138).
2. The abstentions came from Belorussia, Czechoslovakia, Poland, Saudi Arabia, Ukraine, South Africa, USSR, and Yugoslavia.
3. Numerous, plausible histories of this idea exist. For example, see Lauren (1998/2003). For a more recent history that emphasizes its usage in post-1989 political discourse, see Moyn (2010). For an introductory presentation of the necessarily contingent and contested character of human rights, see Sarat and

Kearns (2002). For a reasonable attempt to categorize usages of "human rights" as a concept that lacks the paradoxical features I associate with it, see Marie-Benedicte Dembour, who offers an illuminating grid for understanding the different ways in which agents deployment conceptions of human rights, in, What Are Human Rights? Four Schools of Thought (2010, pp. 1–20). The title of her article refers to "schools of *thought*" (my italics), but she identifies them according to the practical motivations of their agents. The schools named and discussed are those of "natural scholars," "deliberative scholars," "protest scholars," and "discourse scholars."

4. For example, in his "Four Freedoms" speech of 1940 and his articulation in his State of the Union Address of 1941 of a second Bill of Rights for Americans to complement the United States' Constitution of 1789 and the attending Bill of Rights of 1791.

5. The proclivity to treat "human rights" as a coherent, practical, and conceptual object informs the interpretive framework of the major "human rights" journals and appears in the most sophisticated, recent treatments of some of the subjects indicated by its invocation (see Kateb, 2011; Meister, 2011).

6. In this article, Habermas seems engaged in a debate with John Rawls's political theory of human rights, which appeared in the latter's last original. *The Law of Peoples* (1999). Of course, Habermas has discussed the idea of human rights in his earlier works. For example, see Habermas (1996, esp. 3.1), which reappears in slightly modified form in his *The Inclusion of the Other: Studies in Political Theory* (Cronin & de Greiff, Eds., 1996/1998). Also see his "Remarks on Legitimation Through Human Rights," in his book, *The Postnational Constellation: Political Essays* (Habermas, 2001), reprinted as "On Legitimation Through Human Rights," in *Global Justice and Transnational Politics* (Cronin & de Greiff, Eds., 2002).

7. This is the subtitle of Power and Allison's edited collection.

8. The consignment of critical interpretation of the conception of human rights as currently used to the analytical dustbin is recommended by Raymond Geuss, in his account of human rights as "white magic." See his penetrating discussion of this and other topics in his book, *History and Illusion in Politics* (2001, p. 152). I do not presume to refashion criticisms of "rights talk" that have been lodged since the eighteenth and nineteenth centuries and have continued to be made in the twentieth and twenty-first centuries against natural rights – namely, those by the traditional conservative, Edmund Burke; the utilitarian institutionalist, Jeremy Bentham; and the anti-liberal, anti-capitalist, and communist theorist, Karl Marx, or natural law theorists – against the logical or political coherence and practical value of an idea of secular, equal rights for human beings. Aspects of these criticisms – in their own right or recast by deconstructionist, pragmatist, poststructuralist, postcolonial, feminist, or simply realist thought – surely have significant value as warnings about abusive interpretations of what we presuppose as the conceptual framework for human rights. The seminal analytical account of these problematic features of natural or human rights discourse in the last 55 years remains that of H. L. A. Hart (1984). For a natural law perspective on human rights, see Glendon (1991). But human rights as a feature of political discourse is not unusually utopian; it simply has become, as has been noted, the *esperanto* of global political ethics.

9. For examples of philosophical analyses, see the work of Jurgen Habermas and John Rawls – discussed below. The ethnographic treatment of human rights discourse has become a cottage industry for anthropologists, and the results have been highly instructive. For good compendiums of recent works, see *American Anthropologist* (2006), which includes articles by Jane K. Cowan, Mark Goodale, Sally Engle Merry, Annelise Riles, and Richard Ashby Wilson, and *Human Rights: An Anthropological Reader* (2009). However, many of these professional anthropologists, once they engage in theorizing about the conceptual status of human rights, too readily affirm a division between the approaches of apodictally minded political philosophers and empirically minded ethnographers. See particularly the pieces by Goodale and Cown in Goodale (2006). Doing so begs too many questions about what human rights consist of and why. See my discussion below.

10. For recognition of the signal function of human rights in international political ethics (see Beitz, 2009, p. 1).

11. These remarks were catalyzed by the neo-realist, critical, and analytical criticism of human rights discourse of Raymond Geuss (2001, pp. 138–146, *nb* 144, 152). They are more directly focused than his were on various discursive attempts to make human rights a moral and political force for justice.

12. See the work of Lynn Hunt, Costas Douzinas, Upendra Baxi, and many others. My previous treatment of this aspect of human rights appears in my piece, "Human Rights as an Ethics of Power" in *Human Rights in the 'War on Terror'* (2005).

13. That said, the human rights theorist Upendra Baxi has called our current environment "post-human." See *Human Rights in a Post-Human World* (Baxi, 2007), a collection of pieces that update and rely upon his previous book *The Future of Human Rights* (2000).

14. It is possible to find traces of the ethical and political aspirations associated with "human rights" in major documents written in pre-Roman or non-Western times. See those noted in Ishay (2004). But to extend the notion of human rights to include all of those sources blurs the boundaries between human rights discourse as codified in international covenants and conventions and every moral idea notably articulated in the history of the human race.

15. On ancient Greek ideas of virtue, see Guthrie (1971) and with conceptual specificity and historicity by Plato, in his dialogue, *Protagoras*. Also, see Dover (1974). For a recent formulation of the virtue of human dignity in naturalistic terms, see Kateb's *Human Dignity*.

16. This is not to say that "humanitarian interventions" may have political value, but using this term to identify deeply political actions gauged to alter the political conduct of power in particular societies converts a term of international political ethics into rhetorical legerdemain. See my, "Is 'Humanitarian Intervention' a Hoax?" Also, see note 46, infra.

17. See the articles in Wilson (1997) and Cowan, Dembour, and Wilson (2001).

18. Eduardo Rabossi and Richard Rorty, in the latter's "Human Rights, Rationality, and Sentimentality," in *On Human Rights* (1993, pp. 111–134).

19. The radical contrast between *zoe* – a natural function – and *bios* – a human creation is put to interesting use by the Italian theorist Giorgio Agamben. But while

he draws it from Aristotle, Aristotle's texts and theories do not warrant the categorical division between the two that Agamben finds so crucial for his theory of *homo sacer* and the post-totalitarian politics of "the camp." See his *Homo Sacer: Sovereign Power and Bare Life* (1998).

20. For a useful narrative that relates these nineteenth century struggles to the discourse of human rights (see Ishay 2004).

21. The notion of "dignity" as a foundation for contemporary human rights discourse has been championed by Habermas, on Kantian grounds (supra, note 6), and Jeremy Waldron, on utilitarian grounds. See Waldron's "Dignity and Rank" (2007). But this effort to democratize "standing" across borders still misses the matters of power and context raised here.

22. For interesting analyses of the idea, see Jeffrey Isaac (1996) and James D. Ingram (2008).

23. For a clear and useful attempt to articulate normative standards for the politics of human rights promoted by "the international community," see Beitz's *The Idea of Human Rights.*

24. See Michael Goodhart's *Democracy as Human Rights.*

25. Thus see, for example, Isaiah Berlin (1969), Maurice Cranston (1962, 1983), Rawls (1999), and Michael Ignatieff (2000).

26. Rawls, *The Law of Peoples*, p. vi.

27. Rawls, *The Law of Peoples*, p. 10.

28. Rawls, *The Law of Peoples*, p. 93.

29. Rawls, *The Law of Peoples*, pp. 4, 27, 65, 78–81.

30. Rawls, *The Law of Peoples*, p. 80.

31. While Rawls's book received immediate criticism upon publication in professional circles because of disappointing those of his followers who had hoped he would extend the difference principle to the international arena, its greater attention to culture and political differences as considerations equal to those of economic inequality is not inconsistent with the middle ground carved out by *A Theory of Justice* and *Political Liberalism*, only now the subject domain has changed. Indeed, it has received renewed scholarly attention (see Martin & Reidy, 2006).

32. For Beitz's specific analysis of Rawls's view of human rights in *The Law of Peoples*, in which he spells out his debt to Rawlsian liberalism and criticism of the stipulative role and meaning of human rights in Rawls's book, see *The Idea of Human Rights*, pp. 96–102.

33. In Beitz's words (*The Idea of Human Rights*, p. 128), "… a practice of human rights … might be described as 'statist' in at least two senses: its standards apply in the first instance to states, and they rely on states, individually and collectively, as their principal guarantors … The practice of human rights as it has been developed so far can only be understood as a revisionist appurtenance of world order of independent, territorial states."

34. Samantha Power, who previously worked under Ignatieff at Harvard and is now a member of President Obama's foreign policy team, vigorously advocates American military intervention to avoid humanitarian catastrophes – in, for example, Sudan and Libya.

35. For a critique of Ignatieff's conception of human rights that also places it in a broader, theoretical context, see Wallach (2005).

36. See Martha Nussbaum's "Capabilities and Human Rights" (2002) and her recent attempt to popularize her perspective, *Creating Capabilities: The Human Development Approach* (2011).

37. There have been numerous studies of Sen's work over the past decade, particularly in the work of his Nobel Prize in Economics decade. A recent collection of particular note is *Measuring Justice: Primary Goods and Capabilities* (2010).

38. In this vein, Sen's contributions to the development of the UNDP's *Human Development Index* has provided a highly useful tool.

39. See Sen's *Development as Freedom*, "Elements of a Theory of Human Rights", and *The Idea of Justice*.

40. For articles about this debate, see *Measuring Justice*.

41. See Sen's "Democracy as a Universal Value" and *The Idea of Justice* (pp. 324–328).

42. It is worth noting how readily concerns about human rights in American society, which prides itself and its liberalism as being their unmatched champion, regularly makes considerations of state trump human rights in practical determinations of foreign policy. Recently, journalists have noted how the Obama administration has downplayed insistence by the United States on human rights or democracy in the politics of the countries with which it has diplomatic relations. But it is not clear that this marks a reduction of the United States's government's devotion to human rights or the emergence of a more parched conception of them – particularly if one considers the record of previous American administrations. The marginal role of human rights in President Obama's political rhetoric is less a move away from interest in human rights or democracy than an illustration of how devotion to human rights by the American government only emerges when it comports with strategic interests. For agitated journalistic commentary, see Sarah E. Mendelson (2009) and Joshua Kurlantzick (2010).

43. For an extremely useful narrative account of the role of NGOs in efforts to promote international human rights and justice, see William Korey (1998).

44. The United States Institute of Peace, "Haiti: The Republic of NGOs?" April 10, 2010.

45. President Obama actually used the phrase, "responsibility to protect," in his letter to Congress seeking their support for his arguably illegal use of executive power to authorize the use of American military power to enforce a "no-fly" zone in Libya – something his secretary of defense had previously and publicly argued against.

46. See *Responsibility to Protect: Report of the International Commission on Intervention and State Sovereignty* (IDRC Books, 2002), principally the work of Gareth Evans (2009). Another major architect from the academy was Thomas G. Weiss, who has written a primer for understanding R2P (as it has come to be called): *Humanitarian Intervention – Ideas in Action*, with a foreword by Gareth Evans (2007). Not surprisingly, this project has its supporters and critics. For examples of the former, see Cooper and Kohler (2009) and Bass (2008). For the latter, see Pattison (2010).

47. For example, American humanitarian organizations began to enhance their capacity for helping the people of Iraq *before* the American invasion of March 2003. See *The New York Times*. Similarly, in the near term aftermath of the downfall of Saddam Hussein's regime, American troops in Iraq were given three weeks of training in human rights laws and norms – a program that was disbanded not long after.

48. By invoking the term *demoi*, I do not mean to associate my argument with the neo-Habermasian theory of global *demoi* intelligently put forth by James Bohman (2007).

49. This linkage is a staple of the official discourse of American foreign policy, whether it involves (episodically) chastising the politics of the People's Republic of Iraq or justifying the invasions of Afghanistan and Iraq. There have been recent efforts to join democracy and human rights as part of a critical political theory, but this work often begs the question of the relationship between democracy and human rights in discourses of public legitimation.

50. From the second clause of the preamble to *The Universal Declaration of Human Rights*.

REFERENCES

Agamben, G. (1998). *Homo Sacer: Sovereign power and bare life* (D. Heller-Roaze, Trans.). Stanford: Stanford University Press.

Balfour, I., & Cadava, E. (2004). The claims of human rights: An introduction. *South Atlantic Quarterly, 103,* 293.

Bass, G. J. (2008). *Freedom's battle: The origins of humanitarian intervention.* New York, NY: Knopf.

Baxi, U. (2007). *Human rights in a post-human world.* New Delhi: Oxford University Press.

Baxi, U. (2000). *The future of human rights.* New Delhi: Oxford University Press.

Beitz, C. R. (2009). *The idea of human rights.* Oxford: Oxford University Press.

Berlin, I. (1969). Two concepts of liberty. *Berlin, Four Concepts of Liberty.* New York, NY: Oxford University Press.

Bohman, J. (2007). *Democracy across borders: From* demos *to* demoi. Cambridge, MA: MIT Press.

Brown, W. (2004). "The most we can hope for": Human rights and the politics of fatalism. *South Atlantic Quarterly, 103,* 461–462.

Burnyeat, M. (1994). Did the ancient Greeks have a concept of human rights? *Polis, 13,* 1–11.

Chandler, D. (2001). The road to military humanitarianism – How the human rights NGOs shaped a new humanitarian agenda. *Human Rights Quarterly, 23*(3), 678–700.

Connolly, W. E. (1974/1983). *The terms of political discourse* (2nd ed.). Princeton, NJ: Princeton University Press.

Cooper, R. H., & Kohler, J. V. (Eds.). (2009). *The responsibility to protect: Global moral compact for the twenty-first century.* New York, NY: Palgrave Macmillan.

Cowan, J. K., Dembour, M.-B., & Wilson, R. A. (Eds.). (2001). *Culture and rights: Anthropological perspectives.* Cambridge: Cambridge University Press.

Cranston, M. (1962). *Human rights today.* London: Ampersand Books.

Cranston, M. (1983). *Human rights*. Cambridge, MA: American Academy of Arts and Sciences.

Dembour, M-B. (2010). What are human rights? Four schools of thought. *Human Rights Quarterly, 32,* 1–20.

Dover, K. J. (1974). *Greek popular morality in the time of Plato and Aristotle*. Berkeley, CA: University of California Press.

Evans, G. (2009). *The responsibility to protect: Ending mass atrocity*. Washington, DC: Brookings Institution Press.

Finnis, J. A. (1998). *Aquinas*. Oxford: Oxford University Press.

Gallie, W. B. (1955–1956). Essentially contested concepts. *Proceedings of the Aristotelian Society, 56,* 167–198.

Geuss, R. (2001). *History and illusion in politics*. Cambridge: Cambridge University Press.

Glendon, M. (1991). *Rights talk: The impoverishment of political discourse*. New York, NY: The Free Press.

Goodale, M. (2006). In focus: Anthropology and human rights in a new key. *American Anthropologist, 108,* 1–83.

Goodale, M. (2009). Introduction. In: M. Goodale (Ed.), *Human rights: An anthropological reader*. Wiley-Blackwell.

Goodhart, M. J. (2005). *Democracy as human rights: Freedom and equality in the age of globalization*. New York, NY: Routledge.

Guthrie, W. K. C. (1971). *The sophists*. Cambridge: Cambridge University Press.

Habermas, J. (1996). *Between facts and norm: Contributions to a discourse theory of law and democracy* (W. Rehg, Trans.). Cambridge, MA: MIT Press.

Habermas, J. (1996/1998). The inclusion of the other: Studies in political theory. In: C. Cronin & P. de Greiff (Eds.), *Human rights: Global and internal*. Cambridge, MA: MIT Press (Especially Part IV).

Habermas, J. (2001). Remarks on legitimation through human rights. *The postnational constellation: Political essays* (M. Pensky, Trans.). Cambridge, MA: MIT Press.

Habermas, J. (2010). Human dignity and the realistic utopia of human rights. *Metaphilosophy, 41,* 464–480.

Hart, H. L. A. (1984). Are there any natural rights? In: J. Waldron (Ed.), *Theories of rights*. New York, NY: Oxford University Press.

Hunt, L. (2000). The paradoxical origins of human rights. In: J. N. Wasserstrom, L. Hunt & M. B. Young (Eds.), *Human rights and revolutions* (pp. 3–18). Lanham, MD: Rowman & Littlefield.

Hunt, L. (2008). *Inventing human rights*. New York, NY: W. W. Norton.

IDRC Books. (2002). *Responsibility to protect: Report of the International Commission on Intervention and State Sovereignty*. Ottawa: IDRC Books.

Ignatieff, M. (2000). *Human rights as politics and idolatry*. Princeton, NJ: Princeton University Press.

Ignatieff, M. (2004). *The lesser evil: Political ethics in an age of terror*. Princeton, NJ: Princeton University Press.

Ingram, J. D. (2008). What is a "right to have rights"? Three images of the politics of human rights. *American Political Science Review, 102,* 401–416.

Isaac, J. (1996). A new guarantee on earth: Hannah Arendt on human dignity and the politics of human rights. *American Political Science Review, 90,* 61–84.

Ishay, M. (2004). *The history of human rights: From ancient times to the globalization era*. Berkeley, CA: University of California Press.

Kant, I. (1980). Perpetual peace: A philosophical sketch. In: H. Reiss (Ed.), *Kant: Political writings*. Cambridge: Cambridge University Press.

Kateb, G. (2011). *Human dignity*. Cambridge, MA: Harvard University Press.

Kennedy, D. (2004). *The dark sides of virtue: Reassessing international humanitarianism*. Princeton, NJ: Princeton University Press.

Korey, W. (1998). *NGOs and the universal declaration of human rights: A curious grapevine*. New York, NY: St. Martin's Press.

Kurlantzick, J. (2010). The downfall of human rights. *Newsweek*, March 1.

Lauren, P. G. (1998/2003). *The evolution of international human rights: Visions seen*. Philadelphia, PA: University of Pennsylvania Press.

Martin, R., & Reidy, D. A. (Eds.). (2006). *Rawls's law of peoples: A realistic utopia?* Oxford: Blackwell.

Marx, K. (1978). On the Jewish question. In: R. Tucker (Ed.), *The Marx-Engels reader* (2nd ed.). New York, NY: W. W. Norton.

Meister, R. (2011). *After evil: A politics of human rights*. New York, NY: Columbia University Press.

Mendelson, S. E. (2009). Dusk or dawn for the human rights movement. *The Washington Quarterly*, *32*, 103–120.

Moyn, S. (2010). *The last utopia: Human rights in history*. Cambridge, MA: Harvard University Press.

Nussbaum, M. (2002). Capabilities and human rights. In: C. Cronin & P. de Greiff (Eds.), *Global justice and transnational politics* (pp. 117–149). Cambridge, MA: MIT Press.

Nussbaum, M. (2011). *Creating capabilities: The human development approach*. Cambridge, MA: Harvard University Press.

Ottaway, M., & Carothers, T. (2000). *Funding virtue: Civil society and democracy promotion*. Washington, DC: Carnegie Endowment for International Peace.

Pattison, J. (Ed.) (2010). *Humanitarian intervention and the responsibility to protect: Who should intervene?* New York, NY: Oxford University Press.

Power, S., & Allison, G. (Eds.). (2000). *Realizing human rights: Moving from inspiration to impact*. New York, NY: St. Martin's Press.

Rawls, J. (1999). *The law of peoples*. Cambridge, MA: Harvard University Press.

Rieff, D. (2002). *A bed for the night: Humanitarianism in crisis*. New York, NY: Simon & Schuster.

Rorty, R. (1993). Human rights, rationality, and sentimentality. In: S. Shute (Ed.), *On human rights – Oxford amnesty lectures* (pp. 111–134). New York, NY: Basic Books.

Sarat, A., & Kearns, T. R. (2002). The unsettled status of human rights: An introduction. In: A. Sarat & T. R. Kearns (Eds.), *Human rights: Concepts, contests, and contingencies* (pp. 1–24). Ann Arbor, MI: University of Michigan Press.

Sen, A. (1999a). Democracy as a universal value. *Journal of Democracy*, *10*, 3–17.

Sen, A. (1999b). *Development as freedom*. New York, NY: Knopf.

Sen, A. (2004). Elements of a theory of human rights. *Philosophy and Public Affairs*, *32*, 315–356.

Sen, A. (2009). *The idea of justice* (pp. 228–238). Cambridge, MA: Harvard University Press.

Sen, A. (2010) *Measuring justice: Primary goods and capabilities*. Cambridge: Cambridge University Press (edited by Harry Brighouse and Ingrid Robeyns).

Stammers, N. (2009). *Human rights and social movements.* London: Pluto Press.

Waldron, J. (2007). Dignity and rank. *European Journal of Sociology, 48*(2), 201–237.

Wallach, J. R. (2005). Human rights as an ethics of power. In: R. A. Wilson (Ed.), *Human rights in the 'war on terror'.* Cambridge: Cambridge University Press.

Weiss, T. G. (2007). *Humanitarian intervention – Ideas in action.* Cambridge, MA: Polity Press.

Wilson, R. A. (1997). Introduction. In: R. A. Wilson (Ed.), *Human rights, culture and context: Anthropological perspectives.* London: Pluto Press.

FINDING A PLACE FOR MARGINAL MIGRANTS IN THE INTERNATIONAL HUMAN RIGHTS SYSTEM

Leila Kawar

ABSTRACT

This chapter examines how international human rights law is shaping the politics of immigration. It argues that migrant human rights are neither conceptually nor practically incompatible with an international order premised upon state territorial sovereignty, and that the specific aesthetics of the contemporary international human rights system, namely its formalistic and legalistic tendencies, has facilitated its integration with a realm of policymaking traditionally reserved to state discretion. An exploration of two areas in the emerging field of migrant human rights traces the multi-scalar transnational legal processes through which these norms are formulated and internalized.

INTRODUCTION

In the "golden period" of human rights (Falk, 2009) that followed the end of the Cold War, a number of citizenship and immigration scholars

Special Issue: Human Rights: New Possibilities/New Problems
Studies in Law, Politics, and Society, Volume 56, 67–90
ISSN: 1059-4337/doi:10.1108/S1059-4337(2011)0000056006

announced that international human rights norms would soon transform the politics of migration. Arguing provocatively against Arendt's claim that "rights of man" are nil if not encoded in citizen rights by nation-states, they posited that the spread of human rights discourses would create a new place for "guests and aliens" within the law. The "transnationalization" of the legal regime most intimately tied to the principles of state territorial sovereignty was seen to herald a new world order in which human rights would replace citizenship as the primary marker of political affiliation.

While some of these analyses centered on the discursive implications of changes in national laws allowing migrants access to social services programs (Layton-Henry, 1990; Soysal, 1994), others were more juridically oriented, arguing that international legal regimes would imminently overpower restrictionist immigration laws. Among the more ambitious of these transnationalist claims was Saskia Sassen's suggestion that the distinction between the citizen and the alien was being eroded as part of a more general reformulation of territory, authority, and rights that she linked to structural changes in the global economic system (1996). Sassen argued that in the new transnational order based on human rights, and enforced through international law, even unauthorized migrants would be able to claim rights to residence and to family reunification. David Jacobson made similar claims (1996), arguing that the contemporary phenomenon of intensive transnational migration undermines the relevance and legitimacy of nationally based models of membership. According to Jacobson, international human rights codes and institutions provide a new model that is more appropriate to current conditions. He suggests that the judiciary is playing a crucial role in this development by encouraging individuals and NGOs to make claims on the basis of international human rights instruments.

However, not all scholars have been so optimistic about the capacity of human rights norms to transform immigration policies. One set of criticism is based on a perceived irreconcilability at the conceptual level between human rights and immigration control. The contemporary international human rights system, whether embodied in the United Nations (UN) or in regional treaty-based structures, is built upon agreements between nation-states who enjoy complete sovereignty in matters of citizenship. Because they exist only upon the concession of nation-states, the rights of aliens bear the heavy mark of the state's immigration powers and are destined to remain "stratified and reversible" (Joppke, 2010). Obligating states to grant rights to immigrants is conceptually incompatible with a fundamental premise of the international system.

A related set of criticisms is empirically based and focuses on the manner in which national judiciaries have integrated human rights principles into immigration law. As a matter of practice, judicial decisions do grant rights to immigrants but they do so on the basis of national law or international treaties that states find it in their interests to sign. Looking at this empirical record, scholars have variously argued that judicial recognition of immigrant and refugee rights has been animated by the commitment of the judiciary either to norms of equal protection (Guiraudon, 2000) or to principles of reasoned decision making (Dauvergne, 2008). Not only are references to human rights absent from most of these decisions, but analysis of the existing jurisprudence also suggests that human rights advocates are most likely to win their cases when they frame them not as immigration cases, but rather as administrative law cases or civil rights cases (Motomura, 2008). Based on the results of these empirical studies, and with the benefit of hindsight, it seems clear that transnational theorists overestimated the power of international human rights norms to transform immigration jurisprudence.

Nevertheless, I argue in this chapter that it is too soon to categorically dismiss the potential for international human rights norms to shape the set of rights accorded to marginal migrants. As Derrida reminds us, laws as they are embodied in the Western tradition of state-sanctioned rights are inherently capable of according rights to foreigners and strangers (2000, p. 19). Moreover, the particular epistemic qualities of human rights law, which make this body of law both more and less compatible with the positivist vision of law than critics of transnationalism have acknowledged, also imbue human rights principles with the capacity to infuse a range of other existing legal regimes governing migration. On the one hand, international human rights law has become sufficiently formalized and technocratic so as to be typified by conditional rather than absolute formulations of rights, thus preempting claims of conceptual incompatibility with sovereign authority. On the other hand, when it comes to implementation, the norms contained in international human rights instruments are enforced through a process that is decentralized, diffuse, and fundamentally distinct from the positivist vision of law as the command of the sovereign. This means that international human rights norms may well make their way into migration-related policies even when states refuse to ratify international conventions and even if national courts refuse to cite international principles as direct authority.

I illustrate these claims by examining two sets of transnational processes that have formulated and implemented a human rights approach to marginal migrants: (1) the substantial cross-fertilization between refugee law and human rights law and (2) the as yet less developed but potentially far-reaching cross-fertilization of migrant labor standards and human rights law. Conceptualizing international human rights law as being simultaneously positivistic in its formulation and nonpositivistic in its implementation allows us to see that, contrary to the claims of previous scholarship, the body of law governing marginal migrants is neither categorically opposed to human rights in principle nor incompatible with human rights in practice. Instead of asserting overly broad claims about the sources and scope of migrant rights, what is needed is a close and careful analysis of the transnational chain of actors and activities through which new forms of migrant human rights are being produced. Using two case studies, this chapter traces these processes by which marginal migrants are being constructed through law as rights-bearing individuals.

THE LEGALIZATION OF HUMAN RIGHTS

The contemporary system of international human rights came into being only after the Second World War, based upon the UN Charter, the Nuremberg and Tokyo war crimes trials, and the Universal Declaration of Human Rights. Within this system, the principal enforcers of human rights law are nation-states. The approach to human rights that the international "community" initially adopted was primarily aspirational. "The rules were largely declaratory and precatory, and the few mechanisms created had virtually no enforcement" (Koh, 1999, 1408).

It was not until the mid-1960s that international institutions began to undertake a "gradual assumption of responsibility" for developing and implementing human rights law (Alston, 1992). Spurred by the influx of newly independent states, the UN finally adopted the two conventions that together form the International Bill of Rights as well as the Convention on the Elimination of All Forms of Racial Discrimination. Initial steps were also taken toward strengthening the international institutions that would enforce this new body of law. In the 1970s, the UN Commission on Human Rights, which had been largely inactive for its first 20 years of existence, was given the power to examine complaints filed against states by individuals and groups and was also empowered to initiate inquiries into "thematic" – as opposed to country specific – violations (Steiner & Alston, 2008).

The political climate of the late 1970s proved propitious for the expansion and legalization of human rights. Political rights in particular received increased attention from activists looking for a "neutral" alternative to the perceived excesses of both authoritarian and totalitarian states, coinciding with shifts in US foreign policy rhetoric during the post-Vietnam Carter Administration that created openings for the institutionalization of human rights structures within the UN. The higher profile given to human rights issues by the Carter Administration and several of its allies "contributed to a climate in which task expansion was almost an imperative" (Alston, 1992, p. 361). The result was that a bureaucratic momentum in support of international human rights was set in place, allowing the legalization of human rights to further develop (Falk, 2009).

Despite the return to Cold War diplomacy during the 1980s, this process of legalization continued. The UN General Assembly enacted a series of human rights conventions aimed at eliminating discrimination against women, prohibiting torture, and protecting the rights of children. As these treaties acquired sufficient state ratifications to enter into force, committees to monitor their implementation came into being. These monitoring committees were staffed with technical experts who tended to represent their expertise more than the priorities of their countries of origin when reviewing reports on treaty compliance submitted by ratifying countries (Haas, 2008).

In the post-Cold War period, the declared victory of the capitalist West and the collapse of the Communist block created a normative vacuum on the world stage, strengthening international institutions and giving renewed energy to international human rights law. New structures, such as the Office of the High Commissioner on Human Rights and the Ad-Hoc International Criminal Tribunals, were created. The UN sponsored a series of major international conferences focused on human rights, most significantly the 1993 World Conference on Human Rights in Vienna. The commitment of the Ford Foundation to funding human rights NGOs injected additional energy into this increasingly professionalized field (Cummings, 2007; Keck & Sikkink, 1998). Recent studies suggest that human rights treaty-based institutions, which initially had difficulty being taken seriously, are gaining increased attention, with national delegations preparing lengthy reports assessing the national implementation of international human rights law (Merry, 2007).

The aggregate effect of these developments is that the international human rights system had come to be characterized by a degree of *legalization* that those present at the birth of the UN might not have anticipated. An ever-widening set of moral claims is formulated as positive human rights law (Wilson, 2007). Specialized jurists cultivate technical expertise and seek to develop a coherent and justiciable legal regime (Goodale, 2007). Committees of experts interpret human rights instruments using specialized procedures, striving for perfection of form rather than representing the interests of their states of origin. The actors that produce international human rights knowledge and the transnational continuum of activities – at various levels of scale – that connects them have come to be characterized by "a certain aesthetic of information" that is profoundly legalistic (Riles, 2000, p. 2).

The conditional formulations of rights contained in contemporary international human rights conventions are typical of this legalistic aesthetic. The 1948 Universal Declaration of Human Rights had adopted an aspirational and idealistic framing of rights, but the provisions in subsequent treaties have been drafted so that rights are qualified and balanced against other interests by phrases such as "as appropriate" or "as soon as possible" (Merry, 2006). Legalization is also apparent in the epistemic culture that has emerged among those engaged in implementing treaty norms. In contrast with previous less professionalized models of political solidarity activism, the current model of human rights activism is based on classifying claims in terms of legal standards and on making them quantifiable and verifiable (Tate, 2007, p. 118). At the international level, the human rights system has undergone a similar professionalization and institutionalization. As participation in human rights treaties has grown exponentially and the proliferation of treaty bodies has continued, these norm-declaring sites have consolidated and specialized their internal procedures so that technical expertise is brought to bear on an ever-wider array of claims (Crawford, 2000, p. 3).

But is international human rights law really law? If we rely on a positivist vision of the sovereign issuing commands that the subjects are obliged to obey, then international law does not look particularly law-like in its implementation. Even as international human rights law has become increasingly technical and legalistic in its formulation, state-to-state enforcement mechanisms seldom have the power to mandate compliance with international principles and most enforcement remains declaratory rather than judicial in character.

Yet, the dearth of international enforcement mechanisms does not mean that international law is not observed. As Harold Koh explains, it is primarily through a process of "interaction, interpretation, and internalization," in which nongovernmental activists play a key role, that international norms are implemented (Koh, 1999, p. 1417). Human rights entrepreneurs mobilize popular opinion and political support so that international norms become socially, politically, and legally internalized, with the result that they are eventually incorporated into the domestic legal system through executive action, legislative action, judicial interpretation, or some combination of the three.

Koh gives the example of the nongovernmental International Campaign to Ban Landmines, which successfully pushed for an international convention on this issue. Activists then leveraged the moral authority of international norms to lobby US legislators and administrators to enact a moratorium on the sale of landmines and to develop new technologies to aid in demining, even though the United States had not yet signed the convention. This kind of transnational process is also visible in the development and legal internalization of international human rights norms that resulted in the outlawing of the juvenile death penalty (Smith, 2007). International norms have the potential to spread and take root once their domestic internalization acquires sufficient momentum. Koh suggests that just as federal automobile standards over time conditioned drivers not to drive without a seatbelt, in part through the industry's adoption of buckle-up alarms and in part through a process of socialization whereby wearing seatbelts came to be viewed as an integral part of what it meant to be a law-abiding person, so too, international legal standards come to be internalized through multisited processes of institutionalization and socialization. This conception of law's capacity for social internalization is similar to what sociolegal scholars have analyzed in terms of the ideological dimension of legality.

Bringing this approach to her study of transnational human rights activism against gendered violence, Sally Engle Merry suggests that the significance of the legal standards contained in the Convention on the Elimination of All Forms of Discrimination Against Women (CEDAW) lies in their capacity to coalesce and express particular cultural understandings, so that people come to understand themselves in terms of these legal categories (Merry, 2007). Merry shows how these standards have been used by local activists to structure domestic political discussions, even in states that have not officially ratified the treaty, about the need to criminalize domestic violence (Merry, 2006). Although national law also has this constitutive quality, the production of new cultural categories is the primary means of norm enforcement within the international human rights system.

An epistemology of international human rights law that characterizes it as legalized but not centrally commanded renders visible the diverse processes of knowledge construction that have allowed human rights for marginal migrants to be formulated and implemented. Working through this conceptual lens allows us to see how innovative legal forms emerge and make their way into practice through a multisited and multiscaled chain of actors and activities that cannot easily be compressed into the confines of either an institution or a professional network (Wilson, 2007). It is a form of legality that "depends deeply on its texts" (Merry, 2007, p. 183) even if compliance with international law depends not on sovereign states enforcing rules but rather on the potential of these norms to bring about an internalization of new cultural and political categories.

As the following two case studies of "migrant rights as human rights" will demonstrate, broad political constraints also play a part in this process. The formulation and implementation of human rights for marginal migrants is a site of political contestation; it is neither automatic nor inevitable. In the case of the integration of refugee law with international human rights law, this process is fairly advanced. In the case of migrant worker rights, new legal forms are developing but much remains to be done in terms of implementing these human rights standards.

A HUMAN RIGHTS APPROACH TO REFUGEE PROTECTION

The international refugee law regime elaborates a specific, albeit narrow, place for foreign migrants within international law. States commit themselves not to send foreign migrants back to a country where they have a well-founded fear of persecution on account of race, religion, nationality, membership in a particular social group, or political opinion. According to the Universal Declaration of Human Rights, everyone has the right to seek and to enjoy asylum from persecution, but asylum remains a sovereign prerogative and there is no subjective right to be granted asylum. Moreover, unlike human rights law, refugee law does not attempt to set a corrective agenda, tell another country how to act, or propose plans for eradicating particular practices. "Refugee law does not seek to reform states and does not address root causes. Its role is palliative; it represents the interests of the individual in dissociating herself from her community and her state" (Anker, 2002, pp. 153–154).

As with the international human rights system, the origin of international refugee protection was closely tied to the Second World War. An International Refugee Organization was created in 1944 to assist and protect those displaced by the war. The purpose of the 1951 Geneva Convention on Refugees, drafted under the auspices of the UN, was to transfer this responsibility to states. As it was written, the Convention only applied to those who had become refugees prior to 1951 as a result of events linked to Second World War. Fifteen years later, the 1967 UN Protocol on asylum, signed in New York but known as the "Bellagio Protocol," expanded the refugee regime so that it became a weapon of the Cold War to be wielded against Communist states, much as human rights were also being instrumentalized by the super powers at this time.

Beginning in the late 1970s, advocates in Western countries became active in pushing to sever the connection between refugee law and foreign policy and to develop a more legalistic approach for refugee status determination. In the United States, this activism resulted in the passage of the Refugee Act of 1980, which explicitly aimed to bring US law more fully in line with the five grounds for persecution found in the 1967 Protocol. Similar activism took place in European countries, coinciding with the sharp increase in the number of asylum applicants, attributable in part to the closure of other routes to legal immigration in the mid-1970s (Martin, 1990). Nevertheless, during much of the Reagan Presidency, refugee law as it was implemented retained an overtly Cold War approach. Asylum seekers from Communist states seeking asylum in the United States, rather than having their claims examined individually, were presumed to have a well-founded fear of persecution. As human rights law became increasingly legalized, the contrast with the Cold War approach to refugee status determination appeared increasingly pronounced.

Yet, over the past several decades, human rights and refugee protection have become significantly more interconnected. Starting in the mid-1980s, we see the infusion of international refugee law with human rights norms, a process that continues to shape the substance of refugee protection. The cross-fertilization of refugee law and human rights law has brought about important changes in how violence and persecution are understood, both within the law and within the sphere of cultural understandings that guide policymaking and public discussion.

One component of this process has been the transformation of the United Nations High Commissioner for Refugees (UNHCR) into an active generator of legal norms. During its first three decades, the organization's knowledge and dissemination functions remained underdeveloped. But as the Cold War drew to a close, the Executive Committee of UNHCR grew increasingly active in issuing interpretations of international refugee law as part of an ongoing dialog with a growing circle of experts and advocates (Lambert, 2009). Feminist approaches to refugee law were particularly influential in this process of legal development (Bonnerjea, 1989). The transnational women's network that developed in the mid-1980s around the theme of "violence against women" (see Keck & Sikkink, 1998) converged at the UNHCR, among many other sites. In 1985, the same year as the Nairobi UN Conference on Women, advocates were successful in pushing the UNHCR Executive Committee to mention in its conclusions the need to extend the protection of the Convention to women facing violence for having violated the traditions of their societies (Kelly, 1993, p. 659).

In, 1991, UNHCR went a step further issuing guidelines that drew directly on the CEDAW Committee's published 1990 report interpreting gender-based violence as a human rights violation (p. 660). The UNHCR *Guidelines on the Protection of Refugee Women* were careful to emphasize that it is national law, not international law, that determines what legal assistance an individual receives, where she will live, and what assistance will be provided. But they direct UNHCR staff to work with public officials in countries of asylum in order to:

> Promote acceptance in the asylum adjudication process of the principle that women fearing persecution or severe discrimination on the basis of their gender should be considered a member of a social group for the purposes of determining refugee status.... [And] promote acceptance of the notion that sexual violence against women is a form of persecution when it is used by or with the consent or acquiescence of those acting in an official capacity to intimidate or punish. (1991, p. 19)

Similarly worded principles establishing the normative validity of gender-based grounds for asylum were subsequently included in the concluding documents issued at a series of UN conferences that took place in the early 1990s, as well as in the 1994 report of the UN Special Rapporteur on Violence Against Women (Anker, 2002, p. 142).

Having established gender-based violence as both a human rights violation and a form of persecution within international refugee law, activists then turned toward the task of bringing these principles home to the administration of national asylum systems. In Canada, a test case organized by a coalition of Canadian refugee advocates and international women's human rights NGOs served as a focus for intensive administrative lobbying efforts to recognize gender-based violence as persecution (Kobayashi, 1995). The Canadian Immigration and Refugee Board was responsive to these arguments, and in 1993 it issued guidelines for refugee status determination that drew on the text of the 1991 UNHCR guidelines. The Canadian *Guidelines on Women Refugee Claimants Fearing Gender-Related Persecution* translate the general principles developed by UNHCR two years earlier into a "framework of analysis" for asylum adjudicators. Using a visual flowchart to guide adjudicators, the text outlines specific criteria for assessing the particular circumstances that have given rise to the claimant's fear of persecution and lists considerations that might support a gender-based asylum claim, such as whether the social position of women in the country of origin is such that it "engenders the degree of discrimination likely to amount to persecution" (Immigration and Refugee Board, 1993, p. 8).

The Vienna Conference on Human Rights in the summer of 1993 provided a site for advocates and policymakers involved in the development of women's refugee norms to exchange ideas and share strategies (McClymont & Golub, 2000, p. 52). In the following years, advocates in Belgium and France joined in efforts to achieve recognition of asylum claims brought by women fleeing traditional practices. At the same time, US advocates successfully lobbied the director of the Immigration and Naturalization Service to issue a memorandum to asylum officers, endorsing the possibility of using gender-based grounds to grant asylum (Anker, 2002, p. 136). The "Coven Memo" draws explicitly on the text of the Canadian guidelines and goes on to further elaborate some of the ways in which women might be seen to breach social mores (marrying outside an arranged marriage, wearing lipstick, etc.) resulting in persecution.

While the Canadian and US guidelines had moved toward internalizing a human rights approach to international refugee norms, legalization was taken a step further as courts recognized gender-based asylum claims, and as jurisprudence in this area became increasingly principled. In the 1996 *Kasinga* decision, concerning the tribal practice of female genital cutting, the US Board of Immigration Appeals made an effort to enunciate justiciable principles that would delimit the scope of gender-based grounds for asylum while at the same time recognizing the legitimacy of a human rights approach to refugee law. The concurring opinion by Board Member Lory D. Rosenberg was particularly innovative, stating that, "The reason the persecution would be inflicted ... is because of the persecutor's intent to overcome [Kasinga's] state of being non-mutilated and accordingly, free from male-dominated tribal control, including an arranged marriage" (In re Kasinga, 21 I. & N. Dec. 357, 365 (US BIA 1996)). The opinion thus took an important step toward translating gendered violence into refugee law's conceptual categories.

In the *Shah and Islam* decision three years later, concerning wives refusing to adhere to traditional norms, the British Law Lords went on to consider how broader patterns of discriminatory treatment structurally enabled the specific violence the applicants feared from their husbands (Regina v. Immigration Appeal Tribunal, ex parte Shah, [1999] 2 All E.R. 545 (H.L.) (UK)). When articulating a definition of persecution that could encompass gender-based claims, the Law Lords took notice of the *Kasinga* decision as well as other nonbinding international precedents and also cited the gender guidelines developed by the UK Refugee Women's Group (Anker, 2002, p. 137). The decision's analysis of persecution refers to two distinct legal components: serious harm and failure of state protection. However, the Law Lords called on adjudicators to go beyond conventional juridical analysis to undertake a "global appraisal of an individual's past and present situation in a particular cultural, social, political and legal milieu" and emphasized the need to bear in mind the "broad humanitarian purpose" of refugee law (Regina v. Immigration Appeal Tribunal, ex parte Shah, [1999] 2 All E.R. 545, 561 (H.L.) (UK)). In doing so, the decision grounded refugee law in juridical terms while endorsing a nonpositivistic style of legal interpretation that remained open to accommodating future developments in human rights norms.

Administrative bodies, courts, advocates, and legal scholars continue to engage in dialog with one another across national borders on the topic of gender-based persecution. They borrow, adapt, and build on each other's legal innovations. The principles developed in early cases involving gender-based persecution have subsequently been extended to new fact patterns and to cases involving related forms of gender-based persecution (the Center for Gender and Refugee Studies at UC Hastings provides an exhaustive summary of the current law on gender-based persecution, see http://cgrs.uchastings.edu/law/). And through this transnational process of legal development, a complex and rich body of "transnationalized" international law has come into being, for which international human rights law provides the unifying theory (Anker, 2002). There is now clear understanding that human rights principles give meaning to the "right to enjoy asylum" (Lambert, 2009).

The grounding of refugee law interpretation in a human rights paradigm takes place despite the absence of a supervisory legal body for refugee law and despite the fact that foreign jurisprudence and legal instruments are rarely taken as directly authoritative, even when they are cited extra-nationally. Although litigation has played some role, administrative agencies are probably more significant in internalizing gender-based refugee principles. Most significant of all has been the role of NGOs. The international women's human rights movement opened a space in which this development and dissemination of rights for a particular subset of marginal migrants could occur.

A HUMAN RIGHTS APPROACH TO MIGRANT LABOR STANDARDS

The development of a rights-based approach to migrant labor regulation represents another path by which marginalized migrants are finding a place within the international human rights system. Large-scale migrant labor flows have been a perennial feature of capitalist economies. States in need of migrant labor have facilitated these migrant labor flows, either by concluding bilateral guest worker agreements with migrant sending countries or by adopting a policy of noninterference with labor recruitment carried out by the private sector. The International Labour Organization (ILO) is charged with assisting states in organizing labor migration. In 1947, the ILO's competence over the situation of migrants "in their quality as workers" was formally recognized by the UN (Hasenau, 1991).

The origins of international migrant labor standards date to the period immediately following the First World War when pressure from workers' organizations and the shock of the Soviet Revolution pushed the victorious powers to establish an international organization with the mandate of securing common action on matters affecting conditions of employment. The newly created ILO almost immediately undertook the task of encouraging bilateral guest worker agreements in order to replace chaotic prewar labor recruitment practices and provide a solution to postwar Europe's intensified manpower needs (Hasenau, 1991, p. 689). Early recommendations stipulated that the recruitment of migrant workers should be permitted only by mutual agreement between countries concerned and after consultation with employers' and workers' organizations of the industries concerned (Hasenau, 1991, p. 689). Demonstrating a similarly corporatist approach, unemployment benefits would be accessible to migrant workers solely on condition of reciprocity, so as to protect social security schemes in destination countries from being flooded with an influx of less able workers.

After the Second World War, ILO practices moved away from supporting a regime of bilateral agreements and placed greater emphasis on establishing flexible universal standards. The ILO's 1949 Migration for Employment Convention covered all migrant workers, without condition of reciprocity, so long as they possessed the proper work and residence permits. Supplementary provisions added in 1975 recommended that states provide full social security benefits and that migrant workers be allowed to change employers. Yet, reflecting the pro-restrictionist position typical of the labor movement at the time, this move toward principles of equal treatment was accompanied by an increasing focus on suppressing clandestine migration. Undocumented migrants, identified by the ILO as "illegal workers," continued to be excluded from coverage under migrant labor conventions. Moreover, workers in sectors without labor union representation, including seasonal agricultural workers and domestic workers, also remained outside the ILO's corporatist regulatory model.

In the mid-1970s, the ILO's exclusive competence over international migrant labor standards was challenged from within the UN General Assembly. Developing countries with high levels of emigration were eager to address issues of migrant worker rights through the UN rather than the ILO, both because they viewed the symbolism of human rights as an effective mechanism for shaming the racist practices of destination countries and because their governments were averse to addressing migrant rights through an organization that was viewed as overly influenced by oppositional labor unions (Bohning, 1991, p. 700). Moreover, the ILO's recent emphasis on curtailing clandestine migration was unattractive to developing economies such as Mexico and Morocco that depended on high levels of emigration to supply employment opportunities and remittances (Bohning, 1991, p. 700). When in 1978 the General Assembly established a working group to undertake the drafting of a UN Migrant Worker Convention, representatives of these countries took the lead in submitting an initial draft text that featured strong declaratory statements against the racist environment faced by their nationals in Europe and the United States (Lonnroth, 1991, p. 732).

As the drafting process continued throughout the 1980s, however, the text of the UN Migrant Worker Convention acquired elements of the legalistic aesthetic that has come to typify the contemporary international human rights system. The first steps in this direction were taken by delegates from small-sized, social democratic Mediterranean and Scandinavian states (the so-called MESCA group), who came to embrace the Convention drafting process as an opportunity to create a "serious, well-functioning human rights instrument" that would further the overall legalization of the international system that these states relied upon to protect their own security (Lonnroth, 1991, p. 733). Their approach focused on making the legal document as useful as possible for the individual migrant worker rather than adopting the collective rights framework endorsed by developing countries. They also moved away from the initial draft text's more radical statements of absolute rights, replacing these with provisions in which rights are qualified by the state's reserved authority to regulate admission and regularization.

In the final phases of the Convention's drafting, legalization developed a life of its own. German legal experts pointed out lacunae and legal errors as well as contradictions within the text, even though it was clear from the beginning that Germany was unlikely to sign the Convention (1991, p. 734). Similarly, there was widespread belief that the United States would not sign and ratify the Convention in the immediate future, but US delegates nevertheless strove to make the draft meet high legal standards and to make its content as close to its interests as possible "in order to create prerequisites for an eventual ratification at some later stage" and in order to prevent the instrument from becoming a mere political device (1991, p. 734). These drafters acted as positivist legal technicians, softening differences between the various delegations, proposing compromises, and alternative formulations that would take into account the various interests and thereby make the negotiations progress while ensuring that the text remained cohesive and noncontradictory.

The Convention that was finally enacted by the General Assembly in December 1990 illustrates how human rights can be made compatible with migrant labor issues in a manner that produces legally enforceable standards. The text moves away from the ILO's corporatist framework by conceptualizing an individual migrant worker whose rights are not dependent on his or her representation by traditional labor organizations (Bohning, 1991, p. 703). Basic civil and political rights to liberty, free expression, and privacy were reformulated in the specific context of labor migration, thereby articulating rights to freedom of movement, guaranteed days of rest, control over personal documents, advance information about terms of employment, etc. In addition, the Convention's balance of sovereign territorial authority and individual human rights signals an attempt to produce a text that would be taken seriously by ratifying states (Bosniak, 1991). Thus, while the Convention emphasizes that states must treat individuals with dignity and human respect even if they are undocumented, it contains no provision enunciating a right to enter any other country. Rather than a statement of vision, the Convention aims to be a legally enforceable document that could also provide a conceptual base for the future development of migrant worker rights.

Yet progress was initially slow in further developing the Convention's principles. Over the 10 years following its enactment by the General Assembly, only 11 countries ratified it. In large part, this was due to the fact that the drafting process had been state-centric and no broad social movement had done the work of shifting consciousness among politicians and the public toward support of the Convention or in favor of migrant worker rights more generally. In order for these rights to be implemented in the form of either enforceable administrative guidelines or judicial principles, they would need to be embraced by a transnational constituency of human rights entrepreneurs who could propel the internalization of international norms at the local level.

A transnational movement in defense of migrant worker rights did eventually emerge in the 1990s through a process of coalition building and as the result of the changing political dynamics produced by economic globalization. On the one hand, migrant workers in the informal sector, who had been excluded from the traditional labor regulations, mobilized through a panoply of geographically diverse grassroots organizations (D'Souza, 2010). Inspired by the rights-based discourse popularized by the women's movement and indigenous people's movement, associations of migrant domestic workers were particularly active in framing their struggles in the language of universal human rights (Freeman, Roberts, Tretjak, & Wiener, 2003). On the other hand, the trade union movement, which had previously been hostile to migrant workers and uninterested in organizing workers in the informal sector, moved toward adopting a human rights approach to migrant labor issues. Labor federations in Europe and North America rejuvenated their organizing agenda to reverse declining union density, reconsidered their views on the ability of the state to completely control migration in an era of economic internationalization, and became normatively committed to the idea that migrants have rights that are impeded by tough immigration control measures (Haus, 2002).

International human rights conferences during the 1990s provided important sites for networking among activist organizations. Migrant worker activists and their supporters held meetings, distributed information, and were successful in including language on migrant workers into the final conference documents (Grange & d'Auchamp, 2009, p. 83). The discussions generated at these international conferences also served to anchor the issue of migrant human rights on the agenda of the UN Commission on Human Rights, which was itself becoming increasingly participatory as NGO consultative status was opened to national and regional NGOs after 1996. In the late 1990s, the Commission initiated an Intergovernmental Working Group on the Human Rights of Migrants as well as a Special Rapporteur on the issue. These structures in turn provided additional sites for engagement between intergovernmental organizations and NGOs and thus paved the way for the creation in 1998 of a "Global Campaign for Ratification of the Convention on Rights of Migrants" (Grange & d'Auchamp, 2009, p. 84). As a result, by the beginning of the new millennium, the emerging coalition of grassroots associations campaigning for migrant worker rights was reinforced not only by trade union activism at the national and international level but also by international human rights NGOs and religious organizations such as the World Council of Churches and Caritas.

This transnational campaign on behalf of the Convention has propelled a dissemination of the concept of migrant worker rights, even in states that show little interest in signing or ratifying the Convention. In Europe, a Platform for Migrant Worker Rights was launched in 2002 to lobby EU policymakers, and awareness-raising campaigns have been successful in eliciting calls for ratification and statements in support of the Convention's principles from the European Commission and the European Parliament (MacDonald & Cholewinski, 2009). During the same period, US-based NGOs who participated in the Global Campaign have drawn on the Convention's provisions when filing statements and shadow reports on the protection of migrant workers' human rights in both the Human Rights Committee and the Inter-American Commission on Human Rights (Smith, 2007, p. 306). Similarly, a "Human Rights Tribunal" condemning violations of migrant domestic workers' rights under the Convention was organized in 2005 by a coalition of local and international NGOs in New York City (p. 311). The Global Campaign has thus constructed a new "norm-creating forum" (Koh, 1999) for promoting a human rights approach to migrant labor issues.

One of the sites where this rights-based approach has been most visibly developed is, somewhat surprisingly, within the ILO itself. Beginning in the late 1990s, the organization leant its institutional support to the Global Campaign as part of a more general infusion of human rights concepts into its work (Bohning, 1991). As a result, nongovernmental participants in the Global Campaign exercised significant influence over the drafting of the ILO's *Multilateral Framework on Labour Migration* (Grange & d'Auchamp, 2009), which compiles an exhaustive list of international best practices for the implementation of migrant worker rights. Among the rights-oriented practices that are singled out as models for other countries is the policy of the Philippines Overseas Employment Administration requiring legally enforceable work contracts and monitoring recruitment agencies to ensure their compliance, as well as New Zealand's policy of providing information on labor rights in several languages and organizing English language classes for migrant workers (International Labour Office, 2006, p. 50). In addition, over the past 10 years, the ILO has played an important role in developing effective and useful programs to protect migrant workers by organizing regional workshops with trade unions and with the government ministries concerned with migrant workers (D'Souza, 2010).

The ILO's most recent contribution in this area has been to undertake the drafting of a new convention on the rights of domestic workers, scheduled to be completed in July 2011. The text draws on legislative language developed in recent years by migrant domestic workers and their supporters in a variety of national contexts, including the "Freedom Charter for Domestic Workers" passed in 2007 by the Philippines Senate and the "Domestic Workers Bill of Rights" passed in 2010 by New York State (D'Souza, 2010). The Domestic Worker Convention aims to further articulate provisions contained in the Migrant Workers Convention, detailing specific ways in which these principles can be made meaningful in the context of migrant domestic work. For example, elaborating on the principle of equal standards for workplace safety, the ILO Convention's draft text specifies that destination countries should "provid[e] for a system of visits to households in which migrant domestic workers will be employed and develop a network of emergency housing" (International Labour Office, 2010). Migrant domestic workers have traditionally been exempted from minimum labor standards and principles of equal treatment, and are among the most vulnerable migrant workers. These marginal migrants have now become the subject of human rights oriented legal development.

In sum, the process of legally implementing the norms contained in the UN Migrant Workers Convention is still in its early stages. There has been some progress made in disseminating the Convention's norms in destination countries and advocates are optimistic about the prospects for further progress even though this process is taking place largely in the absence of any directly binding legal authority. Because the Convention has not been ratified by many migrant destination states, lobbying efforts before legislatures and administrative agencies appear to hold more potential than litigation for realizing migrant workers' human rights. At this point, migrant worker rights have a foothold within the international human rights system but their legal development remains far from complete.

CONCLUSION

The transnational process through which human rights are being developed for marginal migrants is still in its early stages. It has not received the attention nor produced the sometimes spectacular policy outcomes that have resulted from other transnational processes, such as those that have added a strong security dimension to the politics of immigration (Bigo, 2001; Guiraudon & Joppke, 2001) or those that have paired migration with discussions of economic development (Castles & Wise, 2008). It is these latter framings of immigration that have dominated the ongoing development of EU immigration and asylum policy, seen most clearly in the 1999 Tampere Programme and its regulation-centered rather than rights-centered approach. A number of interstate dialogues, such as the UN-sponsored Global Forum on Migration and Development or the Transatlantic Council on Migration, have also made highly visible links between migration and either development or security. Indeed, in Europe, international cooperation between border enforcement officials was so effective that it provided the initial impetus for developing a European migrant rights NGO network, which aimed to contribute a rights-based perspective to counteract the security emphasis of EU policymaking (Guiraudon, 2002).

The dominance of the security and development frames within policy circles demonstrates just how difficult it is in the current macropolitical context of aggressive neoliberal globalization to develop and enforce the rights of marginal migrants. The lukewarm reception accorded to the Convention on the Rights of Migrant Workers has been due at least in part to the fact that its enactment by the General Assembly coincided with a period of rampant globalization in which the forces of capital have found it in their interest to maintain a mobile but highly vulnerable labor force (Taran, 2009).

These inhospitable conditions have compounded the inherent tensions of the international human rights system arising from international commitments to the protection of state sovereignty as well as to universal individual rights. Although this tension is present throughout the human rights field, in the area of international migration the conflict is all the greater. As legal scholar Linda Bosniak explains, when it comes to questions of migrant rights, "human rights interests contend not merely with states' relative jurisdictional independence from international authority but also with a central substantive aspect of sovereignty: states' plenary territorial powers, one attribute of which is their virtually uncontested authority to control the admission and exclusion of aliens and to confer nationality – to, in effect, prescribe the composition of the national community" (Bosniak, 1991, p. 752). According to Bosniak, migrant rights present the ultimate "hard case," the fact that migrant rights appear at all in international human rights law demonstrates the power of universal human rights principles.

In addition to telling us something about the power of human rights discourse, the development of migrant human rights provides insight into the culture of the contemporary international human rights system. As previous sociolegal work has pointed out, human rights laws are developed and internalized through a process that is transnational rather than simply international. Normative development is the result of "conversation, interplay, and dialogue" between public officials and a range of other actors who struggle to practice human rights according to their own vision (Speed, 2008). In the field of migrant human rights, we can see this in the way that grassroots campaigns by migrant domestic workers and their supporters have called on the spirit of the Convention on the Rights of Migrant Workers to take their claims to the streets as part of efforts to educate the public about the Convention (Smith, 2007). A recent study of the attempt in one US city to pass a local ordinance inspired by international human rights conventions demonstrates a similar dynamic whereby grassroots groups use human rights norms writ large as a tool for educating the public (Merry, Levitt, Rosen, & Yoon, 2010). The authors see this grassroots form of implementation as holding substantial transformative promise, especially in a political context where – as in the case of the Convention on the Rights of Migrant Workers – the US government has shown no interest in placing itself under the control of international law.

While grassroots movements are critical to the internalization of international human rights principles, the power of transnational legal processes derives from a symbiotic relationship between actors at different levels. In this respect, these processes diverge greatly from the legal positivist ideal of clear hierarchy. Widespread mobilization occurs when actors in a range of locations, and operating at a range of scales, are joined in a single "community" (Boyle, 2002). UN institutions provide one possible node in this network of mobilization, but so do other sites of activity. Anthropologist Winifred Tate describes the landscape of the international human rights system as "ephemeral, developing through the specific temporal windows of conferences, commissions and meetings" (Tate, 2007, p. 191). In the case of the Global Campaign for Ratification of the Migrant Rights Convention, a web portal (december18.net) proved to be a crucial site at which multilateral and intergovernmental agencies, international NGOs, national and regional NGOs, and grassroots groups could share information and coordinate strategies.

At the same time that the internalization and enforcement of migrant human rights principles has not proceeded according to a positivist vision of law, the process of formulating both migrant worker rights and refugee protections has been highly legalistic. A fundamental component of the contemporary epistemology of human rights is its legalization (Wilson, 2007). This tendency toward formalism and technical expertise can serve instrumental purposes, allowing for consensus to develop and thus for new rights to be established in international human rights texts (Riles, 2000). It allowed the Convention on the Rights of Migrant Workers to come into being. And rights for migrant workers have previously made an appearance in other international human rights instruments, similarly qualified by the principle of sovereign territorial authority (for a comprehensive survey, see Slinckx, 2009).

But the legalization of human rights can also make it easier for those with power to wield them against the less powerful, finding legalistic justifications to suspend rights when it suits their ends. National security has proved to be a particularly useful justification for weakening the human rights prohibition on torture, even before the era of the so-called "war on terror" (Asad, 1997). These national emergency exceptions have also found their way into refugee law, so that even if there is no doubt that an individual has a well-founded fear of persecution on account of one of the five grounds, he or she is ineligible for asylum if there is even a purely financial connection to a group that has been declared a "terrorist organization."

The tendency to blur human rights with humanitarianism is also a danger of legalization, especially in the current political context in which "good migrants" are sharply distinguished from "bad migrants." When legal arguments on behalf of gender-based asylum claims adopt a pragmatic and instrumental tone, they emphasize that granting asylum to women fleeing traditional customs "won't open the floodgates" to all of the poor and oppressed in the world (see Miller Bashir, 1997). The legalistic qualities of international law ensure that few rights are absolute.

The challenges of implementing the Convention on the Rights of Migrant Workers also point to the ambiguous nature of legalized formulations of human rights. As Bosniak astutely points out, the difficulty in enforcing the Convention is practical, since undocumented migrant workers are unlikely to be able to claim their rights when by doing so they risk bringing themselves to the attention of immigration enforcement officials (Bosniak, 1991, p. 765). If marginal migrants seeking to have human rights standards upheld are pitted alone against the state, the interests of the sovereign are bound to shape how law is applied in practice.

The reformulation of migrant rights as human rights is very much an ongoing political process. Marginal migrants are far from fully embedded within the individualistic and universalistic legal categories of human rights law. A conceptual distinction between the "deliberative" approach to human rights, which locates human rights discourse in the context of contemporary power structures, and the "protest" approach to human rights, which sees human rights as relatively more conducive to counter-hegemonic struggles, may be helpful in further theorizing the possible routes available to this unsettled field (Dembour, 2010). Whether migrant human rights are best conceptualized as part of the current neoliberal deliberated consensus of late modernity, or whether they are best understood as the result of protest, and thus subject to further expansion by social justice and migrant solidarity movements remains to be seen.

REFERENCES

Alston, P. (1992). The commission on human rights. In: P. Alston (Ed.), *The United Nations and human rights: A critical appraisal*. New York, NY: Oxford University Press.

Anker, D. (2002). Boundaries in the field of human rights: Refugee law, gender, and the human rights paradigm. *Harvard Law Review, 15*, 133–154.

Asad, T. (1997). On torture, or cruel, inhuman and degrading treatment. In *Human rights, culture and context*. Sterling, VA: Pluto.

Bigo, D. (2001). Migration and security. In: V. Guiraudon & C. Joppke (Eds.), *Controlling a new migration world*. New York, NY: Routledge.

Bohning, R. (1991). The ILO and the new UN convention on migrant workers: The past and future. *International Migration Review, 25*(4), 698–709.

Bonnerjea, L. (1989). *Shaming the world: The needs of women refugees*. London: Change.

Bosniak, L. (1991). Human rights, state sovereignty and the protection of undocumented migrants under the international migrant workers convention. *International Migration Review, 25*(4), 737–770.

Boyle, E. H. (2002). *Female genital cutting: Cultural conflict in the global community*. Baltimore, MD: Johns Hopkins University Press.

Castles, S., & Wise, R. D. (2008). *Migration and development: Perspectives from the south*. Geneva: International Organization for Migration.

Crawford, J. (2000). The UN human rights treaty system: A system in crisis? In: P. Alston & J. Crawford (Eds.), *The future of UN human rights treaty monitoring*. New York, NY: Cambridge University Press.

Cummings, S. L. (2007). The internationalization of public interest law. *Duke Law Journal, 57*, 891–959.

D'Souza, A. (2010). *Moving towards decent work for domestic workers: An overview of the ILO's work*. Geneva: International Labour Organization.

Dauvergne, C. (2008). *Making people illegal: What globalization means for migration and law*. New York, NY: Cambridge University Press.

Dembour, M.-B. (2010). What are human rights? Four schools of thought. *Human Rights Quarterly, 32*(1), 1–20.

Derrida, J. (2000). *Of hospitality* (R. Bowlby, Trans.). Stanford, CA: Stanford University Press.

Falk, R. (2009). *Achieving human rights*. New York, NY: Routledge.

Freeman, A., Roberts, K., Tretjak, K., & Wiener, C. (2003). *Left out: Assessing the rights of migrant domestic workers in the United States, seeking alternatives*. Berkeley, CA: Boalt Hall International Human Rights Clinic.

Goodale, M. (2007). The power of right(s): Tracking empires of law and new modes of social resistance in Bolivia (and elsewhere). In: M. Goodale & S. E. Merry (Eds.), *The practice of human rights* (pp. 130–162). New York, NY: Cambridge University Press.

Grange, M., & d'Auchamp, M. (2009). Role of civil society in campaigning for and using the ICRMW. In: P. de Guchteneire, A. Pecoud & R. Cholewinski (Eds.), *Migration and human rights: The United Nations convention on migrant workers' rights*. New York, NY: Cambridge University Press.

Guiraudon, V. (2000). *Les politiques d'immigration en Europe: Allemagne, France, Pays-Bas*. Paris: L'Harmattan.

Guiraudon, V. (2002). European integration and migration policy: Vertical policy-making as venue shopping. *Journal of Common Market Studies, 38*(2), 251–271.

Guiraudon, V., & Joppke, C. (2001). Introduction. In *Controlling a new migration world* (pp. xi, 256p.). New York, NY: Routledge.

Haas, M. (2008). *International human rights*. New York, NY: Routledge.

Hasenau, M. (1991). ILO standards on migrant workers: The fundamentals of the UN convention and their genesis. *International Migration Review, 25*(4), 687–697.

Haus, L. A. (2002). *Unions, immigration, and internationalization: New challenges and changing coalitions in the United States and France*. New York, NY: Palgrave Macmillan.

Immigration and Refugee Board. (1993). *Guidelines on women refugee claimants fearing gender-related persecution*. Ottawa: IRB.

International Labour Office. (2006). *ILO multilateral framework on labour migration: Non-binding principles and guidelines for a rights-based approach to labour migration*. Geneva: International Labour Organization.

International Labour Office. (2010). *Decent work for domestic workers: Report IV(1)*. Geneva: International Labour Organization.

Jacobson, D. (1996). *Rights across borders : Immigration and the decline of citizenship*. Baltimore, MD: Johns Hopkins University Press.

Joppke, C. (2010). *Citizenship and immigration*. Malden, MA: Polity.

Keck, M. E., & Sikkink, K. (1998). *Activists beyond borders*. Ithaca, NY: Cornell University Press.

Kelly, N. (1993). Gender-related persecution: Assessing the asylum claims of women. *Cornell International Law Journal, 26*, 625–674.

Kobayashi, A. (1995). Challenging the national dream: Gender persecution and the Canadian immigration law. In: P. Fitzpatrick (Ed.), *Racism, nationalism and the rule of law*. London: Dartmouth.

Koh, H. H. (1999). How is international human rights law enforced? *Indiana Law Journal, 74*, 1397.

Lambert, H. (2009). International Refugee Law: Dominant and Emerging Approaches. In: D. Armstrong (Ed.), *Routledge Handbook of International Law* (pp. 344–354). New York: Routledge.

Layton-Henry, Z. (1990). Citizenship or denizenship for migrant workers? In: Z. Layton-Henry (Ed.), *The political rights of migrant workers in Western Europe*. New York, NY: Sage.

Lonnroth, J. (1991). The international convention on the rights of all migrant workers and their families in the context of international migration policies: An analysis of ten years of negotiations. *International Migration Review, 25*(4), 710–736.

MacDonald, E., & Cholewinski, R. (2009). The ICRMW and the European Union. In: P. de Guchteneire, A. Pecoud & R. Cholewinski (Eds.), *Migration and human rights: The United Nations convention on migrant workers' rights*. New York, NY: Cambridge University Press.

Martin, D. A. (1990). Reforming asylum adjudication: On navigating the coast of Bohemia. *University of Pennsylvania Law Review, 138*, 1247.

McClymont, M., & Golub, S. (2000). *Many roads to justice: The law-related work of Ford Foundation grantees around the world*. New York, NY: Ford Foundation.

Merry, S. E. (2006). *Human rights and gender violence: Translating international law into local justice*. Chicago, IL: University of Chicago Press.

Merry, S. E. (2007). Human rights law as a path to international justice: The case of the women's convention. In: M.-B. Dembour & T. Kelly (Eds.), *Paths to international justice*. New York, NY: Cambridge University Press.

Merry, S. E., Levitt, P., Rosen, M. S., & Yoon, D. H. (2010). Law from below: Women's human rights and social movements in New York City. *Law and Society Review*, *44*(1), 101–128.

Miller Bashir, L. (1997). Female genital mutilation in the United States: An examination of criminal and asylum law. *American University Journal of Gender and Law*, *4*, 415–454.

Motomura, H. (2008). Immigration outside the law. *Columbia Law Review*, *108*(8).

Riles, A. (2000). *The network inside out*. Ann Arbor, MI: University of Michigan Press.

Sassen, S. (1996). *Losing control? Sovereignty in an age of globalization*. New York, NY: Columbia University Press.

Slinckx, I. (2009). Migrants' rights in UN human rights conventions. In: P. de Guchteneire, A. Pecoud & R. Cholewinski (Eds.), *Migration and human rights: The United Nations convention on migrant workers' rights*. New York, NY: Cambridge University Press.

Smith, R. (2007). Human rights at home: Human rights as an organizing and legal tool in low wage worker communities. *Stanford Journal of Civil Rights and Civil Liberties*, *3*, 285–315.

Soysal, Y. N. (1994). *Limits of citizenship: Migrants and postnational membership in Europe*. Chicago, IL: University of Chicago Press.

Speed, S. (2008). *Rights in rebellion: Indigenous struggle and human rights in Chiapas*. Stanford, CA: Stanford University Press.

Steiner, H., & Alston, P. (2008). *International human rights in context: Law, politics, morals*. New York, NY: Oxford University Press.

Taran, P. A. (2009). The need for a rights-based approach to migration in the age of globalization. In: P. de Guchteneire, A. Pecoud & R. Cholewinski (Eds.), *Migration and human rights: The United Nations convention on migrant workers' rights*. New York, NY: Cambridge University Press.

Tate, W. (2007). *Counting the dead: The culture and politics of human rights activism in Colombia*. Berkeley, CA: University of California Press.

United Nations High Commissioner for Refugees. (1991). *Guidelines on the protection of refugee women*. Geneva: UNHCR.

Wilson, R. (2007). Tyrannosaurus Lex: The anthropology of human rights and transnational law. In: M. Goodale & S. Merry (Eds.), *The practice of human rights*. New York, NY: Cambridge University Press.

WHY THE UNDERUTILIZATION OF CHILD RIGHTS IN GLOBAL MOBILIZATION? THE CASES OF FEMALE GENITAL CUTTING PRACTICES AND USER FEES FOR EDUCATION[1]

Elizabeth Heger Boyle and Hollie Nyseth

ABSTRACT

Support for child rights is widespread, and the 1989 Convention on the Rights of the Child is the most widely ratified treaty ever. Surprisingly, however, we find that child rights discourse is not integrated as a core element of mobilization around either the eradication of female genital cutting practices or the provision of free primary education. Analyzing history and the content of child rights claims related to these issues, we unpack this puzzle. In the process, we illuminate the constraints on mobilizing strategies in general and some difficulties inherent in using child rights discourse in particular.

Special Issue: Human Rights: New Possibilities/New Problems
Studies in Law, Politics, and Society, Volume 56, 91–119
Copyright © 2011 by Emerald Group Publishing Limited
ISSN: 1059-4337/doi:10.1108/S1059-4337(2011)0000056007

As the newest elaboration of rights in international law, child rights have the potential to transform the lives of young people around the world. Support for child rights is widespread, and the 1989 Convention on the Rights of the Child (CRC) is the most widely ratified treaty ever. In this chapter, we examine the history of two issues related to child rights: the provision of free primary education and the eradication of female genital cutting practices (FGCs). We find, surprisingly, that child rights discourse has not been integrated as a core element of mobilization around either of these issues. Analyzing history and the content of child rights claims related to these issues, we unpack this puzzle. In the process, we illuminate the constraints on new mobilizing strategies in general and some difficulties inherent in using child rights discourse in particular.

We begin by discussing the trajectory of children in international law. Next, we introduce the roles of history and agency in global mobilization on behalf of children. We then turn to our two cases. We find that path dependency in the core themes of global social movements can prevent them from focusing on child rights as an organizing strategy. That is, historical events and choices shape social movements' contemporary arguments. We find that child rights may also be purposely sidelined, at least for certain issues. We conclude with a discussion of how our cases in combination reveal the promises and problems of a child rights discourse.

THE HISTORY OF INTERNATIONAL LAW
PERTAINING TO CHILD RIGHTS

Early mobilization for child rights was a reflection of new social challenges brought about by industrialization (Fuchs, 2007). With the founding of the League of Nations in 1919, for the first time an international governmental organization (IGO) began to coordinate child welfare initiatives. The Covenant of the League assigned special responsibilities for the protection of children, and the League dedicated efforts to finding homes for World War I orphans (Boyle, Smith, & Guenther, 2006). The League also spurred the creation of networks of child rights activists around the globe and launched the International Labor Organization (ILO), which, since its inception, has sought to limit child labor. The League adopted a Declaration on the Rights of the Child in 1924 that pertained primarily to economic and social rights.

In 1946, the League of Nations was replaced by the United Nations (the UN), which quickly adopted the Universal Declaration of Human Rights (the UDHR). The UDHR proclaims that every human being has certain rights and asserts that all children should enjoy the same social protections as adults (UDHR, Article 25). A decade later, in 1959, the UDHR was followed by a revised Declaration on the Rights of the Child, which contains the principle of nondiscrimination, the right to a name and nationality, the right to nutrition and housing, the right to treatment of handicaps, the right to education, protection from exploitation, and several other special protections. Like its predecessor, the 1959 Declaration focuses on economic rights that are related to survival. It has been signed by 176 nations, and the day of its adoption is now recognized as National Children's Day.

In the decades that followed the 1959 Declaration, other important child-related treaties were adopted. In 1966, the United Nations adopted two binding human rights conventions – the International Covenant on Civil and Political Rights (ICCPR) and the International Covenant on Economic, Social, and Cultural Rights (ICESCR). Civil and political rights include freedom of speech and religion, due process, and rights related to voting. Economic, social, and cultural rights include rights to education, health and a minimum standard of living.[2]

Although children were not the focus of the ICCPR or the ICESCR, both apply to all human beings and consequently to children. Furthermore, each convention also specifically includes provisions relevant to children. Article 10 of the ICESCR asserts that families should protect children, especially from economic and social exploitation. It also recognizes the right to education and requires signatories to improve child health. Children are also entitled to all rights in the ICCPR and several provisions apply specifically to them. Article 14 of the ICCPR concerns juvenile justice, and Article 24 states that children have the right to be free from discrimination, to be registered with a name at birth, and to have a nationality. The two cases we focus on in this chapter – FGCs and free education – fall predominantly into the category of economic, social, and cultural rights, although some civil and political rights are relevant to them.

Other historic treaties focus directly on children. The 1962 UN Convention on Consent to Marriage, Minimum Age for Marriage, and Registration of Marriages urges State Parties to set a minimum age for marriage. Most states have set this age between 14 and 18 (Boyle, et al., 2006). The 1972 ILO Convention Concerning Minimum Age for Admission to Employment requires states to pursue national policies to abolish child labor and raise their minimum ages of employment. It also sets the minimum age for admission to hazardous employment at the age of 18. Both of these treaties received only moderate support; neither was initially ratified by a majority of states.[3]

The crowning achievement for child rights in the twentieth century was the adoption of the CRC by the UN General Assembly in 1989. Unlike the earlier Declarations on the Rights of the Child, the CRC is binding on signatories and includes a monitoring system to encourage state compliance. The Convention received overwhelming support. It has now been ratified by 193 states; only two states have yet to ratify it (the United States and Somalia).

The CRC defines a child as a person under 18 years old (CRC, Article 1). The articles of the CRC are guided by the following four general principles: nondiscrimination (CRC, Article 2), the best interests of the child (CRC, Article 3), the right to life, survival, and development (CRC, Article 6), and the right to participate and be heard (CRC, Article 12). Both civil and political rights and economic, social, and cultural rights are included in the Convention, which makes the CRC a unique document in international law. Furthermore, while early child rights documents framed children as victims, the CRC frames children as agents. For example, it requires states to allow children to have a voice in any decisions that affect them.

Many regional bodies have also created documents that delineate and regulate child rights. The Organization of African Unity was the first regional organization to adopt a binding instrument that focused exclusively on the rights of the child – the African Charter on the Rights and Welfare of the Child – in 1990. The Council of Europe also created several specific conventions regarding child rights issues, and the Association of Southeast Asian Nations has drafted child rights agendas and documents. In general, there are numerous regional and bilateral treaties that add detail to the regulation of global child rights.

PATH DEPENDENCY, INTENTIONALITY, AND THE UNDERUTILIZATION OF CHILD RIGHTS DISCOURSE

Given the strong and growing support for child rights in international law, one might expect a child rights discourse to be prominent in contemporary social movements related to children. Instead, at least in the two cases addressed here, the idea of child rights is present but marginal. To understand why, in this section, we first turn to theories of organizational change and theories of activist strategizing. We then consider how the specific nature of child rights make them a useful framework in some ways, but less useful in other ways. These general discussions lay the groundwork for interpreting mobilization against FGCs and mobilization against user fees in education in the subsequent sections. Throughout this chapter, we use the term "discourse" to refer to institutionalized ideas that are taken for granted and deployed without much reflection.[4] We use the terms "frame," "framing," and "framework" to refer to strategies that are consciously selected by individuals after a consideration of those strategies' likely resonance and impact.[5]

History and Change

The organizational change literature explores the relationship between structure and action. Much work in this area recognizes the constraints that history places on organizational reform. At its founding, an organization is especially influenced by the larger environmental context (Stinchcombe, 1965). Cues from the environment help new organizations respond to uncertainty in roles and relationships internally as well as deal with clients and competitors externally (Hager, Galaskiewicz, & Larson, 2004). This historical environmental "imprinting" affects organizations' abilities to adapt to new circumstances in the future. For example, Kelly (2010) found that corporate noncompliance with legal maternity leave requirements was often the result of a failure to update policies. Rather than purposely violating the law, many corporate officers were drawing, without conscious reflection, on older guidelines. Studies of organizational change demonstrate that, to understand the current condition of any social institution, its history must be systematically taken into account (see also Durkheim, 1977[1904–1905], p. 15)

Scholars have also shown the effect of history on social phenomena outside the organizational context. Savelsberg (2004) found that historical contingencies had a path-dependent effect on Germany's criminal justice system. Boli-Bennett and Meyer (1978) determined that national constitutions are driven as much by the historical period in which they are drafted as by the characteristics of the particular nations that adopt them. The US intelligence community followed the logics of the Cold War many years after that historical era had ended (Emirbayer & Johnson, 2008). Social movement strategies and their legitimacy also have an historical legacy (Rojas, 2006). Advocates draw on existing templates and scripts to determine how to proceed (compare Hallett & Ventresca, 2006). These tools may empower social movements by making mobilization simpler, but they also represent an impediment to new strategies. As this suggests, it is important to study the history of child-related social movements in order to understand the extent to which they currently use child rights discourses.

Contemporary Strategic Action

The strategies of previous activists set the stage for contemporary activists, but the latter still play a leading role in moving their agendas forward. Strategies and discourses are not immutable, nor are current activists' actions predetermined. Keck and Sikkink (1998) pioneered the study of bottom-up approaches to human rights advocacy. They focus on the power of ideas and norms rather than more traditional forms of power (see also Boli & Thomas, 1999). Keck and Sikkink (1998) coined the term "transnational advocacy networks," which include nongovernmental actors of all stripes (professionals, academics, international nongovernmental organizations [INGOs], foundations, religious organizations, etc.) who work transnationally on an issue and who are bound together by shared values and a common discourse. At the core of these networks are dense exchanges of information. Keck and Sikkink (1998) identify four specific strategies that advocacy networks employ to promote their causes: providing information about a particular issue, using symbols to make a compelling case for action and persuade people an issue is important, utilizing leverage through moral shaming and material threats, and keeping track of accountability by overseeing the implementation of international laws. From this perspective, child rights discourse will be the most useful when they can assist in creating symbols, providing information or leverage, or ensuring accountability.

The Content of Child Rights Discourse

There are several reasons to expect advocates and organizations to utilize a child rights framework. First, child rights have received nearly unanimous support worldwide. As previously mentioned, the CRC is the most widely ratified human rights treaty. Additionally, the CRC's inclusion of both civil and political rights and economic, social, and cultural rights increases its applicability to multiple issues; and child-centered demands have a greater potential for building intercultural consensus (Fernando, 2001).

Furthermore, treating children's issues as rights rather than sympathetic causes imbues them with more power. Because of their perceived dependency, children pull on the heartstrings of the public, particularly when they are threatened with bodily harm (Keck & Sikkink, 1998). Most people agree that children deserve special protections. The earliest child rights discourse played into these sentiments. For example, Eglantyne Jebb, the author of the 1924 Declaration on the Rights of the Child and the founder of Save the Children, stated "We cannot leave defenseless children anywhere exposed to ruin – moral or physical. We cannot run the risk that they should weep, starve, despair and die, with never a hand stretched out to help them" (Save the Children, 2010).

The 1989 Convention on the Rights of the Child moved away from sympathy as the primary reason for helping children and instead emphasizes childrens agency and legal rights. It makes child rights more comparable to adult rights. Importantly, under this newer framing, upholding rights is itself the end. As our cases illustrate, "helping" children often becomes a means to some other goal, such as national economic development. When this occurs, the commitment to help children may disappear if that help is not clearly contributing to the larger goal, or if some alternative way of achieving the larger goal is championed. However, if children are entitled to help because it is their right, that help must be provided regardless of its impact on some other outcome. Arguably, therefore, legal *rights* provide children with more reliable access to entitlements.

These and other aspects of child rights have influenced the decision of several human rights networks to adopt a child rights framework. For example, the NGO Group for the Convention of the Rights of the Child consists of over 75 national and international nongovernmental organizations that advocate child rights. This transnational advocacy network originally formed during the drafting of the CRC, and today its member organizations are independently involved in a variety of child rights issues, such as the rights of indigenous children and child pornography (www.childrightsnet.org). The NGO Group also forms subgroups and taskforces that work on child campaigns related to the CRC. In addition, the campaigns for child soldiers and child trafficking both frame their respective issues as child rights issues, and their activism has been reflected in two optional protocols to the CRC (Breen, 2003). Thus, there are some realms in which child rights discourse has taken off.

Despite their promise, child rights are not without criticisms and complexities. Ideas of childhood and children influence which rights people believe children have, and they also influence whether or not people support the notion of child rights in general. Broadly, no one would claim to be in favor of harming children, and virtually everyone concedes that children should have some protections. Beyond this limited consensus, activists, scholars, and national and international organizations have raised several issues in relation to child rights. Common questions regarding child rights and the CRC ask whether another framework is better suited to serve children because children are incapable of fully exercising their rights, whether child rights infringe on parental rights and responsibilities, and whether the CRC is based on western notions of children and childhood.

One of the arguments against children's rights is that they are not an appropriate or useful framework. The claim is that a framework of duties and responsibilities would be more widely understood and better serve children. For example, O'Neill (1988) argues for the examination of the obligations that parents, teachers, and the community at large have toward children. Similarly, Benporath (2003) believes that the focus should be placed on the obligations of parents rather than the rights of children. To him, using a rights framework is dangerous because it creates the risk of obscuring the vulnerability of children and erroneously presents children as capable of making decisions.

A related perspective suggests that children are not fully competent and thus are unable to make educated choices on their own behalves. In other words, children's participation in decision-making concerning their futures may sometimes actually be deleterious to their best interests. These critics often point to examples where children's choices are harmful. Does an anorexic teenager have the right to refuse treatment, or do her parents have the right to decide what is in her best interests? Does a 16-year-old have the right to have an abortion without consulting her parents? Clearly there are some limits. A recent Joint Statement (2008) of ten IGOs suggested that minors could never consent to FGCs. In the area of education, most countries have had compulsory attendance statutes for decades – children cannot choose to stay home from school (Benavot & Resnick, 2006). As these examples suggest, the CRC does not give children the complete freedom to make choices concerning their welfare, but the amount of freedom children have is often debated.

Another common issue regarding children's rights pertains to those who make decisions on behalf of children – parents and guardians. By far, the objections to child rights and the CRC that draw the most public attention are those concerned about the impact of child rights on parental rights. Critics often express concern that the CRC gives the CRC Committee authority over parents and families in deciding how to raise children (Blanchfield, 2009; Guggenheim, 2005). Similarly, critics point to several articles they see as undermining the rights of parents, such as Article 14 (freedom of thought, conscience, and religion) or Article 16 (the right to privacy); although it is noteworthy that Article 5 of the CRC requires states to respect the responsibilities, rights, and duties of parents.

Lastly, critics of child rights and the CRC point to western bias. This argument is not particular to children's rights but rather is a common criticism of human rights in general (Mutua, 2002). However, specific children's rights are also sometimes viewed as steeped in western ideals and norms. For example, Article 18 of the CRC, which provides that both parents have responsibilities for raising children, adheres to a western notion of a nuclear family rather than a structure in which extended kin also care for children (Libesman, 2007). The near universal ratification of the CRC is a counter to this criticism.

The critical perspectives of child rights covered in this section are not mutually exclusive. Many conflicts between children's and parents' rights also include debates over cultural relativism, or the idea that everyday activities should be understood within the terms of specific cultures. For example, the question of whether a teenager should be free to choose his or her own religion elicits debates regarding the right to culture, the conflict between children's and parents' rights, and western notions of freedom of belief. Indeed, even this one example illustrates that conflicts over children's rights are multifaceted and complex. Such complexities often fuel controversies and reflect the intricate web of actors and ideas at work in any situation.

In the next two sections, we develop female genital cutting and free primary education as two cases related to child rights. FGCs came to international prominence as a stark example of women's inequality. Anti-FGC activists asked that restrictions be placed on the decisions that adult family members make on behalf of their children. Free primary education first entered the international arena as a means for states to modernize and develop and thereby solve the problem of poverty. Activists opposed to requiring families to share in the cost of their children's education argued that providing free education was the responsibility of states. Although both of these issues could generate strong and sympathetic child rights claims due to the vulnerability and innocence of children and the general support for children's development, for the most part mobilization around them reiterated feminist and development claims, respectively, instead.

FEMALE GENITAL CUTTING PRACTICES

Although child rights are often mentioned in passing in discussions of FGCs, mobilization is currently organized more around a women's rights discourse. An analysis of the history of mobilization against FGCs suggests both institutional and intentional reasons for this. Institutionally, anti-FGCs mobilization is marked by path dependency; that is, early successes and failures shaped later mobilizing discourses. At the same time, the unique characteristics of FGCs may have led activists to intentionally forego a child rights approach. We begin this section by providing background information about FGCs. Next, we trace the issue's evolution at the international level. We then focus on the characteristics of FGCs that may prompt a strategic decision to downplay child rights discourses. We find that the failure to place child rights at the center of anti-FGCs mobilization is partly a matter of timing and partly because modern notions of child rights do not have the same symbolic impact as a child victims frame. However, there is some evidence that the anti-FGCs advocacy network will make child rights a more prominent framework in the future.

Background

FGCs include a wide range of practices that are almost always performed on children at or before puberty. All involve partial or total removal of the external female genitalia or other injury to the female genital organs (Joint Statement, 1997). Most FGCs occur in a geographic band within Africa that runs from the Horn of Africa south through parts of Kenya and Tanzania and then westward through the center of the continent to Senegal and Guinea-Bissau (Joint Statement, 2008). There are many countries in Africa where FGCs are extremely rare, and FGCs do occur in some countries outside of Africa, such as Yemen (WHO, 2011). Migration from cultures that practice FGCs has increased the prevalence of FGCs in other parts of the world, but overall levels of the practices in other countries are very low (see discussion in Boyle & Corl, 2010).

There are serious health consequences associated with FGCs that vary based on the type of procedure (Toubia & Izett, 1998).[6] Infibulation, which involves the removal of the clitoris and labia and a suturing of the wound so that only a small opening remains for fluid to pass through, has the most serious health consequences (see, e.g., WHO, 2006: infibulation increases the risk of stillbirths by 50 percent over uncircumcised women). Fortunately, infibulation represents only a small percentage of FGCs. Hemorrhaging is a serious risk for all forms of FGCs (Toubia & Izett, 1998).

Labeling FGCs is controversial. The label includes many different practices, which tend to be known locally by unique terms. When FGCs first came to the attention of colonial authorities, the practices were referred to primarily as "female circumcision." In some communities (e.g., in parts of Kenya), girls and boys were circumcised in cohorts when they reached a certain age. Male and female circumcisions were viewed as complimentary, and this is likely where the term "female circumcision" emerged (see Kenyatta, 1938/1978). Activists took issue with this term, arguing that the health consequences of FGCs were more severe than the consequences of male circumcision. To dramatize the health consequences, they began to call the practices "female genital mutilation" (Hosken, 1981). States initially resisted this label, but the most recent Joint Statement (2008) from IGOs concerned with the practices uses it. Ethnographies and policy reports suggest that the use of the term "mutilation" in local communities marks anti-FGCs activists as outsiders and raises resistance to their message (see, e.g., Prazak, 2007). We adopt the term "female genital cutting" as a middle ground.

Institutional History of Anti-FGCs Discourses

In the 1950s and 1960s, international organizations were unwilling to get involved in FGCs eradication efforts within countries. African women's requests for intervention at the time went largely unheeded (Boulware-Miller, 1985). In the 1970s, prominent western feminists, including Fran Hosken, Mary Daly, and Gloria Steinem, took up the issue and were ultimately successful in shaming IGOs to become more involved (Boyle, 2002). These activists argued that FGCs were a sadistic tool of patriarchy, symbols of women's subordination, and part of a global patriarchal conspiracy. For example, Hosken (1979) argued:

> Men in Africa, whether illiterates or intellectuals, know very well that they derive power from castrations of women's sexuality. It is a matter of political control. The fear of female sexuality is after all shared by men around the world (p. 4).

Thus, a discourse of sexism was the first to prompt an international response to FGCs. This discourse has changed some in the intervening decades, but its core point – that FGCs are an egregious example of women's inequality – has remained the central theme of most anti-FGCs activism.

From the outset, many African women rejected this discourse (Berkovitch & Bradley, 1999). At the international women's conference in Copenhagen in 1980, a group of African women boycotted the session featuring Hosken, calling her perspective ethnocentric and insensitive to African women (Kouba & Muasher, 1985). In 1993, when Walker published *Possessing the Secret of Joy*, a fictional account of an African woman's circumcision experience, Dawit and Merkuria (1993, p. A27) criticized it for failing to treat African women as efficacious and self-aware individuals. In their view, Walker "portrays an African village, where women and children are without personality, dancing and gazing blankly through some stranger's script of their lives." Nevertheless, *Warrior Marks*, Walker's coauthored nonfictional account of female genital cutting, and a related documentary film, soon followed the novel (Walker & Parmar, 1993). African women had not been as successful as western feminists in getting IGOs to act. Initially, they were also unsuccessful in getting those feminists to recalibrate arguments concerning patriarchy. It seems that, at the time, the success of the radical language among western women outweighed its costs.

Indeed, despite the criticism, feminist rhetoric spurred international organizations into action. In 1979, the Convention on the Elimination of All Forms of Discrimination against Women was opened for ratification, and this coincided with several anti-FGCs activities. The World Health Organization took up the issue of FGCs and, in that same year, held a conference in Khartoum on "traditional practices harmful to the health of women and children" (Slack, 1988). African nations formed the transnational Inter-African Committee on Traditional Practices Affecting the Health of Women and Children. Furthermore, a United Nations subcommittee began to study the issue.

Although IGOs developed a willingness to work against FGCs, they did not adopt the feminist rhetoric that was the impetus for their involvement. Instead, as the names of the Khartoum Conference and African Committee suggest, they framed their anti-FGCs messages in terms of health. Historically, FGCs eradication efforts were associated with colonialism (see, e.g., Natsoulas, 1998). IGOs may have adopted the health frame because it called for narrow, targeted intervention while a gender inequality frame implied the need for a broader reworking of social relations. The broader frame may have triggered negative recollections of the social engineering that characterized colonialism.

Feminists went along with this reframing in the short term, but continued to push for a return to a broader gender inequality discourse. For example, in a 1981 report, Hosken combined notions of health and the rights of women:

> The mutilation of the genital organs of the female body for any reason whatsoever is a
> fundamental offense against the human rights of all women in general and specifically

against the female children and women who are mutilated. The RIGHT TO HEALTH is
a basic human right that cannot be abridged (1981, p. 489, emphasis in original).

Hosken's language also illustrates how early activist evocations of global
patriarchy began to be replaced with the discourse of women's rights as
human rights. Rather than focusing on oppression by males, activists began
to focus on the empowerment of women (see, e.g., Coomaraswamy, 1999).
Nevertheless, gender inequality continued to be the core theme of anti-
FGCs activists.

Furthermore, the media, which was beginning to pick up on the issue of
FGCs, tended to prefer frames that emphasized women's victimization rather
than their empowerment. Abe Rosenthal at *The New York Times* began
featuring in-depth special reports on the practice in 1992. In 1994, CNN aired a
film of a 10-year-old girl being circumcised by a barber in Cairo while the city
was hosting the International Conference on Population and Development. The
timing of the telecast maximized international attention, and outraged public
reaction soon followed. Newspaper reports from all over the world disparaged
the practice and the Egyptian government for its inaction (Boyle, 2002).

In 1996, media coverage of FGCs peaked with the coverage of the asylum
case of Fauziya Kassindja (Boyle & Hoeschen, 2001). When She was 19,
Kassindja fled Togo and entered first Germany and then the United States
illegally to escape circumcision. She had been in a US prison for a year
waiting for her asylum hearing when *New York Times* reporter, Celia
Dugger, heard of her situation and began writing about it (Kassindja &
Bashir, 1998). The CNN film, the Dugger articles, and related media news
stories were influential in getting both Egypt and the United States to take
stronger stands against FGCs (Boyle, Songora, & Foss, 2001). Although all
of the news stories focused on gender inequality, they tended to emphasize
women's oppression more than women's rights.

Meanwhile, nation-states appeared to prefer the health discourse over the
women's inequality discourse. When they began to take actions against
FGCs in the mid-1990s – in response to informal activist pressure, media
coverage, and the requirements of IGOs and powerful states – states tended
to use Health Ministry decrees to restrict FGCs within their borders (Boyle &
Preves, 2000). Up to this point, the formal discourse of FGCs as a health
problem took precedence over western feminists' preferred inequality theme.

At the same time, while some of those promoting the inequality discourse,
especially within the media, continued to emphasize patriarchy and
oppression, other activists were becoming more sensitive to how different
structures of inequality intersected. The latter group, which included many
academic feminists, had become concerned about the ethnocentric tone of

anti-FGCs discourse and was interested in building alliances between western women and women from the communities where the practices took place (see, e.g., Parker, 1995).

The CRC had opened for signatures in 1989 and had garnered tremendous international support. Among all international treaties, it came the closest to directly banning FGCs, requiring that "State Parties ... take all effective and appropriate measures with a view to abolishing traditional practices affecting women and children" (Article 24(3)). The CRC also targeted child abuse and the torturing of children. Nevertheless, it was barely a footnote for any of the parties involved in eradicating FGCs, including activists in Africa and elsewhere, IGO officials, journalists, and government elites.[7] All parties seemed to be focused on whether health or women's rights was the appropriate framework to move efforts forward.

The framing quandary was resolved by IGOs agreeing to shift toward the women's rights framework in their interventions. In 1995, the World Health Organization, UNICEF, the UN Family Planning Association, and the UN Development Program issued a draft Joint Statement indicating that, moving forward, they would rely primarily on a women's rights discourse to combat FGCs. There were several reasons for this change in their framing. The Joint Statement noted that much of the medical discourse had become exaggerated and was therefore counterproductive within communities where FGCs occurred. In addition, the Statement claimed that medicalization had undercut the urgency for eliminating FGCs by making FGCs medically safer. Officials within these IGOs believed that FGCs had to be eliminated because of their impact on women's sexuality even if their health consequences were minimized. Although the Joint Statement did not mention it specifically, another factor was likely the greater cultural sensitivity of the gender inequality discourse, which had evolved considerably since the 1970s. Finally, successful mobilization and intense media coverage may have provided the momentum for IGOs to frame their opposition to FGCs more broadly. The issuance of the final Joint Statement in 1997 coincided with heightened public interest in FGCs (Boyle & Hoeschen, 2001). Since that time, these organizations have continued to use a women's rights discourse supplemented by targeted health justifications.

The most recent Joint Statement of these IGOs, issued in 2008, gave greater attention to child rights than past documents:

> Seen from a human rights perspective, [female genital mutilation] reflects deep-rooted inequality between the sexes, and constitutes an extreme form of discrimination against women. Female genital mutilation is nearly always carried out on minors and is

therefore a violation of the rights of the child. The practice also violates the rights to health, security and physical integrity of the person, the right to be free from torture and cruel, inhuman or degrading treatment, and the right to life when the procedure results in death (2008, p. 1).

Now that challenges to the women's rights discourse have subsided at the international level, it is possible that activists will begin an active search for new frames to reignite interest in FGCs. The new Joint Statement may be an indication that child rights will receive more attention in this advocacy network in the future. It is also possible that advocates will take the path of least resistance and continue using the discourse that has historically been associated with anti-FGCs mobilization.

This historical analysis provides insight into why anti-FGCs mobilization has largely bypassed a child rights discourse to date. The first successful mobilization predated the CRC and was closely linked to a resurgence in feminism, imprinting the idea of women's inequality on the movement. Later, advocates became caught up in a conflict over the women's inequality frame and the health frame preferred by IGOs. This conflict ended in a compromise rather than a new frame.

The case of FGCs illustrates another factor that may have been historically important as well. Unlike women, children tend not to mobilize in large numbers on their own behalf, at least not at the present time. This is partly because of their dependency on adults and partly because childhood is a transitional life course phase that people leave after a relatively short period. Because of its liminality, childhood does not evoke a strong sense of identity in individuals. In practical terms, this means children have not become a strong advocacy group on their own. If they had or if they do, they might prompt more reframing in the anti-FGCs movement.

FGCs, Child Rights, and Strategic Decision-Making

History points to path dependency in the discourse of arguments against FGCs. At the same time, some activists were undoubtedly consciously considering a child rights framework. However, there are several unique aspects of FGCs that might have prompted these individuals ultimately to forego that frame, and we discuss those here.

One possibility is a concern that child rights discourse is western, and could therefore be ineffective in communities where FGCs occur. The language in the CRC that is deemed to apply to FGCs (the "harmful traditional practices" clause) was the subject of some disagreement among

European and African country representatives. When the CRC was drafted, representatives from Italy and the Netherlands requested that Article 24(3) specifically reference FGCs. The representative from Senegal argued that the language should remain general so that the provision would apply to all countries – not only African countries (Smith, 1995). The Senegalese representative won the argument and the language remained broad. The argument itself may signify that there would be unwillingness by African countries to ratify the CRC if an explicit anti-FGCs provision were included.

At first blush it seems unlikely that a concern about ethnocentrism would block a child rights discourse. After all, the early vehement feminist rhetoric came under consistent attacks for its ethnocentrism, but it nonetheless persisted. Studies show the discourse of women's rights is not particularly effective at the community level. Women in communities where FGCs occur do not necessarily see the practices as a rights issue. They are much more likely to cite physical pain or medical consequences when they make a decision not to circumcise a daughter (Boyle & Carbone-López, 2006). Many react negatively to discourses suggesting that they are mutilated and that they wish to mutilate their daughters – especially when those discourses come from outside their communities or from paid consultants within the community (see, e.g., Prazak, 2007).[8]

However, on closer examination, an important difference in concerns over ethnocentrism emerges. Feminism was a newly reemerging and encompassing discourse in the 1970s. At that point, it emphasized the presumed similarities across women – an "essentializing" perspective that is no longer dominant today. By the late 1980s, when children's rights were codified into international law, there was a greater awareness of how different structures of inequality intersect (such as global economic inequality and gender) and more sensitivity to the difficulties of speaking for all women (or girls). Thus, by the time child rights emerged as a viable frame, activists may have become more sensitive to western bias. Since FGCs tend to occur in communities where elders are especially revered, activists may have also feared that the notion of child rights would be interpreted as anathema to their cultural values.

A second reason that activists may have intentionally avoided child rights is to avoid vilifying mothers. A women's rights framework groups women and girls together, but a child rights framework can place women and girls in opposition to one another in the case of FGCs. This is true because mothers are almost always the ones responsible for perpetuating FGCs. The protection of women is the core point of a feminist approach; a child rights frame would not only go in a new direction but also potentially undermine the feminist discourse.

Yet another reason, and the last that we will discuss in this chapter, is that activists might downplay a child rights justification for eliminating FGCs because it is useful for them to portray children as victims. In contemporary international law, the child rights framework not only protects children who are victims of abuse but first and foremost calls for the recognition of children's agency. Portraying young girls as victims has been highly effective in generating outrage over FGCs. It creates powerful symbols, which are the first step in generating pressure for state reforms. Girl victims are the core elements of anti-FGCs activists' symbolic framing, but that framing is not entirely consistent with a child rights framework.

Given the widespread support for the CRC, the vulnerability of children, and the strong negative reactions by some to the sexism and patriarchy discourses, it is surprising that child rights did not become a more dominant discourse for the anti-FGCs advocacy network. Child rights are often raised in connection with FGCs, but women's rights are typically more prominent. This otherwise puzzling pattern is consistent with a notion of imprinting – that environments set discourses when mobilization first occurs at the international level and are subsequently difficult to change. Of course, while the overarching framework for the anti-FGCs social movement remained consistently focused on women's inequality, some strategies did change. For example, the label for FGCs and the weight assigned to health problems varied over time. Nevertheless, the initial successful discourse related to patriarchy created a strong guiding theme to which later activists frequently returned. The advocacy network participants may also have consciously decided to downplay child rights out of a fear that such a frame would appear ethnocentric and because it called for the criminalization of mothers' choices. They may also have seen a child *victim*'s frame as more powerful.

EDUCATION RIGHTS: FREE OR FOR-FEE?

The sparse attention to child rights in the debate over user fees for education is even more surprising than in the realm of FGCs because the relevant right is prominently and explicitly featured in several international laws. The right to free primary education was first articulated in 1948 in Article 26 of the UDHR.[9] The 1966 ICESCR formalized this right to education and created enforcement mechanisms, and the CRC also recognizes the right to free primary education. This contrasts with the one euphemistic clause in the CRC that is deemed applicable to FGCs. Since free primary education has arguably been a cornerstone of human rights for decades, we would expect activists, NGOs, and others in advocacy networks to draw upon a child rights discourse in the pursuit of free primary education for children. Yet, this generally has not been the case. Child rights-related discourse regarding free primary education was minimal in the 1980s and 1990s when user fees were becoming commonplace (Tomaševski, 2003).

In this section, we examine potential reasons for this lack of child rights discourse in the fight for free primary education and argue that both institutional and agentic reasons are at play. We first trace the history of global education discourse to illustrate that organizations and transnational advocacy networks often become locked in an early discourse due to imprinting. We then explore reasons that activists may have explicitly chosen not to utilize a child rights framework.

History of Global Education Policies

International mobilization on behalf of education became prominent in the wake of the Universal Declaration of Human Rights. The United Nations Educational, Scientific and Cultural Organization (UNESCO) was the leader at this time and framed education as a global development issue that could pave the way to modernity for newly independent states (Benavot & Resnick, 2006; Chabbott, 1999). Government investments in education were mainly targeted toward developing skilled populations to drive industria-lization, as the dominant global discourse on education focused on a means/ end rationality that suggested that education was good for national economies (Chabbott, 1999, 2003).

In the 1970s, education as a right received scant attention, and countries began to cut back on education spending (Mundy, 1998). UNESCO was unable to negotiate countries' conflicting goals and began to be overshadowed by other multilateral organizations, such as UNICEF and the World Bank, which were even more strongly linked to a development discourse. UNICEF defined education as a basic need essential to eliminating poverty (Mundy, 1998). This view explicitly emphasized a discourse that had already taken shape during the 1950s and 1960s: the functional aspect of education was more important than education as a right. Overall in this period, western donors saw education as an instrument rather than a goal and saw health reform as a more effective way to eliminate poverty (Mundy, 1998).

Meanwhile, low interest rates coupled with high inflation had led international financial institutions, such as the World Bank and the International Monetary Fund (IMF) to invest in developing countries in the late 1970s. When interest rates started rising, borrowers began to default on those loans. As a solution, World Bank President Robert McNamara, US Treasury Secretary James Baker, US President Ronald Reagan, and UK Prime Minister Margaret Thatcher devised what later became known as the "Washington Consensus," which promoted neoliberal economic ideas, such as an emphasis on restricted state spending, market solutions to problems, and privatization, to address this debt crisis in developing countries (Babb & Carruthers, 2008). User fees for public services, such as education, water, and health care, were a key feature of the promoted policies. The global financial institutions linked the implementation of neoliberal economic reforms to the receipt of loans during this period. The term for this reform was "structural adjustment." The goal was to increase total wealth in the global system, which would benefit everyone in the long run.

By the end of the 1980s, World Bank policies were defining education systems in less developed countries (Benavot & Resnick, 2006). They helped neoliberal approaches to education to spread globally. With the imposition of fees for primary education, there was a move away from the requirements of international law. Yet, this discourse initially received little comment because it remained consistent with previous discourses that emphasized the functional aspect of education and saw it as a means to development rather than a right in and of itself.

By 2000, 77 of 79 countries studied for a World Bank report had adopted some type of user fee for primary education (Kattan & Burnett, 2004). Thirty-eight percent of countries had tuition fees for education, and countries also sometimes had fees for textbooks, compulsory uniforms, parent–teacher associations, and/or activities. A number of scholars have written about the effect of these policy changes on education outcomes. Mutangadura, Blau, and Lamb (2002), for example, found that higher levels of debt were associated with lower primary-to-secondary transition rates and lower levels of secondary school enrollment in countries in Africa. Makene (2007) found that some parents would enroll only a portion of their children in school because of school fees in Tanzania. Furthermore, gross enrollment rates, which had grown from 45 to 80 percent between 1960 and 1980, declined to 72 percent between 1980 and 1992 in Sub-Saharan Africa (Fredrikson, 2009). Overall, it is clear that user fees kept at least some of the poor from sending their children to school. If education had been viewed as a right rather than as a functional aspect of development, the World Bank and the IMF likely would not have seen it as replaceable. But, since education was largely valued for its development functions, it was seen as optional. There were multiple strategies to promote development.

Opposition to User Fees for Education

Although INGOs had been mobilizing around education-related issues for over a century, the rise of user fees and other neoliberal approaches to state policies brought them together in a transnational advocacy network that called for more expansive education policies (Mundy, 1998; see also Boyle & Kim, 2009; Schafer, 1999).[10] This opposition to the financial institutions' loan conditionalities was intense and rested on charges of perpetuating poverty in poor countries rather than on child rights. In other words, the advocates of free education utilized the World Bank's own language to critique it. While some activists did utilize child rights discourse, the vast majority of them relied on a development discourse.

Nevertheless, the presence of this increasingly vocal and organized civil society network at the global level may explain why the World Bank was willing to work with UNESCO, UNICEF, and the United Nations Development Fund at the World Conference on Education For All in Jomtien, Thailand in 1990. Many INGOs participated in the conference, and it resulted in the 1990 World Declaration on Education for All ("Jomtien Declaration"). However, while the Jomtien Declaration reaffirmed education as a human right, it did not utilize child rights discourse (Tomaševski, 2003). Instead of affirming that education should be free and compulsory, the Declaration referred to societal responsibility and public–private partnerships (Tomaševski, 2003).

By 1995, a growing chorus of criticisms over World Bank policies could no longer be ignored (Gertler & Glewwe, 1992; Harrigan & Mosley, 1991; Ogbu & Gallagher, 1991; Sadasivam, 1997; World Bank, 1994). Much of this criticism came from INGOs that highlighted the negative impact of loan conditionalities on the achievement of universal primary education (Mundy, 2006). However, this advocacy was once again largely framed in the context of development, as many development INGOs had begun to open or expand their education programs (Mundy & Murphy, 2001). Oxfam, ActionAid, and Education International each launched independent advocacy campaigns that targeted the Jomtien Declaration commitment made by governments. In 1999, they combined efforts to form the Global Campaign for Education, which highlighted the negative impact of IMF conditionalities on the funding and the quality of education (Mundy & Murphy, 2001). Rights discourse was not absent from the Global Campaign for Education (Chabbott, 2003). But, like previous efforts, a focus on poverty and other development discourse was more prominent (see Mundy & Murphy, 2001).

Pressure continued, and in response, the World Bank backtracked from some of its hard-line positions. In 2000, the Millennium Development Goals built on and strengthened the Jomtien Declaration (see http://www.un.org/millenniumgoals/). The 2000 World Education Forum in Dakar also reaffirmed commitment to achieving education for all by 2015. The Dakar Framework for Action, which was adopted at the forum, links education to the rights of the child. However, development discourse is much more prominent than rights discourse, and child rights are not a key aspect of the document.

In 2001, the World Bank indicated to countries that it did not support user fees for education (see, e.g., Makene, 2007), which eliminated the need for further strategic action on this point by the advocacy network. Although pressure was eventually successful in influencing the World Bank to change its policies to be consistent with the goal of achieving free universal primary education, it is surprising that child rights discourse did not play a larger role in this story. We offer several explanations for this finding. First, free primary education emerged as an issue of development. Sometimes education was linked to the *right* to development, but it was seldom linked specifically to child rights during the 1950s and 1960s. Just like the organizations mobilizing against FGCs, organizations that focused on education stayed largely within their initial frameworks. Activists often utilized the discourse and strategies of previous activists; in this way, prior activist discourse became an institutional constraint. This certainly was not always the case, but a development discourse dominated.

User Fees, Child Rights, and Strategic Decision-Making

While the strategies of activists likely became institutionalized at the organizational level, activists were also agents who exercise considerable choice over their frameworks. Some activists no doubt consciously chose to utilize a development frame rather than a child rights frame as a response to the development discourse of the World Bank and other international financial institutions. User fees were a strategy that went beyond children; these fees were also applied to water, health care, etc. Thus, activists for multiple causes were against user fees, and a development frame encompassed the concerns of these potential allies better than a specific child rights frame. Furthermore, activists ultimately succeeded in changing the World Bank's stance on user fees for education. They likely stayed close to what they believed resulted in success.

The lack of child rights discourse may also reflect a concern about perceived western bias. Free education has been seen as a method of ending child labor (Mundy & Murphy, 2001), but concerns over child labor are viewed by some as especially ethnocentric (see discussion in Myers, 2001). In particular, critiques are levied that the child rights discourse surrounding child labor is linked to a western view of childhood. While western societies often rigorously separate childhood from adulthood, many other societies equip children to play a mature role in the family by adolescence and expect children to contribute to family livelihood (Myers, 2001). For some families, these contributions from children are necessary to maintain their standard of living. Thus, while the link between labor and education was present in early development discourse, the link was much more controversial when framed interms of child rights. Activists may have chosen to avoid such controversy by choosing to employ development discourse rather than child rights frame.

The case of user fees in education is unique among child rights issues. Unlike anti-FGCs policies, international law was very clear, and UNESCO was involved early on in promoting free education for children. Problems arose when other IGOs began promoting the idea of school fees. States could and did argue that they had no choice but to implement user fees. Ultimately, activists responded by creating a transnational advocacy network that shamed international financial institutions but focused on development rather than child rights.

SUMMARY

Based on just two case studies, we cannot say with certainty the extent to which child rights are marginalized in transnational advocacy networks. Nor can we say that child rights will not be used more in the future. What our case studies do reveal are several difficulties with a child rights discourse that cut across very different issues.

For both FGCs and education cost sharing, we found that historical imprinting impeded a shift in strategies to embrace a child rights frame. The Keck and Sikkink transnational advocacy network model describes the stages of mobilization (symbolism, information, leverage, and account-ability) but says little about the specific strategies deployed within each stage of advocacy and how these might vary across issues. Our cases suggest that these strategies build on the strategies of prior activists, which constrain the extent to which new discourses, such as a child rights discourse, can be fully integrated. The type of information provided in the cases of free primary education and FGCs tended to follow models developed in earlier periods. Advocates could have emphasized information on how user fees and FGCs violated child rights and utilized strategies highlighting the vulnerability of children and their development needs and rights, but they tended to underutilize these arguments. Instead, they focused on perpetuating poverty in poor countries and women's inequality, respectively. It appears that activists make certain assumptions about information's relevance and centrality based on the patterns established by prior activists. Child rights could be a more persuasive framework for both FGCs and education user fees than the frames that are currently dominant, but advocacy networks tend not to deploy them as a core element of mobilization.

In addition to framing, the deployment of symbols appeared to be constrained by historical patterns. Education issues developed during the 1950s and mostly within the confines of IGOs, where deference is shown to states and shaming tactics are circumscribed. Attention to FGCs, in contrast, emerged outside traditional state power structures in the books and articles of "radical" feminists who were struggling mightily to gain the attention of global elites. Their stories, which shocked and appalled, brought approbation but also captured people's attention. These very different strategies continue to be deployed by the respective advocacy networks without much apparent assessment of whether they are in fact the best strategies in the contemporary period.

This lack of attention to child rights arguments seemed based, at least in part, on the fact that children themselves rarely form active interest groups. As long as children are unlikely to mobilize on their own behalves, they are unlikely to shift the teleological processes that keep discourses on a particular track. The creation of child rights may eventually prompt more identity construction around the status of "child" and ultimately more mobilization. In the case of FGCs, there are signs that IGOs are beginning to mobilize a child rights frame on behalf of children. Indeed, if history is the only or the major impediment to child rights, then time will eventually correct the oversight.

More troubling are the substantive weaknesses of the approach. In both of our two cases – despite their differences – it appeared that a child rights frame would exacerbate rather than alleviate allegations of western bias. Furthermore, particularly in the case of FGCs, a child rights perspective, which emphasizes the agency of children, threatened to undermine the strategic choice to symbolize FGC as victimizing children. In the case of education, arguments regarding user fees were caught up in larger discussions of the purpose of the state and the need for public goods. Child rights proved too narrow to deal with this broader concern.

It has been 22 years since the CRC was adopted by the United Nations and it appears that the treaty has been underutilized. This is unfortunate for many reasons. Many saw the CRC as a way to bolster economic, social, and cultural rights more generally (see Fernando, 2001). The ICESCR has received considerably less support than the related ICCPR. The United States has ratified the ICCPR but not the ICESCR, for example. Advocates for greater economic rights and reduced inequality thought that providing these rights to children could be a first step in expanding them more broadly. The lack of reliance on child rights in the user fee case – education is defined as an economic right – suggests that this bootstrapping is not going to happen.

The underutilization of child rights is also unfortunate for children themselves. As we discussed throughout this chapter, if something is a right, then it becomes an end in itself. Placing children's issues into other frameworks runs the risk that they will be abandoned when other outcomes, such as health or economic development, are achieved.

NOTES

1. This chapter is based in part on work supported by National Science Foundation (NSF) Grant No. 0921767. Any opinions, findings, and conclusions are those of the authors and do not necessarily reflect the views of the NSF.

2. The United States ratified the ICCPR in 1992. It has not ratified the ICESCR. The Convention on the Rights of the Child is unique for bringing these two types of rights together in a single treaty. Two schools of thought have guided the logic of child rights as it has evolved. One school, child liberation, suggests that children are entitled to self-determination and are granted rights for the same reasons as adults (Farson 1974). This school believes that children should have a full range of rights. The other school, child protection, claims that children primarily need nurture and protection. Advocates of this view are less willing to grant children the same level of civil and political rights that child liberationists support (Hawes, 1991).

3. Ratifying the Minimum Age Convention was a prerequisite for ratifying the 1999 Convention on the Worst Forms of Child Labor. There was thus a flurry of ratifications of the older treaty at the turn of the millennium, and today a majority of countries have ratified it.

4. Discourse is special terminology and language that creates identities, explains behaviors, and defines structures in specific domains (Chabbott 2003). People use discourse to convey abstract concepts, and over time, people often forget the origins of these concepts. The concepts are then seen as facts and taken for granted as always having existed. Thus, discourse is a way in which identities, behaviors, and structures become institutionalized (Chabbott, 2003).

5. Framing refers to the practices whereby individuals and groups identify, interpret, and express social and political grievances and goals. Specifically, social

movement frames identify a problem, its source, and possible solutions (Benford & Snow, 2000).

6. Keck and Sikkink (1999) note there are certain situations in which transnational advocacy networks have organized most effectively. For example, mobilization of nontraditional power has been most effective with issues that involve bodily harm to individuals who are perceived as vulnerable or innocent. For example, FGCs involve bodily harm to children, who are traditionally seen as vulnerable and innocent.

7. France was an exception. It prosecuted parents under child abuse statutes (Winter, 1994).

8. For more information on this aspect of mobilization against FGCs, see a recent article by Boyle and Corl (2010).

9. This section on education user fees draws on an earlier analysis of the literature on international governmental organizations in the education field (Kim & Boyle, forthcoming).

10. These policies also led to a decrease in international aid for education (Mundy, 1998).

REFERENCES

Babb, S. L., & Carruthers, B. G. (2008). Conditionality: Forms, function, and history. *Annual Review of Law & Social Science, 4*, 13–29.

Benavot, A., & Resnick, J. (2006). Lessons from the Past: A comparative socio-historical analysis of primary and secondary education. In: J. E. Cohen, D. E. Bloom & M. B. Malin (Eds.), *Educating all children: A global agenda* (pp. 123–229). Cambridge, MA: American Academy of Arts and Sciences.

Benford, R. D., & Snow, D. A. (2000). Framing processes and social movements: An overview and assessment. *Annual Review of Sociology, 26*, 611–639.

Benporath, S. R. (2003). Autonomy and vulnerability: On just relations between adults and children. *Journal of Philosophy of Education, 37*(1), 127–145.

Berkovitch, N., & Bradley, K. (1999). The globalization of women's status: Consensus/dissensus in the world polity. *Sociological Perspectives, 42*, 481–498.

Blanchfield, L. (2009). The United Nations Convention on the Rights of the Child: Background and policy issue. Congressional Research Service. Available at http://fpc.state.gov/documents/organization/134266.pdf

Boli, J., & Thomas, G. M (Eds.). (1999). INGOs and the organization of world culture. In *Constructing world culture: International nongovernmental organizations since 1875* (pp. 1–12). Stanford, CA: Stanford University Press.

Boli-Bennett, J., & Meyer, J. W. (1978). The ideology of childhood and the state: Rules distinguishing children in national constitutions. *American Sociological Review, 43*, 797–812.

Boulware-Miller, K. (1985). Female circumcision: Challenges to the practice as a human rights violation. *Harvard Women's Law Journal, 8*, 155–177.

Boyle, E. H. (2002). *Female genital cutting: Cultural conflict in the global community*. Baltimore, MD: Johns Hopkins University Press.

Boyle, E. H., & Carbone-López, K. (2006). Movement frames and African Women's explanations for opposing female genital cutting. *International Journal of Comparative Sociology, 47*(6), 435–465.

Boyle, E. H., & Corl, A. C. (2010). Law and culture in a global context: Interventions to eradicate female genital cutting. *Annual Review of Law & Social Science, 6*, 195–215.

Boyle, E. H., & Hoeschen, A. (2001). Theorizing the form of media coverage over time. *The Sociological Quarterly, 42*, 511–528.

Boyle, E. H., & Kim, M. (2009). International human rights law, global economic reforms, and child survival and development rights outcomes. *Law & Society Review, 43*(3), 455–490.

Boyle, E. H., & Preves, S. (2000). National legislating as an international process: The case of anti-female genital cutting laws. *Law & Society Review, 34*, 401–432.

Boyle, E. H., Smith, T., & Guenther, K. (2006). The rise of the child as an individual in global society. In: S. Alladi Venkatesh & R. Kassimir (Eds.), *Youth, globalization and law* (pp. 255–283). Stanford University Press.

Boyle, E. H., Songora, F., & Foss, G. (2001). International discourse and local politics: Anti-female-genital-cutting laws in Egypt, Tanzania and the United States. *Social Problems, 48*, 524–544.

Breen, C. (2003). The role of NGOs in the formulation of and compliance with the optional protocol to the convention on the rights of the child on involvement of children in armed conflict. *Human Rights Quarterly, 25*(2), 453–481.

Chabbott, C. (1999). Defining development: The making of the international development field, 1945–1990. In: J. Boli & G. Thomas (Eds.), *Constructing world culture: International nongovernmental organizations since 1875*. Stanford, CA: Stanford University Press.

Chabbott, C. (2003). *Constructing education for development: International organizations and education for all*. New York, NY: RoutledgeFalmer.

Coomaraswamy, R. (1999). Reinventing international law: Women's rights as human rights in the international community. In: P. Van Ness (Ed.), *Debating human rights: Critical essays from the United States and Asia* (pp. 167–183). Philadelphia, PA: University of Pennsylvania Press.

Dawit, S., & Merkuria, S. (1993). The West just doesn't get it. *New York Times*, December 7, p. A27.

Durkheim, E. (1977[1904–1905]). *The evolution of educational thought* (P. Collins, Trans.). London: Routledge and Kegan Paul.

Emirbayer, M., & Johnson, V. (2008). Bourdieu and organizational analysis. *Theoretical Sociology, 37*, 1–44.

Farson, R. E. (1974). *Birthrights*. Macmillan Publishing Co., Inc.

Fernando, J. L. (2001). Children's rights: Beyond the impasse. *Annals of the American Academy of Political and Social Science, 575*, 8–24.

Fredrikson, B. (2009). Rationale, issues, and conditions for sustaining the abolition of school fees. In *Abolishing School Fees in Africa: Lessons from Ethiopia, Ghana, Kenya, Malawi, and Mozambique* (pp. 1–XX), edited by the World Bank in collaboration with UNICEF. World Bank.

Fuchs, E. (2007). Children's rights and global civil society. *Comparative Education, 43*(3), 393–412.

Gertler, P., & Glewwe, P. (1992). The willingness to pay for education for daughters in contrast to sons: Evidence from rural Peru. *World Bank Economic Review, 6*, 171–188.

Guggenheim, M. (2005). *What's wrong with children's rights*. Cambridge, MA: Harvard University Press.

Hager, M. A., Galaskiewicz, J., & Larson, J. A. (2004). Structural embeddedness and the liability of newness among nonprofit organizations. *Public Management Review, 6*(2), 159–188.

Hallett, T., & Ventresca, M. J. (2006). Inhabited institutions: Social interactions and organizational forms in Gouldner's *Patterns of Industrial Bureaucracy*. *Theory and Society, 35*, 213–236.

Harrigan, J., & Mosley, P. (1991). Evaluating the impact of World Bank Structural adjustment lending: 1980–87. *The Journal of Development Studies, 27*, 63–94.

Hawes, J. M. (1991). *The child rights movement: A history of advocacy and protection*. Boston, MA: Twayne Publishers.

Hosken, F. (1979). *The Hosken Report: Genital and sexual mutilations of females* (2nd ed). Lexington, MA: Women's International Network News.

Hosken, F. (1981). Female genital mutilation in the World Today: A global review. *International Journal of Health Services, 11*, 415–430.

Joint Statement. (2008). *Eliminating female genital mutilation: An interagency statement*. Geneva: WHO.

Joint Statement of WHO/UNICEF/UN Family Plan. Assoc./UN Dev. Program. (1997). *Joint Statement on Female Genital Mutilation*. Geneva: WHO.

Kassindja, F., & Bashir, L. M. (1998). *Do they hear you when you cry?* New York, NY: Dell Publishing.

Kattan, R. B., & Burnett, N. (2004). *User fees in primary education*. World Bank Report. Available at http://siteresources.worldbank.org/EDUCATION/Resources/278200-10990 79877269/547664-1099079993288/EFAcase_userfees.pdf. Accessed on October 15, 2010.

Keck, M., & Sikkink, K. (1998). *Activists without borders: Transnational advocacy in international politics*. Ithaca, NY: Cornell University Press.

Keck, M., & Sikkink, K. (1999). Transnational advocacy networks in international and regional politics. *International Social Science Journal, 51*(1), 89–101.

Kelly, E. (2010). Failure to update: An institutional perspective on noncompliance with the family and medical leave act. *Law & Society Review, 44*(1), 33–66.

Kenyatta, J. (1938/1978). *Facing Mount Kenya: The tribal life of the Gikuyu*. New York, NY: Vintage.

Kim, M. & Boyle, E. H. (forthcoming). Neoliberalism, comprehensive education norms, and education spending in the developing world, 1983-2004. *Law & Social Inquiry*.

Kouba, L. J., & Muasher, J. (1985). Female circumcision in Africa: An overview. *African Studies Review, 28*, 95–110.

Libesman, T. (2007). Can international law imagine the world of indigenous children? *International Journal of Child Rights, 15*(2), 283–309.

Makene, F. S. (2007). *Tanzanian responses to contradictory requirements in international law on issues relating to children and elders*. Ph.D. Dissertation, Department of Sociology, University of Minnesota.

Mundy, K. (1998). Educational multilateralism and world (dis)order. *Comparative Education Review, 42*(4), 448–478.

Mundy, K. (2006). Education for all and the new development compact. In: J. Zajda, S. Majhanovich & V. Rust (Eds.), *Education and social justice* (pp. 13–38). Netherlands: Springer.

Mundy, K., & Murphy, L. (2001). Transnational advocacy, global civil society? Emerging evidence from the field of education. *Comparative Education Review*, *45*(1), 85–126.

Mutangadura, G. B., Blau, J. R., & Lamb, V. L. (2002). External debt and secondary education in Sub-Saharan Africa: A dynamic analysis. *The Journal of African Policy Studies*, *8*(1), 1–15.

Mutua, M. (2002). *Human rights: A political and cultural critique*. Philadelphia, PA: University of Pennsylvania Press.

Myers, W. E. (2001). The right rights? Child labor in a globalizing world. *The Annals of the American Academy of Political and Social Science*, *575*(1), 38–55.

Natsoulas, T. (1998). The politicization of the ban on female circumcision and the rise of the independent school movement in Kenya. *JAAS*, *33*, 137–158.

Ogbu, O. M., & Gallagher, M. (1991). On public expenditures and delivery of education in sub-Saharan Africa. *Comprehensive Educational Review*, *35*, 295–318.

O'Neill, O. (1988). Children's rights and children's lives. *Ethics*, *98*(3), 445–463.

Parker, M. (1995). Rethinking female circumcision. *Africa*, *65*, 506–524.

Prazak, M. (2007). Introducing alternative rites of passage. *Africa Today*, *53*(4), 18–40.

Rojas, F. (2006). Social movement tactics, organizational change and the spread of African-American Studies. *Social Forces*, *84*(4), 2147–2166.

Sadasivam, B. (1997). The impact of structural adjustment on women: A governance and human rights agenda. *Human Rights Quarterly*, *19*, 630–665.

Savelsberg, J. (2004). Religion, historical contingencies, and institutional conditions of criminal punishment: The German case and beyond. *Law & Social Inquiry*, *29*, 373–401.

Save the Children. (2010). History. Available at http://www.savethechildren.org/site/c.8rKLIXMGIpI4E/b.6229507/k.C571/History.htm. Accessed on October 25, 2010.

Schafer, M. J. (1999). International nongovernmental organizations and third world education in 1990: A cross-national study. *Sociology of Education*, *72*, 69–88.

Slack, A. T. (1988). Female circumcision: A critical appraisal. *Human Rights Quarterly*, *10*, 437–486.

Smith, J. (1995). *Visions and discussions on genital mutilation of girls: An international survey*. Amsterdam: Defense for Children International.

Stinchcombe, A. L. (1965). Social structure and organizations. In: J. G. March (Ed.), *Handbook of organizations* (pp. 153–193). Chicago, IL: Rand McNally.

Tomaševski, K. (2003). *Education denied: Costs and remedies*. London: Zed Books.

Toubia, N., & Izett, S. (1998). *Female genital mutilation: An Overview*. Geneva: WHO.

Walker, A. (1993). *Possessing the secret of joy*. Orlando, FL: Harcourt Brace.

Walker, A., & Parmar, P. (1993). *Warrior marks: Female genital mutilation and the sexual blinding of women*. New York, NY: Harcourt Brace.

WHO. (2006). Female genital mutilation and obstetric outcome: WHO collaborative prospective study in six African Countries. *Lancet*, *367*, 1835–1841.

WHO. (2011). Female genital mutilation and other harmful practices. Available at http://www.who.int/reproductivehealth/topics/fgm/prevalence/en/index.html. Accessed on March 11, 2011.

Winter, B. (1994). Women, the law, and cultural relativism in France. *Signs: Journal of Women in Culture and Society*, *19*, 939–974.

World Bank. (1994). *Adjustment in Africa: Reforms, results and the road ahead*. New York, NY: Oxford University Press.

LAWS CITED

Convention against Torture and Other Cruel, Inhuman or Degrading Treatment or Punishment. (1984). United Nations.

Convention Concerning Minimum Age for Admission to Employment. (1972). International Labor Organization.

Convention Concerning the Prohibition and Immediate Action for the Elimination of the Worse Forms of Child Labor. (1999). International Labor Organization.

Convention for the Elimination of all forms of Discrimination Against Women. (1979). United Nations.

Convention for the Elimination of Racial Discrimination. (1965). United Nations.

Convention on Consent to Marriage, Minimum Age for Marriage, and Registration of Marriages. (1962). United Nations.

Convention on the Rights of the Child. (1989). United Nations.

International Covenant on Civil and Political Rights. (1966). United Nations.

International Covenant on Economic, Social and Cultural Rights. (1966). United Nations.

Universal Declaration of Human Rights. (1949). United Nations.

THE BOTTOM UP JOURNEY OF "DEFAMATION OF RELIGION" FROM MUSLIM STATES TO THE UNITED NATIONS: A CASE STUDY OF THE MIGRATION OF ANTI-CONSTITUTIONAL IDEAS ☆

Robert C. Blitt

ABSTRACT

This chapter is intended to elaborate on the existing academic literature addressing the migration of constitutional ideas. Through an examination of ongoing efforts to enshrine "defamation of religion" as a violation of

☆This chapter is based on presentations made at the America Association of Law Schools 2010 annual meeting, as a guest of the Faculty Scholarship Roundtable Series at John Marshall Law School, and as a guest at Marquette University Law School. I am indebted to Austin Sarat for his patience, and extend thanks to Ben Clarke from the University of Notre Dame Australia as well as to the anonymous external reviewer, both of whom provided insightful and helpful comments on an earlier draft. I am also indebted to the University of Tennessee College of Law for a summer grant that supported a significant amount of the research conducted for this project, to Professor Gary Pulsinelli for his insight into copyright law, and to Jenny Tang for her editorial assistance. The chapter is dedicated with love to Idan Eli.

Special Issue: Human Rights: New Possibilities/New Problems
Studies in Law, Politics, and Society, Volume 56, 121–211
Copyright © 2011 by Emerald Group Publishing Limited
ISSN: 1059-4337/doi:10.1108/S1059-4337(2011)0000056008

international human rights, the author confirms that the phenomenon of migration is not restricted to positive constitutional norms, but rather also encompasses negative ideas that ultimately may serve to undermine international and domestic constitutionalism. More specifically, the case study demonstrates that the movement of anti-constitutional ideas is not restricted to the domain of "international security" law, and further, that the vertical axis linking international and domestic law is in fact a two-way channel that permits the transmission of domestic anti-constitutional ideas up to the international level.

In reaching the findings presented herein, the chapter also adds to the universalism–relativism debate by demonstrating that allowances for "plurality consciousness" on the international level may in certain instances undermine fundamental norms previously negotiated and accepted as authoritative by the international community. From this perspective, the movement in favor of prohibiting "defamation of religion" is not merely a case study that helps to expand our understanding of how anti-constitutional ideas migrate, but also indicative of a reenergized campaign to challenge the status, content, and stability of universal human rights norms.

INTRODUCTION

The study of how and why legal norms move from one jurisdiction to another continues to generate much attention and controversy. Whether borrowed, bricolaged, transplanted, transmitted, or migrated, "foreign" legal norms have gravitated or been actively pulled into the orbit of various states around the globe for hundreds if not thousands of years. The constant evolution and refinement of the associated theories and terms applied to identify and describe this movement testify to the desire for an overarching framework while betraying the academic uncertainty achieved to date (see, e.g., Langer, 2004; Teubner, 1998; and discussion below). For the most part, academic writing has focused on positive examples of norm exchange (see, e.g., Slaughter, 2000; Kommers, 2002) or has taken a value-neutral approach (see, e.g., Watson, 1993) with regard to the content of norms being transmitted. Yet, alongside the promise of benevolent ideas traversing long distances and potentially transcending various cultural and political systems lies a parallel story less told. This is reflected in the movement of anti-constitutional ideas that operate in practice to restrict the currently recognized panoply of human rights principles.

Applying the recent scholarship of Sujit Choudhry and others to an analysis of the international movement in favor of prohibiting "defamation of religion," this chapter suggests that a modest corollary to the theory of "migration of constitutional ideas" is advisable. In the first instance, the effort by a coalition of states to harness the force of international law to secure what amounts to a ban on blasphemy confirms Choudhry's position that the phenomenon of migration is not restricted to positive ideas advancing constitutionalism, but may in fact encompass deleterious norms as well. However, this case study also signals that the existing understanding of migration theory requires elaboration: First, it illustrates that the movement of anti-constitutional ideas is not restricted to the domain of "international security" law. And second, it demonstrates that the vertical axis linking international and domestic law is in fact open to two-way traffic that allows for the transmission of domestic anti-constitutional ideas from the bottom up to the international level, rather than only in a top-down manner.

This chapter also adds to the universalism–relativism debate by demonstrating that allowances for "plurality consciousness" (Menski, 2006) and "equal discursive dignity" (Baxi, 2003, p. 50) in reshaping existing international human rights law may sometimes operate to undermine norms previously negotiated and accepted as authoritative by the international community. In the context of entertaining a prohibition on defamation of religion, an approach based on "plurality consciousness" may result in the perverse outcome of eliminating plurality in practice. From this standpoint, examining the effort to outlaw "defamation of religion" not only expands our understanding of how anti-constitutional ideas migrate but also harbingers an energized campaign to challenge the status, content, and stability of universal human rights norms. Accordingly, the phenomenon of defamation of religion deserves a concerted and clear response by all actors committed to upholding long-standing and universal individual rights including freedom of expression and freedom of thought, conscience, and religion or belief.

The section that follows introduces the debate over approaches to comparativism and the study of how legal norms – specifically constitutional norms – pass from one jurisdiction to another. This survey highlights the recent scholarship around migration of constitutional ideas, emphasizing the theory's openness for identifying anti-constitutional ideas. With this theoretical framework in place, the third section focuses on the origins of "defamation of religion" and the problems associated with municipal enforcement of blasphemy offenses. The fourth section addresses how the defamation concept arrived at the United Nations (UN), tracing its bottom-up migration as well as its increasing legitimization by the UN's various political bodies and reporting mechanisms.

Lastly, the chapter discusses the perspective of the Organization of the Islamic Conference (OIC), the driving force behind support for the creation of an international prohibition on defamation of religion. This analysis will demonstrate that the OIC, partly because of developments at the UN, already considers that the ban has achieved binding status internationally. More specifically, this section will show that the OIC's formulation of the ban is premised upon multiple anti-constitutional ideas that promote discrimination, criminal punishment, and – most troublingly – the upending or distorting of preexisting human rights norms. Examined from this perspective, the OIC's activism on defamation of religion not only enlarges our understanding of how anti-constitutional norms may migrate but also signals the practical risks and limitations of negotiating international norms through a lens of plurality consciousness alone. The consequence of such an approach, if left unqualified and unchallenged, may allow an increasingly assertive relativism based on parochial religious beliefs to overshadow the human rights gains achieved over the past 60 years.

TO TRANSPLANT, TRANSPORT, OR MIGRATE?
THE MOVEMENT OF LEGAL NORMS AND
CONSTITUTIONAL IDEAS

In the afterword to the second edition of his landmark text *Legal Transplants*, Alan Watson (1993) confessed to "gravely underestimat[ing] the extent and impact of legal borrowing" (p. 108). Watson's original study assessed with impressive breadth the practice of legal transplants from as early as the Babylonian Code of Hammurabi, through Roman times to colonial Massachusetts, and up to modern-day Scottish law. Yet, in retrospect, Watson (1993) still felt that he had underestimated the "continual massive borrowing" and its prevalence as a common practice across borders and cultures (p. 107).

Many scholars quickly moved to point out flaws in Watson's reasoning and challenged his metaphor of transplantation. Among them, Pierre Legrand (1997) rejected the possibility of Watson's approach perhaps most vociferously.[1] Legrand's chief criticism posited that transplants were impossible because one nation's law was rooted in its own specific cultural and social context that could not be reproduced elsewhere.[2] Maintaining that law could adapt to new circumstances and take on a life of its own, Watson (1993) allegorized, "A successful legal transplant – like that of a human organ – will grow in its new body" (p. 27).[3] David Nelken attempted to bridge these viewpoints by calling for the rethinking of "the metaphors we use as part of … attempts to theorise processes of legal transfer." Nelken (2001) himself preferred the more open-ended notion of "legal adaptation" and leaving open the possibility of resorting to "different metaphors so as to come to terms with different processes" (p. 30).

Menski frames the above debate as one between "culturalists" like Legrand and "transferists" such as Watson. Culturalists reason that since law reflects a culturally determined construct, one society cannot adopt the laws of another without some strong, shared affinity. In contrast, transferists hold that borrowing can occur despite jurisdictional differences in social, political, and cultural makeup (Menski, 2006, pp. 51–52). Rather than endorsing one metaphor, Menski advances an overarching critique for the enterprise of comparativism as a whole. In Menski's view, existing models are inherently "Eurocentric legal theories [that] claim universal validity while representing only a shrinking part of global humanity" (Menski, 2006, p. 25). Menski's frustration stems from his belief that these models are premised on "assumptions about the superiority of Western laws" and focus "mainly on Western inputs" (Menski, 2006, p. 51). In other words, Menski (2006) acknowledges the possibility of transfer, but decries the fact that "the global movement of legal norms and rules has always been assumed to migrate from the West to the East, from the North to the South, and hardly ever in the reverse direction" (p. 51).

Menski's (2006) solution calls for boosting "voices of the South … now manifested as increasingly self-confident post-colonial assertion of non-Western laws in the countries of the North" (p. 38). Others share this perspective. According to Upendra Baxi (2003), comparative legal studies require an "epistemic break" because the field has failed to provide "equal discursive dignity to non-European-American traditions" (p. 50).[4] For Baxi, the field can no longer "simply thrive on the sound of the trumpet. It needs also, and more than ever before, to listen to the power of lamentation of the millennial losers" (Baxi, 2003, p. 75).

Despite these criticisms that legal transplants are tainted by Eurocentricism, Nelken (2003) aptly concludes, "It can hardly be gainsaid that legal transfers are possible, are taking place, have taken place and will take place. What exactly is happening or is likely to happen in such transfers is another story" (p. 443).[5] This perspective encourages refinement of the theoretical frameworks used to assess how norms move from one jurisdiction to another and invites greater consideration of possible critiques, including those by Menski and Baxi. By accounting for the shortcomings in existing comparative methodology, this chapter acknowledges the necessity of creating space for the postcolonial assertion of non-Western laws and the migration of legal norms from the south to north, but also underscores the need for a theoretical framework that allows for normative unpacking of any possible adoption or transfer of ideas be they malevolent or benign. For example, Watson's theory (1993) affords no normative judgment regarding the transplant of the death penalty for idolatry, sodomy, and witchcraft to the Massachusetts Bay Colony (pp. 65–67); nor does he explore whether its transmission results in positive or negative consequences for the legal culture undertaking the adoption. In the context of globalization, where ideas are able to move at a pace and distance far exceeding anything witnessed in colonial times, these concerns can have serious implications in practice and theory.

Sujit Choudhry's (2006b) more contemporary approach helps move this discussion forward. Choudhry makes the case that the linguistic and theoretical constraints associated with the debate over constitutional borrowing and transplants demand a more encompassing term that can accommodate all the intellectual and practical traffic associated with the movement of constitutional norms. In his view, previous metaphoric devices only carry scholars so far and fall short of offering a comprehensive formula for better understanding the dynamics of comparativism (Choudhry, 2006a, p. 20). In response to this shortcoming, Choudhry advances the term "migration" as a framework that more readily encapsulates a comprehensive research agenda and methodology for identifying how constitutional ideas journey from one jurisdiction to the next.

The metaphor of migration, more so than borrowing, bricolage,[6] or transplant, reflects theoretical refinements particularly useful for the context of this chapter. First, Choudhry (2006a) rightly points out that migration of constitutional ideas "may occur without knowledge or permission of the source jurisdiction. Migration is often covert and illicit" (p. 21). Second, migration, unlike borrowing, "explicitly opens the door to a wider range of uses for constitutional ideas, and for the outcomes of the process of comparative engagement" (Choudhry, 2006a, p. 21). For example, migration has occurred "not only in the context of constitution-making, but also in that of constitutional interpretation" (Rosenfeld, 2001, p. 69).[7] Finally, and perhaps most importantly, Choudhry (2006a) reasons that unlocking this wider spectrum of uses demonstrates that "the constitutional ideas which have migrated are often actually anti-constitutional ideas" (p. 33). Thus,

Choudhry's theory, unlike others, explicitly acknowledges that migration can be harmful as well as beneficial. As Neil Walker (2006) observes, "Unlike other terms current in the Comparativist literature such as 'borrowing,' 'transplant,' or 'cross-fertilization,' [migration] presumes nothing about the attitudes of the giver or the recipient, or about the properties or fate of the legal objects transferred" (p. 320).

Although Choudhry's recognition that the migration of legal ideas is not reserved for the function of benevolent law making or interpretation is a simple but important breakthrough, I argue that existing migration theory does not go far enough. As it currently stands, identification of anti-constitutional ideas is too narrowly focused and too reliant upon post-9/11 "international security" law. Further, the ideas appear to migrate only from the top-down, that is, from the UN Security Council (UNSC) to UN member states.[8] Despite Choudhry's cursory exploration of the anti-constitutional prong of migration theory, his conclusion regarding its implications ring true on a much broader level:

> whereas the migration of constitutional ideas has typically been associated with enhanced respect for human rights and the rule of law, post 9/11 it has arguably resulted in their dilution. Constitutionalism post 9/11 therefore raises the question of whether constitutional convergence is an unqualified good – with strong suggestions ... for the persuasiveness of negative responses. (Choudhry, 2006a, p. 33)

In her analysis of UNSC Resolution 1373, Kim Lane Scheppele (2006) provides a valuable example of how anti-constitutional ideas post-9/11 may travel. She posits that by issuing the resolution, the UNSC essentially facilitated the migration of anti-constitutional ideas into the legal systems of member states under the guise of combating terrorism. As states took measures to implement the resolution, certain governments invoked the resolution to justify infringements on fundamental rights and otherwise act in an anti-constitutional manner (Scheppele, 2006, p. 363).

Though innovative, Scheppele's use of Resolution 1373 as an example of the top-down migration of anti-constitutional ideas is not immune from criticism. Scheppele conspicuously fails to demonstrate that the UNSC intended its resolution to have any anti-constitutional content or effect. Although Resolution 1373 (2001, September 28) required that all states inter alia "[e]nsure that ... terrorist acts are established as serious criminal offences in domestic laws" (para. 2(e)), its implementation was left to the domestic discretion of the member states. The resolution did not explicitly mandate states to trample on recognized human rights obligations. Moreover, within the year that followed Resolution 1373, key UNSC members clearly expressed the expectation that international human rights protections needed to be safeguarded in the international campaign against terrorism. For example, the Organization for Security and Cooperation in Europe's (OSCE) *Charter on Preventing and Combating Terrorism* required that "all counter-terrorism measures and co-operation [be conducted] in accordance with the rule of law, the UN Charter and the relevant provisions of international law, international standards of human rights and ... international humanitarian law" (OSCE, 2002, December 7).

Nothing in this context supports that Resolution 1373 was intended as an anti-constitutional carte blanche inviting states to cast aside fundamental individual rights. Rather, certain regimes twisted the admittedly equivocal UNSC mandate to serve their own anti-constitutional purposes.[9] Therefore, Scheppele's explanation for the migration of anti-constitutional ideas via the UNSC arguably falls flat in so far as the resolution itself lacked any definitive anti-constitutional content at its migratory point of origin. In other words, no anti-constitutional idea ever migrated per se. Instead, a group of states elected to ignore preexisting international human rights law obligations and unilaterally manipulated an otherwise legitimate UNSC directive to serve an anti-constitutional function. Indeed, Scheppele (2006) concedes "those states that started without a strong constitutionalist orientation [were often] quickest to comply with the [UN Security Council Counter-Terrorism Committee] mandates in the most abusive ways" (p. 372). Furthermore, though it required a 16-month time lag, the UNSC ultimately did clarify the oblique nature of Resolution 1373 by resolving that "[s]tates must ensure that any measure taken to combat terrorism comply with all their obligations under international law, and should adopt such measures in accordance with international law, in particular international human rights, refugee, and humanitarian law" (UNSC, 2003, January 20, para. 6). UNSC directives issued subsequently followed a similar format.[10]

Despite this shortcoming, Scheppele's argument provides useful insights for furthering our understanding of migration theory. First, she recognizes the possibility that other aspects of the legal process, including legislation, can be a part of the migration of constitutional ideas. Scheppele (2006) reasons that once the study of constitutional ideas is reframed "in terms of migration, it is no longer inevitable that the primary legal ideas on the move are only *domestic* and *constitutional* legal ideas moving from place to place" (p. 349). Instead, "domestic ideas from fields of legal doctrine other than *constitutional* law may be part of this picture because they too migrate into other fields, including into and out of constitutional law itself" (Scheppele, 2006, p. 349).

Second, and most importantly for this chapter, Scheppele accurately observes that migration need not be driven exclusively by the objective of constitutional betterment. In her words, the post-9/11 wave of migration "is occurring in a very different field, one that has a tendency to *undermine constitutional structures* and protections," by inter alia, "truncating due process guarantees ... restricting individual rights of liberty, speech, association, and privacy" (Scheppele, 2006, p. 351, emphasis added).[11] As will be argued below, these are all "features" (if one can call them that) of the anti-constitutional campaign to brand defamation of religion as a violation of international human rights law.

This chapter picks up where Choudhry and Scheppele leave off. Framing the effort to outlaw defamation of religion on the international level as an example of the migration of anti-constitutional ideas yields several useful refinements on the existing theory, as well as insight into the potentially deleterious effect associated with empowering Baxi's "lamentation of the millennial losers." First, the analysis demonstrates that the migration of anti-constitutional ideas is not restricted to the realm of antiterror legislation, but rather operates equally outside the post-9/11 environment. Second, it illustrates that in addition to the top-down migration of anti-constitutional ideas identified by Scheppele, a parallel bottom-up migratory axis exists for passing domestic anti-constitutional ideas up to the international system for broader dissemination and/or legitimization purposes. Finally, in regard to how the push to prohibit defamation of religion may embody the self-confident postcolonial assertion of a non-Western norm by voices of the South, this chapter contends that consideration of "plurality-consciousness" should not come at the expense of diluting existing international human rights standards. Accordingly, the emerging – and increasingly muscular – "self-confidence" on the part of various "non-Western" states in this area should be viewed with caution. Although "listening" to their lamentations may be a commendable approach, diplomats and human rights activists alike must not automatically accept their proposals as normatively necessary or worthy when they threaten to undermine existing universal norms designed to protect the rights of all individuals equally and without discrimination.

THE ROOTS OF DEFAMATION OF RELIGION AND ITS ANTI-CONSTITUTION LINEAGE

Journey to the Origin of Defamation of Religion: A Blasphemy Primer

Blasphemy in Christian and Muslim Tradition
Although much has been written on the historical development of the offense of blasphemy,[12] this brief section provides a foundation for better

understanding of the challenge posed by defamation of religion as it manifests on the international level. Blasphemy – the crime of challenging the structure and related dogmas of the predominant faith – has existed at one time or another across a variety of legal systems, including Western common law and Islamic sharia law. Until the 17th century, ecclesiastical courts in the West retained jurisdiction over blasphemy offenses. However, in 1643, the English parliament sought to suppress under state law "the great late abuses and frequent disorders in Printing many false forged, scandalous, seditious, libellous, and unlicensed Papers, Pamphlets, and Books to the great defamation of Religion and government" (Meyerson, 2001, p. 303 (Licensing order, June 14, 1643, reprinted in Milton, John, *Complete Prose Works*, Vol. 2)). At the same time, the nation's courts identified blasphemy as a common law offense, reasoning that "to reproach the Christian religion is to speak in subversion of the law" (Taylor's Case, 1676). Consequently, such an expression entailed not only an offence against God and religion but also a crime against the state. This understanding carried over to the United States. For example, in 1650 the state of Connecticut's penal code provided the death penalty for the offense of blasphemy (as well as for sorcery, adultery and rape) (Tocqueville, 1990, p. 37). In 1792, every state in the United States made either blasphemy or profanity, or both, statutory crimes (*Roth v. U.S.*, 1957, p. 482). Inevitably, such laws empowered state officials with broad powers to restrict expression on the basis of vague rules, and operated to restrict not only speech deemed insulting of the predominant faith but also that considered threatening to the state (Mayton, 1982, p. 248; see also Witte, 2008, p. 1589).

A similar pattern of shielding the predominant faith and ruler against perceived challenges emerged early in Islamic history. Although no precise parallel to the Judeo–Christian notion of blasphemy exists under Islam,[13] insulting God, Muhammed, or any other aspect of divine revelation traditionally has amounted to a punishable offense under Islamic law whether framed as apostasy or heresy (Arzt, 1996a, pp. 351–352; see also Hassan, 2006).[14] This practice emerged in part because "no separation between religion and politics or religious and civil authority [existed] in the early days of Islam" (Kamali, 1997, p. 249), leading to the absence of any bright line separation between religion and state (see e.g., Arzt, 1996b, p. 143; Arzt, 1996c; Mayer, 1991).

Despite the historical absence of any separation between mosque and state, some progressive Islamic scholars have posited that the Qur'an in fact entitles an individual to express "what he or she pleases." However, this liberty comes with a sweeping caveat: such expression cannot "involve blasphemy, backbiting, slander, insult or lies, nor seek to give rise to perversity, corruption, hostility or sedition" (Kamali, 1997, p. 12). Given these competing interpretations, the concept of blasphemy in Islam "has always remained open and difficult define, in part because the general approach has subsumed the offense under apostasy" (Kamali, 1997, p. 213).

Blasphemy Today
Invariably, the operation of blasphemy laws, regardless of state venue, has subjected individuals who express viewpoints deemed unfavorable by the ruling regime to grave risk (Levy, 1985, p. 5). For example, William Gott, the last individual in the United Kingdom sentenced to a prison term for blasphemy in 1922, served nine months hard labor for distributing pamphlets describing Jesus Christ entering Jerusalem "like a circus clown on the back of two donkeys" (*Rex v. Gott*, 1922, p. 89).[15] As religion and state slowly decoupled, the offense of blasphemy in the West gradually lost its luster. Prosecutions dwindled during the 20th century (Levy, 1981, p. x),[16] and in 2008 the United Kingdom officially abolished the common law offense of blasphemy (UK Criminal Justice and Immigration Act, 2008, s. 79). Today, blasphemy exists as an offense only in a minority of Council of Europe (CoE) member states and is rarely prosecuted (CoE, 2010, p. 19).[17] The CoE's Venice Commission recently concluded that member states with blasphemy laws remaining in force should take measures to abolish the offense and that similar laws "should not be reintroduced" in the future (CoE, 2010, p. 32).

In contrast to Western experience, the predominant interpretation of Islamic theology still rejects the possibility of any separation between religion and state,[18] and consequently many majority Muslim states today have not experienced a similar decoupling. While the maintenance of an established state religion is not per se incompatible with international human rights law, such official recognition must not result in any impairment of recognized rights, "nor in any discrimination against adherents to other religions or non-believers" (UN Human Rights Committee, 1993, July 30, para. 9). Accordingly, a dilemma arises where states elect to continue to enforce blasphemy prohibitions despite potential problems with existing international human rights norms and sometimes even domestic constitutional safeguards.

Remarkably, these anti-blasphemy laws are in effect not only where the governing constitutional arrangement establishes Islam as the official state religion, but even in states that are officially declared secular or whose constitutions are silent with regard to the role of Islam. As Fig. 1 indicates,

Fig. 1. Spectrum of Constitutional Models Addressing Islam in the Muslim World.
Source: Adapted from Stahnke and Blitt (2005).

the constitutions of most Muslim majority countries account for Islam in one of four ways (Stahnke & Blitt, 2005).[19] In the first instance, the constitution declares that the state is "Islamic" and also proclaims Islam the official state religion. In the second, the constitution forgoes declaring the state "Islamic" but endorses Islam as the state religion. A third classification makes no explicit provision for Islam, opting instead for silence as to what role, if any, religion might play vis-a-vis the state. Finally, the fourth grouping expressly stipulates that the state is officially secular.

Predictably, declared Islamic states such as Saudi Arabia and Pakistan offer up harsh penalties for the offense of blasphemy (U.S. Commission on International Religious Freedom, 2010, pp. 126 (Saudi Arabia) and 96 (Pakistan)). Yet surprisingly, Muslim majority states self-identified as secular (such as Turkey) as well as states without any express constitutional position on the role of religion (such as Indonesia) still criminally prosecute acts and expression deemed blasphemous. Table 1 illustrates the consistency of this practice across a sampling of Muslim majority states that exhibit each of the four constitutional approaches for addressing the role of Islam. Polling data that reflects the public's level of religiosity and attitude toward blasphemy is also provided for additional context.

The country sampling provided in Table 1 demonstrates that although majority Muslim states have deployed a variety of constitutional approaches for addressing the state's relationship with Islam, this theoretical diversity is not mirrored in practice when concerning blasphemy.[20] Rather, there is singular agreement among the majority of Muslim states, from those declared secular to those declared Islamic, that the offense of blasphemy merits state sanction.[21] Moreover, while differentiation may exist in terms of definition and punishment, the similarities coloring how these offenses are conceptualized and enforced across jurisdictions betray blasphemy

Table 1. Muslim Constitutional Models and Governmental/Public Attitudes Toward Blasphemy.

State	Constitutional Model	Do Constitutional Provisions Generally Compare Favorably with International Religious Freedom Standards?[a]	Anti-Blasphemy Law in Force?	Blasphemous Attitudes[b]	Religiosity (% Orthodox)
Iran	Declared Islamic	No	Yes[c]	Moderate[d]	59
Pakistan	Declared Islamic	Yes	Yes[e]	Strong	96
Egypt	Islam declared state religion	No	Yes[f]	Strong	89
Malaysia	Islam declared state religion	No	Yes[g]	Strong	88
Indonesia	No constitutional declaration	Yes	Yes[h]	Strong	83
Turkey	Declared secular	Yes	Yes[i]	Weak	57

[a]This data is based on Stahnke and Blitt (2005).

[b]Data on "blasphemous attitudes" and "religiosity" is based on a survey of the general population provided by Hassan (2006, p. 127). His study compares this information against the UN's Human Development Index data.

[c]Prosecutions are based on sharia.

[d]This finding may be surprising to some. Hassan suggests one possible explanation may stem from decreased public trust in religious institutions because of their fusion with mechanisms of state, thus impacting "the expressions of religiosity at the individual level" (Hassan, 2006, p. 128).

[e]Penal Code of Pakistan, October 6, 1860, Articles 295–298.

[f]Article 98(f) of Egypt's Penal Code "prohibits citizens from ridiculing or insulting heavenly religions or inciting sectarian strife" (USCIRF, 2009, p. 166).

[g]See discussion at Part III(B)(1), below.

[h]See discussion at Part III(B)(1), below.

[i]Criminal Code of Turkey, September 26, 2004, Article 125.

laws as an anti-constitutional idea with grave human rights implications for Muslims and non-Muslims alike. As will be argued below, those governments that have aligned together to drive enactment of a global prohibition against defamation of religion are principally motivated by the desire to retain and expand the legitimacy of these laws.

The Problem with Blasphemy Laws: Anti-Constitutional Ideas Breed Anti-Constitutional Results

Examining the current formulation and enforcement of anti-blasphemy measures in a variety of states provides better understanding of the offense's anti-constitutional nature and the challenge it poses to existing international human rights standards. These states' practices evidence troubling implications for endorsing a parallel norm prohibiting defamation of religion on the international level.

Although this section focuses mainly on Muslim majority states in illustrating the problems associated with anti-blasphemy laws, it is important to stress at the outset that these states do not represent the sole sanctuary for such offenses. A variety of non Muslim states not only support a ban on defamation of religion at the international level, but also endorse similar practices domestically as well. For example, in Russia, a constitutionally secular state, it has become increasingly problematic to criticize Russian Orthodoxy or the Moscow Patriarchate. A recent trial in Moscow found museum curators guilty of incitement to religious hatred for staging an exhibit entitled "Forbidden Art."[22] The artwork that the court concluded resulted in psychological trauma and moral suffering to Christians – and specifically to the Russian Orthodox group that bolstered the charges – included one painting of the crucifixion where the head of Jesus Christ was replaced by the Order of Lenin medal and another where Mickey Mouse's face was affixed to the body of Jesus Christ (*BBC News*, 2010, July 12). Notably, Human Rights Watch stated that the case highlighted the precarious nature of freedom of expression in Russia and decried the use of "anti-extremism laws to silence independent opinion" (Human Rights Watch, 2010, July 12).[23] Despite such instances in Russia[24] and elsewhere,[25] the simple reality remains that those states at the vanguard of support for an international prohibition on defamation of religion are members of the OIC, an inter-governmental organization representing "the collective voice of the Muslim world" (OIC, "About OIC"). Accordingly, an understanding of how blasphemy measures play out in OIC states is critical to fully appreciate the implications an international prohibition on defamation of religion will have in practice.

"Traditional" and "Second-Generation" Blasphemy Offenses in Select Muslim Majority States

Traditional blasphemy offenses were first designed to discriminately protect the predominant faith only. For example, in *Choudhury v. United Kingdom*, members of Britain's Muslim community sought unsuccessfully to prosecute author Salman Rushdie for allegedly blaspheming against Islam in his novel, *The Satanic Verses* (*Choudhury v. UK*, 1991). The unanimous court rejected the argument that the common law offense of blasphemy should be extended to protect Muslims from religious insult and expressed "no doubt that as the law now stands it does not extend to religions other than Christianity" (*Choudhury v. UK*, 1991, p. 447).[26] Yet, from the Islamic perspective, Rushdie had plainly blasphemed. The Islamic Law Academy of the Muslim World League declared Rushdie an apostate and called for the OIC to prosecute and try Rushdie in absentia in an Islamic country under sharia rules. The organization also dismissed Rushdie's expression of regret over the incident as "idle and meaningless" (Kamali, 1997, pp. 297–298).

Although it is difficult to identify a single Western state that continues to actively enforce this type of traditional or "first generation" blasphemy offense, such prohibitions persist in a number of Muslim states today. For example, the declared Islamic state of Pakistan currently penalizes the use of derogatory language "in respect of the Holy Prophet" (Penal Code of Pakistan, 1860, October 6, Article 295-C). Article 298-A of the Penal Code more generally prohibits the "use of derogatory remarks, etc." in respect of Islam's other holy personages (Penal Code of Pakistan, 1860, Article 298-A). Like the now abolished UK common law offense of blasphemy, Pakistan's criminal ordinances are based on the principle of strict liability. In Pakistan, however, punishment is far more severe and allows for the death penalty in certain instances. In its 2008 annual report on international religious freedom, the U.S. Department of State noted that Pakistani authorities "arrested at least 25 Ahmadis, 11 Christians, and 17 Muslims on blasphemy charges" (U.S. Department of State, 2008). As a means of further bulwarking against "blasphemy," the Pakistani government recently announced plans to begin monitoring and blocking Internet content deemed objectionable to the Islamic faith (Shahzad, 2010, June 25; Wright, Champion, & Efrati, 2010). As one commentator rightly observed, the decision "marks another dangerous expansion of the nation's blasphemy prohibitions, which have been used to restrict freedom of expression, thought and religion" (Stahnke, 2010, July 12).

Similarly in Malaysia, where Islam is the official state religion, sharia-derived laws operate to protect only Islam from offense. In practice, this type of "protection" has been invoked zealously, among other things, to prohibit the Malaysian Bar Association from using the word "Allah" on its website (The Becket Fund, 2009, March 23). At the same time, individuals as well as government representatives are free to attack other faiths. For example, Malaysia permits free distribution of inflammatory materials including

Henry Ford's *The Jew* and the notorious forgery, *The Protocols of the Elders of Zion* – books that not only propagate "blasphemy" but more troublingly have been historically responsible for directly inciting violence against Jewish communities around the world (Ben-Ito, 2005; Cohn, 2005). As a testament to the wide legitimacy these books have achieved in Malaysia, they appear for sale even in academic conferences intended to foster greater religious understanding.[27] Aggravating this climate, for over two decades as Malaysia's Prime Minister, Mahathir bin Muhamad consistently promoted an anti-Semitic worldview that permeated the nation's attitude toward Jews and Israel (Schrag, 2003, October 20). Mahathir's hatred was so visceral and deep-seated that his government went so far as to prohibit the screening of Steven Spielberg's 1994 film *Schindler's List*, labeling it "anti-German propaganda" (Yegar, 2006, October).[28] In 2003, Mahathir told an unflinching audience of OIC delegates, "[T]oday the Jews rule this world by proxy. They get others to fight and die for them … . They invented and successfully promoted Socialism, Communism, human rights and democracy so that persecuting them would appear to be wrong (Prime Minister Mohamad, 2003)."[29] This last statement is particularly disquieting as it seems to posit that but for meddlesome "human rights" and "democracy" it would be perfectly acceptable to persecute Jews.[30]

Malaysia's free-wheeling climate of incitement against Judaism contrasts glaringly with its assertions on the UN level that "no one could remain neutral in the fight against intolerance or any form of incitement, including defamation of religions that endangered peaceful and harmonious co-existence among societies and civilizations … . All States should take steps to promote understanding and respect for other religions and cultures and their sensitivities" (UNHRC, 2006, September 22).

Even where states have taken measures to design a more inclusive anti-blasphemy statute, the application of such "second generation" laws often reflects discriminatory enforcement practices that do little to level the playing field for minority or dissenting religious beliefs. For example, Indonesia's Criminal Code provides the following general anti-blasphemy provision:

156.   The person who publicly gives expression to feelings of hostility, hatred or contempt against one or more groups of the population of Indonesia, shall be punished by a maximum imprisonment of four years or a … fine.

156a: By a maximum imprisonment of five years shall be punished any person who deliberately in public gives expression to feelings or commits an act,

      a. which principally have the character of being at enimity [sic] with, abusing or staining a religion, adhered to in Indonesia;

      b. with the intention to prevent a person to adhere to any religion based on the belief of the allmighty [sic] God.

157. Any person who disseminated [sic], openly demonstrates or puts up a writing or portrait where feelings of hostility, hatred, or contempt against or among groups of the population of Indonesia are expressed, with intent to give publicity to the contents or to enhance the publicity thereof, shall be punished by a maximum imprisonment of two years and six months or a ... fine.[31]

Despite their ostensibly general applicability, Indonesia's criminal code provisions have in practice been invoked "almost always" to prosecute crimes involving blasphemy and heresy against Islam, including practices of Muslims deemed to deviate from mainstream Islam (U.S. Department of State, 2008; see also Human Rights Watch, 2009, World Report). Among other instances, blasphemy charges have been leveled at art exhibits containing photographic representations of Adam and Eve (Indo-Asian News Service, 2006, February 3), and have resulted in jail time for various individuals claiming to be reincarnations of the Prophet Muhammad (Gelling, 2007, November 16) and the archangel Gabriel (Wisnu, 2009, June 3). On a much broader scale, the government has severely restricted and even banned certain activities of the Ahmadi community, including public religious worship, as part of a pattern to suppress targeted groups deemed "heretical," "deviant," or heterodox (USCIRF, 2009, p. 171).

Finally, in Turkey, a declared secular Muslim majority state, the offense of blasphemy still remains in play. Article 125 of the Criminal Code of Turkey (2004, September 26) provides a form of penalty enhancement by increasing the minimum sentence for defamation to no less than one year jail time when the alleged act "mention[s] sacred values in view of the religion with which a person is connected" (Article 125(3)). Like Indonesia, Turkey's inclusively drafted anti-blasphemy law misses the mark on enforcement, typically resulting in protection for the predominant religion only.[32] In a replay of the Salman Rushdie affair, Turkey's Religious Affairs Directorate supported charges filed against Turkish-French author Nedim Gursel for insulting Islam in his novel *The Daughters of Allah* (Reuters, 2009, May 26). Although ultimately acquitted (Lea, 2009, June 26),[33] Gursel's case is but one example among dozens where writers, journalists, and editors have faced prosecution under Turkish laws restricting free speech (International Pen, 2009, May 11). In a related case, a Turkish court ordered access to atheist Richard Dawkins' website blocked after Adnan Oktar, author of a 900-page illustrated *Atlas of Creation* that advocates Islamic "creationism," alleged that the site's content amounted to blasphemy (Gledhill, 2008, September 19).[34] As in Malaysia, the *Jyllands-Posten* Muhammed cartoon affair continued to have deep reverberations in Turkey, most recently manifested in the government's threat to veto Anders Fogh Rasmussen's appointment to head NATO because of his unwillingness to apologize for publication of the cartoons during his tenure as Denmark's prime minister (Butler & Yackley, 2009, April 6). In this vein, Turkish government officials also have pressed their European counterparts to review existing European law and take steps to incorporate "defamation of religion" as a criminal offense (Rennie, 2006, March 13).

Assessing the Anti-Constitutional Effect: Discrimination, Inequality, and Restrictions on Freedom of Expression and Religion or Belief
The above examples illustrate that traditional and "second generation" anti-blasphemy measures pose a challenge to basic principles related to non-discrimination and equality as established under international human rights law, and, as is often the case, parallel domestic constitutional norms. These challenges may arise either because the law is facially discriminatory or discriminatory in effect by virtue of its selective enforcement. For example, the UN Special Rapporteur on Freedom of Religion or Belief's 2008 report on the United Kingdom criticized the now repealed common law offense of blasphemy as being "discriminatory because it favours Christianity alone" (Jahangir, 2008, February 7, p. 21, para. 73).[35] Similarly, the Special Rapporteur's 15-year-old conclusions regarding Pakistan remain salient: "State laws related to religious minorities, and more generally speaking the subject of tolerance and nondiscrimination based on religion or belief, are likely to favour or foster intolerance in society ... More generally speaking, blasphemy [legislation] ... should not be discriminatory and should not give rise to abuse. Nor should it be so vague as to jeopardize human rights, especially those of minorities. If offences against belief are made punishable under ordinary law, then procedural guarantees must be introduced and a balanced attitude must be maintained" (Amor, 1996, January 2, para. 82). The government of Pakistan's response to these findings missed the point completely: it reasoned that the blasphemy ordinance did not discriminate because "[t]hose charged under it have been Muslims as well as non-Muslims" (Amor, 1997, November 12, p. 19).[36]

Although discriminatory and unequal treatment should suffice to demonstrate the operation of an anti-constitutional idea at work, there are deeper problems associated with blasphemy prohibitions. When put into practice, these provisions betray a long-standing record of significantly undermining freedom of expression and freedom of thought, conscience, and religion or belief as defined under international human rights law. Consequently, Abdelfattah Amor, the former Special Rapporteur on Freedom of Religion, has emphasized that blasphemy offenses "should not be used to censure all inter-religious and intra-religious criticism," and that "efforts to combat defamation (particularly blasphemy) may be manipulated for purposes contrary to human rights" (Amor, 2000, February 15, p. 25, para. 11). This is not a radical proposition. Writing in 1960, Arcot Krishnaswami, Special Rapporteur for the UN Sub-Commission on Prevention of Discrimination and Protection of Minorities, similarly concluded that in certain instances:

> the laws against blasphemy have been framed in such a manner that they characterize any pronouncement not in conformity with the predominant faith as blasphemous. Under such laws, censorship of books, pamphlets and newspapers, as well as control of the media of mass communications such as films, radio, television and the like, have sometimes been used to limit unduly – or even to prohibit altogether – the dissemination of beliefs other than those of the predominant religion or philosophy. (1960, p. 41)

Thus, half a century ago, Krishnaswami found that blasphemy offenses breed troubling restrictions on an individual's rights to free expression and free belief and that enforcement of these offenses typically disregarded any balancing of legitimate competing interests. Consider here, for example, the strict liability nature of the UK's now defunct blasphemy offense, as well as Pakistan's contemporary and vigorously enforced blasphemy statute.[37] Although Krishnaswami's analysis predates the International Covenant on Civil and Political Rights (ICCPR) and other key international human rights instruments, undue limitations on free expression and free belief remain a pervasive feature of anti-blasphemy laws today. This inescapable reality underscores why advocacy in favor of installing "defamation of religion" on the international level signals the migration of an anti-constitutional norm, poses a threat to existing international human rights law, and accordingly must be rejected.

Cases of blasphemy-inspired constraints on free expression and free belief culled from present-day municipal practice provide a disquieting glimpse into what types of limitations an international prohibition against defamation of religion might serve to legitimate. In Pakistan, for example, blasphemy laws have consistently been used to restrict basic rights of the Ahmadi community (Amor, 2000, February 15, p. 18, para. 79).[38] As it stands, Ahmadis are prohibited from calling their place of worship a "mosque" and from performing any act that may "outrage" the feelings of Muslims (UN Working Group on Minorities, 2004, November, para. 17), "effectively criminaliz[ing] various practices of their faith" (USCIRF, 2010, p. 91). While Pakistan's blasphemy law on paper expresses preferential protection for Islam over other faiths and therefore is facially discrimina- tory, in its application the law is responsible not merely for discrimination but also for aiding and abetting the persecution of religious minorities, including the Ahmadi community.[39]

Blasphemy laws do not only create hierarchies among schools of religious thought, but often target those professing atheistic or nontheistic views for repression as well. As the Special Rapporteur on Freedom of Religion and Belief previously concluded, members of religious minorities, dissenting believers, and nontheists are made to bear the brunt of such laws (Jahangir, 2007, August 20, p. 21, para. 76). For example, in the Sudan, another state that prohibits blasphemy, an association of Islamic clerics issued a *fatwa* declaring that "Communism is blasphemy, [and] whosoever believes in Communism is Kafir [i.e., an unbeliever] even if he observes prayer five times a day" (USCIRF, 2010, p. 143). In a related development, the Sudanese Communist Party's headquarters was attacked following an imam's accusation that it represented "a den of atheism, vice and fornication." In Spain, where the constitutional prohibits an established state church,[40] the government recently filed charges against a popular musician for offending religious sensibilities.[41] Remarkably, the legal action hinges on a satire originally filmed over 30 years ago entitled "How to Cook a Christ" and which was broadcasted on television (stills only) during a 2004 interview with the artist (Gordon, 2010, June 15).

Building on Krishnaswami's conclusions and further underscoring the anti-constitutional nature of blasphemy prohibitions, the UN Special Rapporteur on Freedom of Religion and Belief has observed that such measures "are misused for the purposes of outright censorship of the right to criticism and discussion of religion and related questions." This technique for stifling expression is wielded as "a weapon of war, particularly against vulnerable groups, be they women ... or ethnic or religious minorities ... or simply non-obscurantist intellectual minorities" (Amor, 2000, September 8, p. 24, para. 97). A 2006 report to the UNHRC prepared by Special Rapporteurs Asma Jahangir and Doudou Diène (2006, September 20) acknowledges "there are numerous examples of persecution of religious minorities as a result of excessive legislation on religious offences or overzealous application of laws that are fairly neutral" (para. 42). The report further emphasizes that prohibiting defamation of religion and blasphemy may risk limiting "scholarship on religious issues and may asphyxiate honest debate or research" (para. 42),[42] and that independent research and criticism of certain laws appearing to be in violation of human rights may also risk being labeled defamatory where such practices are sanctioned by religion (para. 43).

Many of the conclusions by the Special Rapporteurs are grounded in treaty provisions intended to safeguard freedom of expression and freedom of religion. According to the UN Human Rights Committee (1993, July 30), Article 18 of the ICCPR:

> protects theistic, non-theistic and atheistic beliefs, as well as the right not to profess any religion or belief. The terms "belief" and "religion" are to be broadly construed. Article 18 is not limited in its application to traditional religions or to religions and beliefs with institutional characteristics or practices analogous to those of traditional religions. (para. 2)

Notably, the Committee has additionally concluded that the existence of an official state religion or ideology does not exempt the state from respecting these fundamental rights, no matter how new or theologically at odds the impugned beliefs may be:

> The fact that a religion is recognized as a state religion or that it is established as official or traditional or that its followers comprise the majority of the population, shall not result in any impairment of the enjoyment of any of the rights under the Covenant ... nor in any discrimination against adherents to other religions or non-believers. (para. 9)

> If a set of beliefs is treated as official ideology in constitutions, statutes, proclamations of ruling parties, etc., or in actual practice, this shall not result in any impairment of the freedoms under article 18 or any other rights recognized under the Covenant nor in any discrimination against persons who do not accept the official ideology or who oppose it. (para. 10)

Clearly, the invocation of freedom of religion as a justification for enacting anti-blasphemy measures must necessarily be rejected. While a state may choose to enshrine an official religion, the scope of protection afforded to the right to freedom of religion or belief, "does not include the right to have a religion or belief that is free from criticism or ridicule" (Jahangir & Diène, 2006, September 20, para. 36). Accordingly, although defamation of a religion may result in insult or hurt feelings, it does not rise to the level of violating actual rights, and specifically the right to freedom of religion: "Freedom of religion primarily confers a right to act in accordance with one's religion but *does not bestow a right for believers to have their religion itself protected from all adverse comment*" (Jahangir & Diène, 2006, September 20, para. 37, emphasis added).

Within the municipal context, prohibitions on blasphemy – whether designed to afford exclusive protection for one faith or couched in the language of inclusiveness – represent an anti-constitutional norm with wide-ranging implications for the principles of nondiscrimination and equality, as well as the rights to freedom of expression and religion or belief. This peculiar, even perverse, dynamic – whereby the law is used to enshrine a particular set of beliefs with enforceable rights that can invoked to discriminate against or otherwise silence individuals and groups alike – becomes even more patent when the debate over blasphemy is shifted to the international level.

AN ANTI-CONSTITUTIONAL IDEA GOES INTERNATIONAL: THE MIGRATION OF DEFAMATION OF RELIGION

A Norm Struggles to Be Born: Defamation of Islam Knocks at the UN's Door

The first reference to defamation of Islam at the UN came in the wake of a 1997 report released by Maurice Glélé-Ahanhanzo, Special Rapporteur on Contemporary Forms of Racism, Racial Discrimination, Xenophobia, and Related Intolerance. Among other sources of discrimination contemplated in the report, the Special Rapporteur devoted a four paragraph section to "Islamist and Arab anti-Semitism" (Glélé-Ahanhanzo, 1997, January 16, p. 13), wherein he cited to an annual worldwide survey on anti-Semitism published by Tel Aviv University. The survey noted that the "use of Christian and secular European anti-Semitism motifs in Muslim publications is on the rise, yet at the same time Muslim extremists are turning increasingly to their own religious sources, first and foremost the Qur'an, as a primary anti-Jewish source" (Glélé-Ahanhanzo, 1997, January 16, p. 14; Wadlow & Littman, 1997). Confronted with this passage, Indonesia's representative to the UNCHR, speaking on behalf of OIC member states, averred, "Apart from the fact that such a statement constituted blasphemy against the Qur'an, the Commission could not allow itself to become a silent spectator of such defamation of one of the great religions of the world." The representative then called upon the Chairman "to condemn that defamatory statement on behalf of the Commission" (UNCHR, 1997, September 3, para. 14). Other OIC member states reiterated this view, and Pakistan's representative demanded that the UNCHR "delete the passage in the report of the Special Rapporteur that constituted an insult to Islam" (UNCHR, 1997, September 3, para. 30). This occasion marked the first time that the Commission considered a proposal to delete part of a Special Rapporteur's ostensibly independent report (UNCHR, 1997, September 3, para. 44). Within eight hours, the UNCHR Chairman read out a proposed draft decision that branded the passage in question an "offensive reference to the Holy Qur'an" and sought to

1. ... express[the Commission's] indignation and protest at the content of such an offensive reference to Islam and the Holy Qur'an,
2. Affirm[] that this offensive reference should have been excluded from the report, and
3. Request[] the Chairman to ask the Special Rapporteur to take corrective action in response to this decision (UNCHR, 1997, April 28, para. 22).

Without further debate or concern for the precedent being established, the Commission – including representatives from United States, Austria, Canada, Denmark, France, Germany, Ireland, Italy, Netherlands, and the United Kingdom – moved to adopt the draft decision without a vote (UNCHR, 1997, April 28, para. 23, 1997, April 18). Shortly thereafter, Glélé-Ahanhanzo (1997, July 8) issued a corrigendum effectively deleting the controversial text from his report.[43] Meeting (1997, November 20) as a group following this incident, the UN's Special Rapporteurs expressed their agreement "that it was inappropriate for the Commission to request a Special Rapporteur to amend his report" and that rapporteurs "should not be requested to amend their reports merely because certain passages were deemed offensive by a particular Member State or group of Member States" (para. 23). This statement had little practical effect, and since 1997 no reference has been made specifically to "Islamist and Arab anti-Semitism" in any UN report.[44]

In a revealing comment on the nature of this controversy, the observer for Indonesia remarked in the UN Sub-Commission on Prevention of Discrimination and Protection of Minorities (1997, December 22) that "[i]t could only be assumed that the motive of those who insulted Islam was to generate conflict with Islamic peoples or even to justify the injustices to which they were currently being subjected" (para. 14). Accordingly, Indonesia – along with other OIC states – maintains the view that no critical comment concerning Islam is justifiable – regardless of whether the forum is academic or the objective pursued is a worthy one, such as the elimination of discrimination. Underscoring this perspective two years earlier, a representative from Iran informed the UN that "[in] the opinion [of] the Organization of the Islamic Conference ... the right to freedom of thought, opinion and expression could in no case justify blasphemy" (UN, 1995, February 3). This adamant position is worth keeping in mind as the following sections analyze the effort to enshrine a prohibition against "defamation of religions" and the OIC's intent regarding the scope and application of such a ban.

The UNCHR Endorses "Defamation of Religion"

Negotiating the First UNCHR Resolution on Defamation of Religions

The uproar over Glélé-Ahanhanzo's report and its final disposition by the UNCHR confirmed the OIC's political influence. Having established a precedent of suppressing "blasphemous" and "defamatory" statements, the OIC turned to the larger task of promoting an international resolution intended to prohibit all forms of expression deemed "defamatory" of Islam. Acting on behalf of the OIC, Pakistan submitted a draft resolution to the UNCHR that sought the Commission's formal condemnation of "defamation of Islam" and to establish a reporting mechanism to address the issue (UNCHR, 1999, April 20). Pakistan's UN ambassador asserted that negative media coverage of Islam amounted to a defamation campaign against the religion and its adherents to which the UNCHR had to react (UNCHR (Amb. Akram, Pakistan), 1999, October 19, para. 1–2). The German ambassador responded that "the draft's overall design was not balanced, since it referred exclusively to the negative stereotyping of Islam, whereas other religions had been and continued to be subjected to various forms of discrimination" (UNCHR, 1999, October 19, para. 3). Pakistan countered by emphasizing that any bid for greater inclusivity "would defeat the purpose of the text, which was to bring a problem relating specifically to [Islam] to the attention of the international community" (UNCHR, 1999, October 19, para. 8).

Subsequent negotiations over the proposed resolution revealed the OIC's focus on securing singular recognition for Islam as the victim of perceived defamatory attacks (UNCHR, 1999, April 28, para. 8). Despite this effort, the final agreed text relegated the term "defamation" to the resolution title only and sought to address all religions generally (UNCHR, 1999, April 30, adopted without a vote). Faced with this outcome, Pakistan hailed the OIC member states' "considerable flexibility" in agreeing to a compromise resolution (UNCHR, 1999, November 17, para. 1). Germany, on behalf of the European Union (EU), stressed its "wish to make it clear that they did

not attach any legal meaning to the term 'defamation' as used in the title"
(para. 9). This discomfort with ascribing legal meaning to the term
"defamation of religion" derived in part from the fact that defamation
law traditionally applies to individuals only rather than to ideas or beliefs. If
expanded to also protect a set of ideas, this concept would risk placing the
protection of certain beliefs above existing individual rights – an outcome
antithetical to the very impetus for international human rights law.[45]
Moreover, unlike legitimate prohibitions on hate speech that are intended
to protect individuals and groups from actual incitement, defamation of
religion would function to insulate improvable ideas even from academic
scrutiny, criticism, or other form of inquiry.

Despite the failure to agree upon a legal definition of defamation of
religion, the UNCHR (1999, April 30) called upon the Special Rapporteurs
on Religious Intolerance and on Racism, Racial Discrimination, Xenophobia, and Related Intolerance to take into account this newly minted chimera
concept during their reporting to the following UNCHR session (para. 6).

The Special Rapporteur on Freedom of Religion Falls Out of Favor
In his first report back to the UNCHR, Abdelfattah Amor, Special
Rapporteur for Freedom of Religion or Belief (2000, February 15), side-
stepped the glaring absence of any operative definition of defamation of
religion, and observed that "religious, especially Muslim, minorities were the
butt of prejudice and stereotyping" (para. 110). At the same time, he also
found "that non-Muslim religious minorities were victims of defamation,
[that] defamation often stems from intolerance and/or inter-religious as well
as intra-religious ignorance, often in the context of an adversarial relationship
between majority and minorities … [and] emphasized that there are growing
problems between traditional majority religions and sects/new religious
movements, as well as between believers and non-believers" (para. 110). In
place of a formal conclusion, Amor instead offered a prescient warning: that
efforts to combat defamation of religion (whatever that might mean) "should
not be used to censure all inter-religious and intra-religious criticism" given
the danger that such efforts – and particularly blasphemy offenses – "may be
manipulated for purposes contrary to human rights" (para. 111).

Amor reiterated his findings with greater detail in a subsequent report to
the UNGA. After conceding the obvious point that negative stereotyping
has an impact on religious groups, Amor (2000, September 8) noted that:

> very frequently, prohibitions against acts of defamation or blasphemy are misused for
> the purposes of outright censorship of the right to criticism and discussion of religion

and related questions. In many cases, defamation becomes the tool of extremists in censoring and maintaining or propagating obscurantism. It becomes a weapon of war, particularly against vulnerable groups, be they women ... or ethnic or religious minorities ... or simply non-obscurantist intellectual minorities. In any event, one must be very cautious in dealing with the question of defamation, displaying intellectual vigilance and wisdom in view of the primary aim of protecting and promoting human rights. (para. 97)

Remarkably, Amor relied on Special Rapporteur mission reports and allegations deriving from Pakistan, Jordan, Bangladesh, Indonesia, and Sudan – all Muslim majority countries – as examples illustrative of the danger associated with domestic bans on defamation of religion (Amor, 1996, 1996, 2000, January 2, November 11, September 8). Yet, this did nothing to deter the same states (in lockstep with their OIC cohorts) from reiterating their support for internationalizing a prohibition against defamation of religion in the years that followed. Rather than contemplating the implications of Amor's findings for the safeguarding of human rights such as freedom of expression and freedom of religion or belief, the OIC member states instead ignored Amor altogether and pushed him out of the reporting mandates generated by subsequent UNCHR resolutions on defamation of religion. As a result, the Commission did not request the Special Rapporteur on Freedom of Religion to report on the issue of defamation until its demise in 2006, when it was replaced by the UNHRC.[46]

This snub did not go unnoticed. In his general report on the elimination of all forms of religious intolerance to the UNGA in 2001, Amor called attention to the fact that UNCHR Resolution 2001/4 on combating defamation of religions "no longer refers to the Special Rapporteur on religious intolerance" (Amor, 2001, July 31, para. 136) despite the fact that defamation "essentially constitutes a violation of freedom of religion and belief" (para. 137). Amor also used the opportunity "to stress the importance of ensuring that efforts to combat defamation are not used as an excuse to restrict freedom of expression and the right to criticize, which would be contrary to human rights" (para. 138).[47]

The UNCHR Looks to the Special Rapporteur on Racism for [Mis] Guidance
After rendering the Special Rapporteur on Freedom of Religion or Belief Persona Non Grata, the UNCHR shifted to the Special Rapporteur on Contemporary Forms of Racism, Racial Discrimination, Xenophobia, and Related Intolerance for its reporting needs. The Committee also narrowly tailored the mandate's purview, obviating any focus on Muslim countries where existing laws prohibiting defamation and blasphemy already restricted

freedom of religion and freedom of expression. Instead – and still acting under the premise of combating "defamation" – the UNCHR tasked Doudou Diène with exploring "physical assaults and attacks" occurring only as against Muslim and Arab "places of worship, cultural centres, businesses and properties in the aftermath of the events of 11 September 2001" (UNCHR, 2002, April 15, para. 12).

Thus, in one sweeping move the UNCHR blurred the line between defamation (an act of oral or written expression) and physical violence and shifted from reporting on defamation of all religions to reporting exclusively on defamation of Islam. As a result, a workable definition for "defamation of religions" became even more remote and the OIC states achieved one of their original aims: a reporting mechanism dedicated solely to defamation of Islam. Diène worked tirelessly to help ensure that the OIC achieved this goal. In his 2003 report presented to the UNCHR, Diène (2003, January 3) asserted without definition or corroboration that an "explicit and public defamation of Islam" represented the "ideological dimension associated with anti-Muslim and/or anti-Arab violence" (p. 2). Further on, he concluded – again without substantive evidence – that media coverage of 9/11 "contributed to a sharp increase in Islamophobia or its acceptance as normal in the West, not only among the common people, but also, and more openly, among certain elites, who at times seemed to adopt it as an ideological or even esthetic position" (para. 31).

Unpacking the substance of Diène's allegations reveals little credibility for his conclusions. One of the so-called "elites" Diène invokes to substantiate his claim is Rev. Jerry Falwell, who also happened to take the following well-publicized – and outrageous – view: "The abortionists have got to bear some burden for [9/11] ... I really believe that the pagans, and the abortionists, and the feminists, and the gays and the lesbians who are actively trying to make that an alternative lifestyle, the ACLU, People for the American Way, all of them who have tried to secularise America, I point the finger in their face and say, 'You helped this happen'" (Goodstein, 2001, September 19).

As another example of the media explicitly and publicly defaming Islam, Diène (2003, January 3) points to the "non-stop pictures of the demonstration of joy of Palestinian crowds after the attacks of 11 September" (para. 33). Here, Diène claims that "[i]n fact, the demonstration filmed in Gaza consisted only of youths and was an isolated incident in the Palestinian territories. However, the record was not set straight afterwards" (para. 33). These assertions are patently false for the following reasons: First, such "incidents" were by no means isolated. Rather, reports of celebrations marking the 9/11 attacks against the U.S. came from a variety of locales in addition to Gaza, including "refugee camps in Lebanon" (Sawer, 2001, September 11, p. A14), "the streets of Nablus" (Holmes, 2001, September 12), in the West Bank, and East Jerusalem (Moreton, 2001, September 16). Second, video footage from at least one of these spontaneous street celebrations makes plain that participants were not limited to youths, but rather included adults – men and women alike – as well (see, e.g., video footage from MSNBC News, FOX News, and CNN).[48] In fact, media reports estimated that these celebrations in some instances attracted thousands of supporters (Gardiner, 2001, September 12, p. A17; Manchester Evening News, 2001, September 12, p. 17).[49] Finally, if Diène had bothered to truly examine the "record," he would have found that the media needed no correction. After being confronted with allegations that the video footage depicting one celebration in East Jerusalem was fabricated, CNN and Reuters both rechecked and confirmed the video's authenticity (CNN, 2001a, 2001b, September 20).[50] Indeed, the episodes of celebrants exalting the 9/11 attacks were so real – and ongoing – that the Palestinian Authority moved to "suppress broadcast images and photos of Palestinians glorifying the terrorist attacks" by informing foreign news agencies and television stations that their safety could not be guaranteed if they opted to disseminate such footage.[51]

Rather than distorting the situation to illustrate defamation of religion (and in the process perpetuating the falsehood that these celebrations were isolated and driven by children), Diène could have simply and accurately pointed out the fact that Palestinian Authority President Yasser Arafat, speaking on behalf of the Palestinian people, almost immediately decried the attacks and expressed condolences "for this terrible incident" (Holmes, 2001, September 12, p. A14), in a statement that was, incidentally, widely covered by the media.

In 2004, Diène (2004, September 13) took the unprecedented step of unilaterally preparing an additional report "analys[ing] further the question of the defamation of religions" in response to burgeoning UN interest in the phenomenon (para. 6). This document, like Diène's previous reports, fails to provide a definition for defamation. Remarkably, the only time Diène uses the term, apart from references back to eponymous UNCHR resolutions, appears in his summary of the differing opinions regarding anti-Semitism and criticism of Israel. Here, Diène (2004, December 13) observes, "For some a distinction must be drawn between objective criticism, which is legitimate, and 'disproportionate' and 'ongoing' criticism, and which in reality concerns defamation, demonization and questioning of the legitimacy of the State of

Israel" (para. 40).[52] More troubling is the fact that Diène asserted a "manifest increase in Islamophobia" (para. 20) despite having received "little in the way of reliable data on manifestations of Islamophobia" (para. 22) and conceding his inability "to submit full numerical data … in view of the difficulty of assessing the reliability of the methodologies and the rigour employed in data collection" (para. 11).

Undeterred by the fact that scant statistical evidence backed up his conclusions – and even while acknowledging that the report was prepared "in the absence of reliable data" (para. 27) – Diène proceeds to speak in loose terms of "significant trends regarding Islamophobia that seem particularly alarming" (para. 27). He further decries the existence of a "clash of civilizations" mentality by making the baffling claim that

> the current rise in Islamophobia is characterized by the interpretation – in particular by politicians and the media – of individual acts as collective behaviour, an interpretation illustrated by such comments as "[film director Théo] Van Gogh's murder is an attack on our values and our civilization." (para. 26)[53]

This bizarre criticism begs the question: would Diène similarly be opposed, for example, to characterizing the assassination of Martin Luther King Jr. as an attack on "our values and our civilization?"

One of the most problematic aspects of Diène's reporting relates to his obfuscation of Islamophobia and defamation of religion. According to Diène, Islamophobia is "a baseless hostility and fear vis-a-vis Islam, and as a result a fear of and aversion toward all Muslims or the majority of them" (para. 13). In his view, Islamophobia also is a form of defamation of religion (Diène, 2007, August 21, para. 14). As a consequence of this conflation, the term "defamation of religion" suddenly includes "typical expression[s] of Islamophobia, [whereby] Muslims are seen as opposed to so-called Western values and often portrayed as enemies and a threat to national values and social cohesion" (para. 15). In other words, Diène legitimates the concept of defamation of religion by shifting its alleged target from a set of beliefs to an individual or group of individuals. The foundational flaw in Diène's support for a ban on defamation of religion lies in his failure to draw a principled distinction between typical cases of unlawful discrimination against an individual, such as "barriers to adequate housing, schooling, employment and, more generally, racial profiling" (para. 16), and the more problematic and overriding objective of quashing expression deemed insulting or offensive to subjective and improvable religious beliefs.

The culmination of Diène's ideologically driven reporting on defamation – which coincidentally further blurs the line between defamation and

Islamophobia – comes in 2006, when the Special Rapporteur tackles what he labels "[t]he most serious manifestation of the deteriorating situation of Arab and Muslim populations generally and Islamophobia in particular" (Diène, 2006, February 13, para. 23): the publication of the cartoons of the Prophet Muhammad in the Danish newspaper *Jyllands-Posten*.[54] Diène considered this event so grave that he allocated nearly half of his 10-page report to the subject.[55] Remarkably, rather than reflect a dispassionate and objective analysis, Diène's assessment of this "most serious manifestation" is beset with gross distortions, hyperbole, and omission.[56] Indeed, a cursory scrutiny of his substandard reporting makes plain the desire to boost the conceptual validity ascribed to defamation of Islam by affixing it to a breathless account of the rising global specter of Islamophobia. Thus, Diène (2006, February 13) recommends that the UNCHR "should draw the attention of [UN] Member States to the link between the upsurge in Islamophobia and the general increase in defamation of religions ... [and] invite the Special Rapporteur to submit a regular report on all manifestations of defamation of religion" (para. 37).[57]

Diène's treatment of the cartoon affair evidences that he will not allow facts to stand in the way of depicting a climate ripe for limiting existing human rights in the name of bulwarking Islam from criticism. Diène asserts that the editorial cartoons exemplify "three worrying trends underpinning resurgent Islamophobia" (para. 23): first, how much the defamation of religions has become trivialized; second, the desire to shape the attitude to religion of a particularly sensitive and vulnerable age group; and finally, the dominant theme of associating Islam with terrorism (para. 23). In the first instance, Diène fails to define what action precisely amounts to defamation of religion. Is it the mere act of drawing a cartoon image – even a flattering one – of the Prophet Muhammed? Or does defamation of religion only transpire on the narrower basis of associating Islam or Muhammed with terrorism? Even without this necessary guidance, Diène is adamant that domestic concerns over an increasing climate of self-censorship in Denmark did not warrant challenging religious beliefs. Instead, he claims that *Jyllands-Posten's* invitation to submit drawings in response to the claim that Danish cartoonists were too afraid to illustrate the Prophet Muhammed trivialized defamation of religion. But viewed against the backdrop of Van Gogh's murder in broad daylight – and in the face of a massive and disproportionate fallout surrounding the "affair" – it would appear that the norm subjected to trivialization was the right to freedom of expression rather than some amorphous conception intended to protect religious dogma at the expense of the former.

Diène's second "worrying trend" inexplicably conflates publication of the *editorial* cartoons with the original impetus for the newspaper's challenge, a complaint by Danish author Kare Bluitgen that no artist was willing to illustrate his children's book on the life of Prophet Muhammed. According to Diène, the *Jyllands-Posten* cartoons intended to influence the attitude of a particularly sensitive and vulnerable age group, namely children, to a certain religion. This characterization is misleading for the simple reason that most children typically do not glance at, let alone study, the editorial page of the local paper. It is also worth noting that nothing in Bluitgen's book, *The Qur'an and the Life of the Prophet Muhammad (Koranen og profeten Muhammeds liv)*, indicates he sought to disparage or attack Islam.[58] Had Diène taken the time to acquire a copy, he would have discovered a text accompanied by "loving illustrations" (Lau, 2006, February 1), "neutral, simple and devoid of associations with terror groups" (Langlands, 2006, February 8). But this extra step would have negated his provocative finding that malevolent forces were operating to deleteriously influence children's opinion of Islam through a medium traditionally reserved for an adult audience.

Finally, Diène's (2006, February 13) assertion that "the dominant theme of the [*Jyllands-Posten*] cartoons is to associate Islam with terrorism" (para. 23) is misleading at best. As an opening salvo, Diène describes one image depicting Muhammed "as a devil holding a grenade" (para. 23).[59] Yet *Jyllands-Posten* never published such an image, prompting one to wonder whether Diène even examined the cartoons himself or simply relied on secondhand accounts.[60] By taking this minimal step, Diène should have realized it was unreasonable to extrapolate a single dominant theme from the collected illustrations. Rather, the cartoons represented a variety of views: Some images were openly critical of the newspaper for undertaking the competition, some addressed the treatment of women under Islam, and others proffered a link between Islam and violence. Although interpreting any art form is ultimately a subjective process, clearly not all of the published drawings included a representation of Muhammed, and only four of twelve depict Islam in a decidedly unfavorable light.[61] Undeterred by these facts, Diène (2003, February 13) uses the link between Islam and terrorism suggested by several of the cartoons to sweepingly conclude, "The cartoons are thus clearly defamatory of Islam" (para. 23).

Diène's overbroad supposition betrays the plain fact that he fails to establish any principled distinction between the image of Muhammed as a peaceful wanderer and the image of Muhammed with a bomb for a turban. From this gaping oversight, it is evident that in Diène's mind the offense of defamation of religion (though still undefined) arises not only from the linkage of Islam with terrorism but also from the mere act of depicting the Prophet Muhammed, even in a flattering light. Thus, Diène concludes that the subsequent efforts by other newspapers to republish the editorial cartoons in a gesture of support for *Jyllands-Posten* amounted to an "intransigent defence of unlimited freedom of expression" (para. 28). Diène's lack of objective detachment parallels his attempts elsewhere to tease out a workable distinction between anti-Semitism and anti-Zionism in the name of legitimating the latter practice (Diène, 2004, December 13, paras. 38–43) and his hypocritical condemnation of the "manipulation and selective quoting of sacred texts, in particular the Koran, as a means to deceptively argue that these texts show the violent nature of Islam" (Diène, 2007, August 21, para. 23). On this latter issue, Diène's own blanket assertions – namely that the dominant theme of the cartoons associates Islam with terrorism and that all of the cartoons are defamatory – demonstrate a modus operandi built upon the same techniques of manipulation and selectivity.

Despite these critical misrepresentations and unsubstantiated normative conclusions – or perhaps precisely because of them – a majority of states in the UNCHR (and later, the UNHRC) eagerly welcomed Diène's work (UNHRC, 2007, Preamble). Subsequent resolutions relied on Diène's findings as a basis for justifying new limitations on freedom of expression. For example, in 2007, the UNGA and UNHRC passed resolutions that expressed "deep concern" over the "the intensification of the campaign of defamation of religions" (UNGA, 2007, February 21, para. 3; UNHRC, 2007, April 30, para. 3). More disconcerting, both resolutions also took the unprecedented step of endorsing any limitation on freedom of expression deemed necessary for ensuring "respect for religions and beliefs" (UNGA, 2007, February 21, para. 3; UNHRC, 2007, April 30, para. 3).[62] It is worth recalling here that the ICCPR does not stipulate or make allowance for any limitation on freedom of expression based on respect "for religions and beliefs." Therefore, these resolutions embodied a blatant effort to expand the scope of permissible limitations on freedom of expression despite treaty guidance to the contrary.[63]

Ten Years of Expanding Legitimacy at the United Nations
By 2010, the concept of defamation of religion had made significant inroads at the UN, yet still remained subject to controversy. Since the first seemingly harmless mention of defamation of religion in the title to a 1999 UNCHR resolution, subsequent annual resolutions have dramatically expanded such

references to where the term is now invoked 10–15 times per resolution (see Fig. 2). Moreover, placement of references to defamation within the text of the resolutions has gradually shifted from relatively innocuous preambulary paragraphs to the more significant operative portions (see Fig. 3). This shift is of particular significance given the fact that the OIC had previously expressly called for the inclusion of "[o]perative provisions prohibiting blasphemy ... in the text of [defamation resolutions]" negotiated at the UN (OIC, 2006, June, para. 23).

Indeed, the matter of defamation of religion has been deemed so weighty that beginning in 2006, attention to it extended beyond the relatively provincial domain of the specialized human rights body and into the larger (and arguably more important) UN General Assembly. As it currently stands, both UN bodies now pass annual resolutions dedicated to combating defamation of religion, and these documents create ongoing obligations for the UN's various reporting bodies, including its Special Rapporteurs, the High Commissioner for Human Rights and even the Secretary General (Fig. 4).

Even in its "soft law" permutation, it is evident that the anti-constitutional norm envisaged by the OIC has gained significant ground in the international

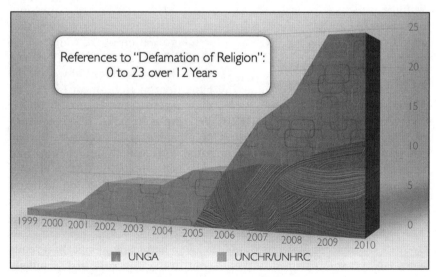

Fig. 2. Norm Creation at the UN: References to "Defamation of Religions" in UN Resolutions, 1999–2010.

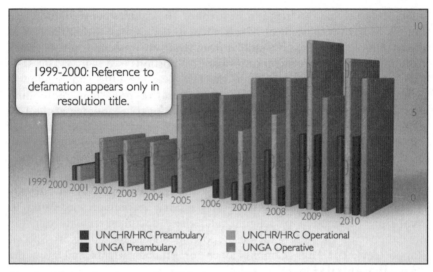

Fig. 3. Norm Creation at the UN: Preambulary and Operational References to Defamation of Religions in UN Resolutions, 1999–2010.

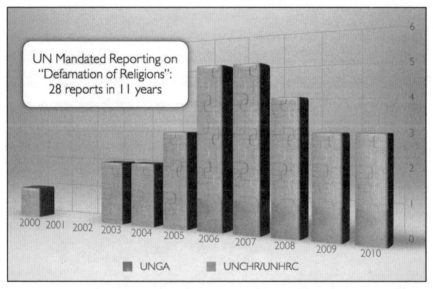

Fig. 4. Norm Creation at the UN: Reporting Requirements Generated by UN Resolutions for Various UN Mandates, 2000–2010 (see Appendix A for a list of reports by mandate-holder).

arena. In the OIC's view, "[t]he succession of UNGA and UNHRC resolutions on the defamation of religions makes it a stand alone concept with international legitimacy. It should not be made to stand out by creating the impression that it somehow encroaches upon the freedom of expression" (Second OIC Observatory Report on Islamophobia, 2009, p. 4). As the following section illustrates, an examination of the OIC's position provides even clearer evidence that the effort to entrench a prohibition on defamation of religion on the international level is steeped in anti-constitutional ideas that challenge the foundation of an international human rights system premised on universality.

THE FAIT ACCOMPLI VIEW FROM THE ORGANIZATION OF THE ISLAMIC CONFERENCE: DEFAMATION OF [CERTAIN] RELIGIONS IS PROHIBITED UNDER INTERNATIONAL LAW

The OIC's advocacy efforts to enshrine a prohibition against defamation of religion at the UN are fueled by the organization's preoccupation with outlawing and punishing defamation of Islam specifically. This fixation has so permeated the organization that its revised 2008 Charter now establishes "combat[ing] defamation of Islam" as one of the organization's central objectives (OIC Charter, 2008, March 14, Article 1(12)).[64] Moreover, the OIC's *Draft Rules Governing Observer Status and Draft Rules For Accession of States To Observer Status* (2006) requires applicant states to submit in writing a commitment to respect the OIC Charter as well as a specific "endorsement of legislations prohibiting defamation of religions in accordance with the principles of international law, and international conventions and resolutions in this regard" (Article 6; Article 3(b)).[65]

Admittedly, the OIC is an Islamic organization and its primary concern may therefore lie in protecting its parochial interests rather than the rights of all individuals to freedom of religion or belief. Nevertheless, the reality remains that active discrimination against religions other than Islam is a consistent theme across the human rights records of many OIC member states.[66] A closer look at the OIC's advocacy favoring a ban on defamation of religion reveals an approach that embodies not one but several anti-constitutional ideas that operate to foreclose the principles of nondiscrimination and equality and undercut universal rights to freedom of expression and freedom of religion or belief. In the first instance, application and enforcement of defamation prohibitions are discriminatory; protections typically apply only to Islam (and in many cases only to a specific interpretation of Islam) and most generously may apply to other select "divine religions." Second, the OIC's requirement for criminalization is at odds with international efforts to limit conventional defamation offenses to civil liability; and third, its desire to protect religious beliefs by manipulating the framework of human rights upends the traditional understanding that rights belong to individuals rather than subjective concepts or beliefs. In addition to the OIC's efforts to legitimate the concept of defamation of religion, the organization's increasingly contrived campaign to label such acts incitement to religious hatred also evidences a desire to place protection of ideas above protection for individuals. This recent twist in rhetoric exemplifies yet another anti-constitutional threat to free expression and freedom of religion insofar as it purports to dilute the existing high bar for a showing of actual incitement, and particularly the necessary requirement of intent.

Defamation Is Prohibited Against Islam [and Possibly Other "Divine" Religions] Only

The OIC Charter makes obvious that its member states ascribe little value to protecting against defamation of religious beliefs other than Islam. This narrow approach – maintained over a decade after the UNCHR originally rejected Pakistan's 1999 proposal for a resolution exclusively decrying defamation of Islam – is a testament to the OIC's tenacity. It also signals that despite a pragmatic willingness to compromise with seemingly more inclusive language at the UN, the OIC remains singularly committed to a hidebound vision intended to afford protection to Islam exclusively. Numerous OIC resolutions single out concern for "defamation of Islam" only. For example, OIC Resolution No. 68/9-P (IS):

1. Endorses the efforts of the member states of the OIC in Geneva to highlight the concerns of the Islamic countries *regarding the defamation of Islam and taking common positions on issue of direct interest to them* in the UN human rights bodies [and]
2. *Commends the initiative by OIC member states in Geneva to oppose the "defamation of Islam"* as reflected in the Commission on Human Rights' resolution on "Defamation of religions" and encourages them to continue this initiative (November 2000, emphasis added).

The OIC has continued to endorse this exclusionary definition of defamation in its 2009 and 2010 resolutions that express "the need to pursue, as a matter of priority, a common policy aimed at preventing defamation of Islam perpetrated under the pretext and justification of the [sic] freedom of expression in particular through media and Internet" (OIC Resolution No. 2/36-Leg, 2009, May, para. 10; OIC Resolution No. 1/37-Leg, 2010, May, para. 10). Similarly, in 2010 while the OIC stressed "the need to prevent the abuse of freedom of expression and press for insulting Islam and other divine religions" it exclusively condemned:

> in the strongest possible terms, all blasphemous acts against Islamic principles, symbols and sacred personalities, in particular, publication of offensive caricatures of Prophet Mohammad (PBUH), all abhorrent and irresponsible statements about Islam and its sacred personalities, and screening of [sic] defamatory documentary about the Holy Quran and dissemination of this hate material under the pretext of freedom of expression and opinion. (OIC Resolution No. 38/37-P, 2010, May, paras. 5 and 6)

Where the OIC does appear to enlarge its interpretation of defamation of religion, it does so only in a very narrow and dogmatic manner. In certain resolutions and related documents, the organization favors repeated use of the term "other divine religions" rather than the more inclusive term "religions" or "all religions." The qualifying term "divine" serves a limiting function, theoretically extending protection against defamation only to those "secondary" religious texts and figures deemed sacred under Islam. This critical – and discriminatory – distinction originates in the Qur'anic mandate that *Ahl al-Kitab* or "people of the book," traditionally understood to include "mainly Christians and Jews" (An-Na'im, 1987, p. 11),[67] are entitled to protection under Islam, whereas nonbelievers are not. Numerous OIC resolutions and reports reaffirm this selective understanding of defamation of religion. For example, the OIC has asserted a "consistent position ... against disrespect and defamation of the *Prophets of the revealed faiths* and the insult of religious symbols" (Second OIC Observatory Report on Islamophobia, 2009, p. 18, emphasis added). Similarly, OIC Resolution No. 34/34-Pol emphasizes:

> the need to prevent the abuse of freedom of expression and press for *insulting Islam and other divine religions* and urges all concerned to block any internet website in their respective area of jurisdiction that are engaged in blasphemous acts of ridiculing and defaming Islam and Prophet Muhammad (PBUH) and to hold the operators of the websites responsible for the consequences that may result from their vicious and malicious campaign and to take necessary legal measures against them. (May 2007, para. 9 (emphasis added); See also OIC Resolution No. 34/36-Pol 2009, May, para. 5)

Likewise, Resolution No. 34/36-Pol "[a]ffirms categorically the firm determination of member states to continue their effective cooperation and close consultations to combat Islamophobia, *defamation of all divine religions*, and incitement to hatred, hostility and discrimination against Muslims" (May 2009, para. 1). More forcefully still, the OIC in 2009 "[s]trongly condemn[ed]" and in 2010 "[n]ote[d] with grave concern" the "increasing trend of Islamophobic measures in the Western countries" and emphasized "the responsibility of those States to *ensure full respect to Islam and all divine religions* and the inapplicability of using freedom of expression or press as a pretext to defame religions" (OIC Resolution No. 2/36-Leg, 2009, May, para. 8; OIC Resolution No. 1/37-Leg, 2010, May, para. 8).[68] These provisions make clear that religions not considered "divine" under Islam – coincidentally, the same religions that are frequent targets of abuse in certain OIC member states – are not deserving of and shall not benefit from protection against defamation.

Arguably, a more contemporary or generous interpretation of "divine religions" might extend recognition of divinity to include all monotheistic faiths (Galston, 1994, October, p. 1853, no. 40).[69] This would enable several additional "preferred" guests to fall within the OIC's penumbra of protection against defamation. However, even such a munificent reading does little to resolve the underlying reality that the official OIC viewpoint operates in a facially discriminatory manner against religions falling outside this penumbra. In other words, faiths deemed apostate, unbelieving, polytheist, or simply unworthy of "divinity" – regardless of whether they may predate Islam (Buddhism or Hinduism) or post-date it (Baha'ism) – are fair game for discrimination. In any case, this exercise of expanding the category of faiths considered "divinely revealed" may be of little practical effect. Consider, for example, that in the Hashemite Kingdom of Jordan "there are two divinely revealed religions, Islam and Christianity" (Jordan, 1999, September 13, para. 33). Judaism, although traditionally viewed by Islam as a protected faith, is given no such recognition under Jordanian law. Likewise, Article 98(f) of Egypt's penal code operates as a de facto prohibition on "defamation of Islam" by criminalizing "disparaging or showing contempt for any divinely-revealed religion" (Egyptian Penal Code, 1937, Article 98(f)).[70] However, the government has routinely tolerated – and arguably facilitated – a media notorious for spewing anti-Semitic ideas and imagery (see, e.g., Anti-Defamation League, 2009; BBC News, 2002, November 7). In a similar vein – and in lockstep with the government – Egyptian *fatwas* unanimously regard Baha'is as unbelievers. Baha'is of non-Muslim descent are considered polytheists because "they believe in a prophet not recognized by Islam, and their sacred scriptures are not of heavenly origin" (Pink, 2003, p. 418). As a consequence, arrests of Baha'is in Egypt are "at least outwardly, driven by the intention to protect 'true religion' and to exclude from the public sphere religions that are not recognized by Islam as revealed religions" (Pink, 2003, p. 430). According to Egyptian human rights NGOs, the term "divine religions" (*al-adyaan al samaawiyya*) contained in Article 98(f), is used "as a means to deny and withhold state protection to members of other religious minorities that do not fall under, or are deliberately excluded from, the three Abrahamic religions of Islam, Christianity and Judaism" (Cairo Institute for Human Rights Studies, 2008, August 29, p. 3).[71] Moreover, the provision is also used "to detain and prosecute Muslims for belonging to minority sects within Islam or for holding or expressing views that deviate from the mainstream interpretation of the Muslim faith" (CIHRS, 2008, August 29, p. 2).

Defamation Demands Criminal Punishment

In addition to exclusively protecting Islam from defamation, the anti-constitutional nature of the offense is exacerbated by the OIC's demand that infringements be addressed through criminal punishment rather than civil liability. The OIC has repeatedly promoted "coordinat[ion] with States as well as regional and international institutions and organizations to urge them to criminalize [defamation of Islam and its values] as a form of racism" (OIC Final Communiqué, 2005, December). It has also "call[ed] upon all States to enact laws to counter [Islamophobia], including deterrent punishments" (OIC Programme, 2005, December), and has demanded that states "take all appropriate masseurs [sic], inter alia, enacting and effective application of necessary laws to render all acts, whatsoever, defaming Islam as 'offensive acts' and subject to punishment" (OIC Resolution No. 1/35-C, 2008, June, para. 7; see also OIC Resolution No. 34/34-Pol, 2007, May, paras. 4 and 11; OIC Resolution No. 26/33-DW, 2005, June, para. 11).

At its most recent Islamic Summit, the OIC called "upon Member States, to take all appropriate measures to consider all acts, whatever they may be, which defame Islam as heinous acts that require punishment" (OIC Final Communiqué, 2008, March, para. 176). In elaborating on "all appropriate measures," the OIC urged states, inter alia, to "[e]nsure the criminalization of all acts of defamation of religions and discrimination on the basis of religion, and to enact the appropriate penalties that represent adequate deterrence against such practices" (Eleventh Session of the Islamic Summit Conference,

2008, March, para. 11(b)). In prepared remarks following the conclusion of a seminar sponsored by the UN Office of the High Commissioner on Human Rights (OHCHR) addressing the issue of defamation of religion, the OIC's deputy permanent representative to the UN did little to hide the organization's disdain for measures falling short of criminal sanction:

> [G]lobal preventive measures such as education, dialogue and etc, as suggested by some ... *have to be considered as supplementary mechanisms for a long term aim. They are not a means to an end by themselves.* Interestingly enough, those who have been active in the area of instigating violence and hatred against Muslims and the religion of Islam are well educated and high caliber artists. They do not need to be lectured about the value of tolerance and co-existing ... They are aware of the weaknesses of relevant international instruments as well as the *incompetence of the world community to bring them to justice.* (Vahid, 2008, October 2, p. 3, emphasis added)

In a similar vein, the Islamic Educational, Scientific and Cultural Organization (ISESCO), a specialized institution of the OIC, has used its mandate to reiterate the OIC's demand for the necessity of criminal sanctions, calling upon the UN "to issue an international law criminalizing all forms of offence against religions under any circumstances" (ISESCO, 2010, September 9).

The overriding emphasis on imposing criminal penalties for the offense of defamation remains a central motif in the OIC's campaign. Most recently within the UNHRC's Ad Hoc Committee on the elaboration of complementary standards,[72] the OIC reaffirmed the need for sweeping criminal sanctions for a variety of defamation-related offenses. For example, the OIC argued that the "scourges" of Islamophobia, Anti-Semitism, Christianophobia and "ideological racism" should "be criminalized in all their manifestations, and made punishable offences in accordance with international human rights law" (UNHRC, 2009, August 26, para. 6(d)). In addition, under the theme "[a]dvocacy and incitement to racial, ethnic, national and religious hatred," the OIC insisted that the following acts "must be criminalized in national laws, and the perpetrators thereof punished, *as well as those instigating, aiding or abetting them*" (para. 20, emphasis added):

(a) Public insults and defamation ... against a person or group of persons on the grounds of their ... religion ... ;
(b) The public expression of prejudice that has the purpose or effect of denigrating a group of persons on the basis of the above-mentioned grounds;
(c) The public dissemination or distribution, or the production of written, audio or visual or other material containing manifestations of [defamation of religion] (para. 20).[73]

Similarly, addressing the theme "discrimination based on religion or belief" within the ad hoc committee, the OIC went even further, calling for states to create criminal liability for a wide range of offenses, including for those who indirectly aid or abet defamation:

(b) Penalization, through the criminal law of States, of public expression ... which depreciates or denigrates a grouping of persons on the grounds of their ... religion ... ;

(c) ...

(d) Legal restriction to public insults and defamation threats against a person or a grouping of persons on the grounds of their ... religion ... ;

(e) Legal prohibition of publication of material that negatively stereotypes, insults, or uses offensive language on matters regarded by followers of any religion or belief as sacred or inherent to their dignity as human beings, with the aim of protecting their fundamental human rights;

(f) *The penalization of the above-mentioned acts by the criminal law of States*, without any discrimination, in order to combat impunity for those who commit, instigate, or aid and abet them directly or indirectly (UNHRC, 2009, August 26, para. 27, submissions received from member states and groups of states).

Significantly, the criminal sanctions for defamation proposed by the OIC as part of a new international protocol mirror the practice already in place in numerous OIC states.[74] Similarly, like the national laws in these states, nowhere in the OIC's long wish list of criminal liability does the organization acknowledge the need for normative standards that would balance protection against defamation with the right to freedom of expression and freedom of religion or belief.

The OIC's insistence on criminal sanction embodies another anti-constitutional aspect of its drive to codify defamation of religion as an offense at international law. Many international NGOs specializing in freedom of expression have long opposed attaching criminal punishment to traditional defamation offenses.[75] Endorsing this effort, a joint statement issued in 2000 by the UN and the Organization of American States (OAS) Special Rapporteurs on Freedom of Expression, together with the OSCE Representative on Freedom of the Media, bluntly concluded that:

> Criminal defamation laws ... are unnecessary to protect reputations. The threat of criminal sanctions – imprisonment and prohibitive fines ... exerts a significant chilling effect on freedom of expression which cannot be justified. Criminal defamation laws are frequently abused, being used in cases which do not involve the public interest and as a first, rather than last resort. Criminal defamation laws should be abolished and replaced with appropriate civil defamation laws. (Canton, Duve, & Hussain, 2000)[76]

Building on this consensus, the most recent report of the UN Special Rapporteur on Freedom of Expression calls on states to reject the criminalization of acts generally considered defamatory and "make civil liability proceedings the sole form of redress for complaints of damage to reputation."[77] The current UN Special Rapporteur on Contemporary Forms of Racism, Racial Discrimination, Xenophobia, and Related Intolerance has also endorsed eliminating the use of criminal penalties for acts deemed defamatory (Muigai, 2010, July 12). For its part, the UN Human Rights Committee has repeatedly called for the decriminalization of defamation offenses, leaving it subject only to civil lawsuits with a cap on any damages awarded.[78] To this end, the most current draft of UNHRC General Comment No. 34 on ICCPR Article 19 reiterates this position. (UN Human Rights Committee, 2010, October 22, para. 49). In more practical terms, the evidence is growing that the trend away from criminalization has taken hold in various parts of the world (Ligabo, 2007, January 2, paras. 55 and 75).

The Prohibition on Defamation Trumps Existing International Human Rights Protections and Norms

The OIC's position on defamation of Islam exposes its desire to protect select religious beliefs at the expense of either diluting or altogether casting aside existing international norms relating to freedom of expression, freedom of religion or belief, and nondiscrimination. The demand to enshrine certain religious dogmas with an absolute right to inviolability upends the foundation of human rights law by allowing protection of subjective beliefs to trump rights ascribed to individuals. The anti-constitutional impact of such an approach is evident from the analysis and findings presented above, including the fallout on the ground in states where blasphemy and similar statutes are actively enforced. In addition, the OIC's more recent attempt to equate defamation of religion with incitement to religious hatred poses a similar anti-constitution challenge, insofar as it seeks to dilute the high bar traditionally ascribed to the ICCPR's mandatory prohibition against "advocacy of national, racial or religious hatred that constitutes incitement to discrimination, hostility or violence" (UNGA, 1976, Article 20(2)).

Curtailing Existing Human Rights in the Name of Religion
As noted above, the Special Rapporteurs on Freedom of Religion and Contemporary Forms of Racism have concluded that "the right to freedom of religion or belief, as enshrined in relevant international legal standards,

does not include the right to have a religion or belief that is free from criticism or ridicule … . Freedom of religion primarily confers a right to act in accordance with one's religion but does not bestow a right for believers to have their religion itself protected from all adverse comment" (Jahangir & Diène, 2006, September 20, para. 36). More recently, the UN Human Rights Committee has reasoned that "[b]lasphemy laws should not be used to prevent or punish criticism of religious leaders or commentary on religious doctrine and tenets of faith" (UN Human Rights Committee, 2010, October 22, para. 50).

Despite these observations, the OIC has repeatedly stressed "the inapplicability of using the [sic] freedom of expression as a pretext to defame religions" (OIC Final Communiqué, December 2005) and decided a priori that "defamation of religions is a part of 'incitement to religious hatred' which invokes permissible limitation to or an abuse of freedom of expression" (Second OIC Observatory Report, p. 14). As part of this effort to enable anti-constitutional limitations on freedom of expression, the OIC in 2008 successfully lobbied for an amendment to the mandate of the Special Rapporteur on the Promotion and Protection of the Rights to Freedom of Opinion and Expression. The move resulted in blurring the long-standing distinction between race and religion by requiring future reports to include:

> instances in which the abuse of the right of freedom of expression constitutes an act of racial or religious discrimination, taking into account articles 19 (3) and 20 of the International Covenant on Civil and Political Rights, and general comment No. 15 of the Committee on the Elimination of All Forms of Racial Discrimination, which stipulates that the prohibition of the dissemination of all ideas based upon racial superiority or hatred is compatible with the freedom of opinion and expression. (UNHRC, 2008, March 28, para. 4)[79]

Subsequent UNHRC resolutions have affirmed this new mandate despite criticism of its implications (UNHRC, 2009, October 12, para. 12, adopted without a vote ("Invit[ing] the Special Rapporteur … within the framework of his mandate, to carry out his activities in accordance with its resolution 7/36."")).[80] The World Association of Newspapers and the World Editors Forum described the resolution as "part of a dangerous, backward campaign to equate critical portrayal of religion with racism," and criticized the UNHRC for "giv[ing] credit to this thesis, which completely undermines the basis of freedom of opinion and expression enjoyed in democracies" (World Association of Newspapers, 2008, April 8).[81] Ironically, the Special Rapporteur on Free Expression used his revised mandate as an opportunity to:

> reiterate that defamation laws may not be used to protect abstract or subjective notions or concepts. These include the State, national symbols, national identity, cultures,

schools of thought, religions, ideologies, or political doctrines. On this basis ... the
concept of "defamation of religions" does not accord with international standards
regarding defamation, which refer to the protection of the reputation of individuals,
while religions, like all beliefs, cannot be said to have a reputation of their own. (La Rue,
2010, June 3)

This forceful stance has done little to obviate the OIC's determination to
enshrine an international prohibition against defamation at the expense of
existing rights. In a recent statement to the UN, the OIC asserted that the
debate on defamation "has been wrongly linked with malafide intentions to
its perceived clash with another fundamental right i.e. freedom of opinion
and expression," and that the organization does "not intend to limit or
circumscribe the right to freedom of opinion and expression but [only]
emphasize the need to create and maintain the delicate balance between the
freedom of expression, respect for religions and hate speech" (Pakistan
Ministry of Foreign Affairs, 2006). Yet at the same time, the OIC continues
to abide by a hamstrung understanding of freedom of expression that
expressly excludes "deliberate and premeditated insults and ridiculing,"
"malicious and insulting attacks," and "ridiculing and insulting interpretation" of Islam.[82]

Inserting the vague concept of requiring "respect for religions" alongside
more clearly defined legal norms also gives rise to concern. The OIC has
condemned one British politician for criticizing Islam as a "vicious and
wicked religion" and a group of cartoonists for ridiculing Muhammed, but
more worrisomely, it invokes these occurrences as sufficient for evidencing
that "the contention that human rights standards should apply only to
individuals is not credible" (Pakistan Ministry of Foreign Affairs, 2006).
Accordingly, from the OIC's standpoint it is relatively easy to make the leap
in favor of attaching rights – including the "right to respect" – to subjective
and improvable religious beliefs, in turn permitting the protection of beliefs
to trump existing individual rights.

Falsely Equating Defamation of Islam with Incitement to Religious Hatred
Perhaps because of the mounting scrutiny over implications associated with
ascribing the offense of defamation to religion (*The Becket Fund*, Spring
2010, p. 1, outlining the drop in support for UNHRC resolutions on
combating defamation of religions), the OIC more recently has begun
channeling its efforts into a campaign to have insults against religion
recognized as incitement to religious hatred.[83] If successful, this recognition
would trigger a mandatory prohibition against such expression under
ICCPR Article 20. The OIC's tactical shift is evidenced in its support for a

UNHRC decision to establish an Ad Hoc Committee on the Elaboration of Complementary Standards (UNHRC, 2009, August 26) tasked with elaborating:

> as a matter of priority and necessity, complementary standards in the form of either a convention or additional protocol(s) to the International Convention on the Elimination of All Forms of Racial Discrimination [CERD], filling the existing gaps in the Convention and also providing new normative standards aimed at combating [*inter alia*] incitement to racial and religious hatred. (UNHRC, 2007, April 23, para (a))

The UNHRC's decision to investigate "gap filling" opportunities related to incitement to religious hatred is remarkable given the fact that similar earlier efforts failed to demonstrate the existence of such gaps. For example, experts appointed by the UNHRC to address the content and scope of substantive gaps in existing international instruments to combat racism, racial discrimination, xenophobia, and related intolerance concluded "that religious intolerance combined with racial and xenophobic prejudices is adequately covered under international human rights instruments."[84] Additionally, the 2007 Study of the Committee on the Elimination of Racial Discrimination made no mention whatsoever of enhancing measures related to defamation or incitement to religious hatred (UNHRC, 2007, June 15).

Pakistan's representations to the Ad Hoc Committee on behalf of the OIC have sought to further blur the distinction between defamation and incitement to religious hatred. Nothing in the OIC's materials or statements evidences an understanding that a lawful limitation on expression cannot simply be a blunt instrument, but rather must satisfy a high threshold before becoming permissible.[85] Likewise, it has ignored the exceptionally high standard that must be triggered before expression may be prohibited on the basis of incitement to religious hatred. This standard requires a case-by-case contextual analysis, consideration of the nature of expression, and, clearly, the requisite finding of incitement.[86] As the UN Human Rights Committee has observed, ICCPR Article 20(2) applies only to acts of "an extreme nature" (UN Human Rights Committee, 2010, October 22, para. 52), a standard that almost certainly excludes from its purview a batch of cartoons reflecting varied opinions about a religious faith.

More directly, the OIC's rhetorical shift away from a stand alone norm prohibiting defamation of religion in favor of incitement to religious hatred does little to hide its overriding goal of shielding Islam from criticism. Repackaging the offense as incitement to religious hatred only serves to situate defamation of Islam within an ostensibly more palatable – and legally grounded – framework. The mandatory criminal offenses recently proposed by the OIC under the banner of "[a]dvocacy and incitement to racial, ethnic, national and religious hatred" – namely, any public defamation of Islam or dissemination of other material manifesting defamation (UNHRC, 2009, August 26, para. 20) – makes plain that the organization is choosing to manipulate the ICCPR's Article 20(2) provision on incitement to achieve its desired prohibition on defamation. In the face of this effort, it is worth recalling that the UN Special Rapporteur on Freedom of Expression has called on governments to "refrain from introducing new norms which will pursue the same goals as defamation laws under a different legal terminology such as disinformation and dissemination of false information" (Ligabo, 2007, January 2, para. 82).

The push to include defamation of religion, still undefined, under the rubric of incitement to religious hostility runs two dangerous risks that underscore the need to maintain a clear distinction between mere criticism of religions or beliefs and actual incitement to religious hatred. First, endorsing a vague and arbitrary standard premised on defamation may lead to abuse on the part of states seeking to protect a privileged faith. Second, diluting the intentionally narrow formula established under ICCPR Article 20(2) may give rise to other states no longer taking seriously their obligation to prohibit advocacy of hatred that actually constitutes incitement, thus leaving more immediately threatening acts unchecked.

The Prohibition on Defamation Is Already Binding International Law

By Hook or By Crook

Whether by means of a specific declaration prohibiting defamation or a protocol to the CERD addressing incitement, the OIC remains fixated on securing an international document that will achieve two objectives: first, provide an imprimatur of international legitimacy for ongoing anti-constitutional efforts to silence perceived criticism or threats against Islam on the municipal level; and second, create a tool for channeling and validating criticism against those states unwilling to enforce such a prohibition within their own jurisdictions.

In 2006, the Pakistani government applauded its own effort to "pursue the inclusion of an operative para[graph] in the UNHRC, adoption of a comprehensive International Communication Order and an international convention/additional protocol to one of the existing instruments against defamation of religions" (Pakistan Ministry of Foreign Affairs, 2006,

March 1).[87] The following year, the OIC called upon the UNHRC "to adopt a universal declaration to incriminate the defamation of religions" and further expressed "the need to effectively combat defamation of religions through the adoption of an international convention in this regard" (Thirty-Fourth Session of the Islamic Conference of Foreign Ministers, 2007, May, para. 5). The UNHRC promptly advanced this demand by establishing the Ad Hoc Committee on Complimentary Standards and empowering it with a "mandate to elaborate ... a convention or additional protocol(s) to the [CERD] filling the existing gaps ... and also providing new normative standards aimed at combating ... incitement to racial and religious hatred" (UNHRC, 2007, April 23, para. (a)). In 2008, with the Ad Hoc Committee's mandate in place, the OIC redoubled its efforts to blur the critical distinction between defamation and incitement by proposing that the committee expressly adopt:

> some sort of additional protocol or universal declaration for codifying freedom of expression in the context of human responsibilities. It may be called an additional protocol or universal declaration on "freedom of expression and human responsibilities" ... a comprehensive framework is needed for analyzing national laws as well as understanding their provisions. This could then be compiled in a single universal document as guidelines for legislation – aimed at countering "defamation of or incitement to religious hatred and violence." (Vahid, 2008, October 2, p. 3)[88]

However, as the work of the Ad Hoc Committee on Complementary Standards bogged down with differences in opinion concerning the existing scope of protection afforded under international law,[89] no consensus emerged over whether gap filling or new normative standards were necessary. Still, Pakistan, on behalf of the OIC, resolutely asserted at the close of the second session in October 2009 that the Committee "was obliged to implement its mandate," and as such, "the Chair needed to formulate the proposals made during the session in the form of draft complementary standards" (Pakistan, 2010, February 17, para. 166) for the purpose of "deal[ing] with this scourge in [a] proposed international legal instrument" (Pakistan, explanatory letter to ad hoc committee on behalf of OIC, 2010, pp. 41–42).

Although the Ad Hoc Committee is expected to reconvene in December 2010, the nature of its final proposals remains to be determined (UNHRC, 2010, April 15). Despite this uncertainty, there are indications that the OIC may choose not to wait for official international validation of its long-desired prohibition. In fact, the OIC has steadily argued that even without additional guidance in the form of a declaration or treaty, an international prohibition on defamation of religion has already taken hold. As one OIC report remarked, "[T]his position has over the past decade repeatedly been observed to command support by a majority of the UN member states – a support that transcended the confines of the OIC member states. The succession of UNGA and UNHRC resolutions on the defamation of religions *makes it a standalone concept with international legitimacy*" (Second OIC Observatory Report on Islamophobia, 2009, May, p. 4, emphasis added). Moreover, the report asserted that "[a]ny denial of these facts constitutes a contradiction of the established position of the international community, the international legitimacy and above all the main provisions of international law and international humanitarian law" (p. 5).

Ultimately, even if it fails to secure an additional protocol or universal declaration, the OIC's public assertions suggest its member states already take succor in the view that prohibiting defamation of Islam has become a legitimate international norm. This presumption in turn may be used to legitimate domestic measures shielding specific religious beliefs from dissent, criticism, or scrutiny that would otherwise infringe existing international safeguards on freedom of expression and freedom of religion or belief.

Trend of Informal Self-Censorship Underscores Migration of the OIC's Anti-Constitutional Idée Fixe
Recent prominent examples of informal self-censorship premised on fear of insulting religious beliefs may also be evidence that the norm prohibiting defamation of religion has already migrated outside the Muslim world. Regardless of the extent to which this trend may be directly attributed to the OIC's international activities, the mere fact that it has emerged supports the organization's claim in favor of international legitimacy. The incidents noted below underscore the shifting and subjective standard being applied to circumscribe the boundaries of free expression. Significantly, this chilling of free expression is not restricted to those states that rely on coercive government power to enforce blasphemy laws. In places such as the United States, these limits are being adopted not by legal proscription, but rather in the face of intimidation and threats of violence; they are driven by fear rather than principled legal analysis. For example, consider Random House's decision to forgo publication of *The Jewel of Medina* in 2008. The publisher decided to pull the plug on this project – a "misty-eyed account of romance between Muhammad and his wife Aisha" (The Economist, 2009, February 14) – after receiving "from credible and unrelated sources, cautionary advice [that the] book might be offensive to some in the Muslim community, [and] could incite acts of violence by a small, radical segment" (The Random House Publishing Group, Medina Letter, undated).[90]

In a similar though more widely covered incident, Yale University Press (YUP) chose to publish *The Cartoons that Shook the World*, a scholarly account of the *Jyllands-Posten* incident, without reprinting the actual cartoons (Cohen, 2009, August 12). In defense of its decision, YUP claimed that extensive consultations "with experts in the intelligence, national security, law enforcement, and diplomatic fields, as well as with leading scholars in Islamic studies and Middle East studies" signaled that republishing the editorial cartoons – as well as other illustrations of Muhammed that had previously been published without issue – "ran a serious risk of instigating violence" (Klausen, 2009, "Publisher's Statement"). It is revealing to note that YUP failed to consult with human rights experts or leading scholars of free expression in making its decision. Additionally, the publisher failed to consider the critical distinction between expression that actually incites violence against the "targeted" group and expression that generates violence as a reaction against those exercising their right to free expression.[91] YUP's decision to forgo an authoritative reproduction of the cartoons, reasoning that the reader can "consult the Internet," is also unsatisfactory. An Internet search for these cartoons reveals considerable confusion over which images *Jyllands-Posten* actually published. For a time, even the BBC was unable to get its facts straight, erroneously claiming that the newspaper published an image representing the Prophet with a pig's snout (Reynolds, 2006, February 6).[92] In short, the Internet is awash with copycat images that often distort the debate. Though referring the reader to Google may be a convenient diversion, it fails to provide authoritative and accurate information that in turn would enable the reader to formulate an informed opinion regarding the controversy.

Comedy Central's handling of the animated series *South Park* is another example of the increasing tendency toward self-censorship surrounding commentary, criticism, and scrutiny of Islam. In July 2001, the television network allowed an episode entitled "Super Best Friends" – which featured an animated Prophet Muhammed alongside the founders of other religious traditions – to air uncut.[93] Five years later, in the wake of the *Jyllands-Posten* controversy, Comedy Central concealed an image of Muhammed identical to the one used in 2001 behind a black bar marked "IMAGE CENSORED" (South Park, April 5, 2006, "Cartoon Wars Part I"; April 12, 2006, "Cartoon Wars Part II"). To the chagrin of many, the network did not similarly question the propriety of depicting of an animated Jesus Christ defecating on President George W. Bush during the same episode.

Most recently in a two-part storyline broadcasted 2010, *South Park* again attempted to include a depiction of Muhammed together with many other religious figures previously caricatured on the show (South Park, April 14, 2010, "200"; April 21, 2010, "201"). In the first episode entitled "200," Comedy Central once again prohibited the screening of the original 2001 image of Muhammed, replacing it with the now familiar "CENSORED" black bar. Following this broadcast, a previously unknown New York-based fringe Islamic group posted a message to its website with the dubious intent of "warning" the *South Park* producers "that what they are doing is stupid and they will probably wind up like Theo Van Gogh for airing this show" (Associated Press, 2010, April 21).[94] Faced with this veiled threat, Comedy Central took the proverbial censor's scissors to episode "201," this time outdoing its previous efforts. Not satisfied with black-barring the image of Muhammed, the network in an unprecedented move bleeped out every spoken reference to "Muhammed" as well as 35 seconds of audio that, according to the producers, "didn't mention Muhammad at all" (Roberts, 2010, April 23; see also Itzkoff, 2010, April 22). As an additional precaution, the network also pulled episodes 200 and 201 from repeat broadcasts on television and refused to make them available for viewing on the *South Park* website.[95]

On Double Standards, Relativism, and the Value of Plurality Consciousness

To summarize the OIC's position, defamation of religion violates international human rights law and demands criminal censure. Respect for select religious beliefs and doctrines (i.e., Islam) necessarily trumps other competing interests such as free expression, freedom of religion or belief, or nondiscrimination. In the context of international law specifically, the OIC additionally claims that defamation of religion also amounts to incitement to religious hatred, even without any requisite finding of intent or actual incitement. These pronouncements are evidenced by the dozens of UN resolutions and reports endorsed by a majority of member states over a decade-long period, as well as from the ongoing work to secure a binding international instrument expressly prohibiting defamation of religion. Driving this point home, one need only look to the august offices of YUP to see that the prohibition on defamation of religion has already gained recognition in practice as a valid basis for limiting free expression.

Despite the OIC's effort to couch the campaign to prohibit defamation of religion in terms of human rights and its tireless pursuit of an international convention or protocol enshrining this view, the organization simultaneously adheres to one seemingly contradictory caveat: it remains fiercely opposed to any international scrutiny of the human rights practices of its member states. The OIC recently called for "the non-use of the universality of human rights as a pretext to [i]nterfere in the states' internal affairs and undermine their national sovereignty" (OIC Resolution No. 1/37-Leg, May 2010, para. 5). This statement plainly evidences the disingenuousness of the OIC's engagement with international human rights mechanisms to advance its case for a ban on defamation of religion. The denial of the universality of human rights also flies in the face of a clear and long-standing consensus among other states. For example, over 20 years ago, OSCE participating states "categorically and irrevocably declare[d] that the commitments undertaken in the field of the human dimension of the CSCE are *matters of direct and legitimate concern to all participating States and do not belong exclusively to the internal affairs of the State concerned*' (OSCE, 1991, October 4, preamble, emphasis added). Based on this undertaking, 56 nations from Europe, Central Asia, and North America committed themselves to no longer "invok[ing] the non-intervention principle to avoid discussions about human rights problems within their countries" OSCE, 2001, p. xvi). Arguably, state parties to the ICCPR and other major international human rights treaties already tacitly or explicitly acknowledge this basic premise.[96]

While the OIC's characterization of human rights engagement as "interference" in internal affairs may be at odds with its decade-long quest for *international* endorsement of a prohibition on defamation of religion, its position establishes a convenient fail-safe for its member states concerned with their own human rights records. On the one hand, if the OIC is unsuccessful in securing an international treaty banning defamation of Islam, its member states retain the ability to reject any international scrutiny of their individual human rights practices. On the other hand, if OIC member states successfully negotiate an international treaty but nevertheless find themselves subject to criticism regarding their own enforcement practices, they reserve the ability to reject any international expression of concern by branding it interference in internal affairs.

To be certain, the proclamation that the universality of human rights is not a legitimate basis for "interference" in internal affairs – made simultaneously with a demand for an international human rights protocol prohibiting defamation – isn't just *chutzpah*, it's the anti-constitutional idea par excellence, amounting to a demand for the creation of an international norm of suspect character along with the ability to enforce it without the restraint of "judicial" (or in this case, international) oversight. Notably, this assault on the validity of the universality of human rights is not an isolated misstep for the OIC. Rather, it fits squarely within a long and steady pattern intended to establish a rival system of international norms detached from the principles originally established by the Universal Declaration of Human Rights (UDHR). This effort can be traced to the OIC's 1990 Cairo Declaration on Human Rights, which espoused an alternate normative framework for constitutionalism steeped in Islamic law (Backer, 2007–2008, p. 43).

For example, Article 22 of the Cairo Declaration provides, "Everyone shall have the right to express his opinion freely in such manner as would not be contrary to the principles of the Shari'a" (Cairo Declaration, 1990, August 5, Article 22(a) and (b)). This single provision has the effect of prioritizing religious norms of indeterminate content above international norms and conventional constitutional rights. But the relativist challenge to the premise of universality contained in the Cairo Declaration is far bolder than a single limitation on one right long enshrined under international human rights law. The final articles of the Cairo Declaration stipulate that:

> Article 24: All the rights and freedoms stipulated in this Declaration are subject to the Islamic Shari'a.

> Article 25: The Islamic Shari'a is the only source of reference for the explanation or classification of any of the articles of this Declaration. (Articles 24 and 25)

With these two provisions, the OIC member states rendered moot the long-standing international consensus that had been painstakingly framed around universal values rather than the doctrinal tenets of one faith.[97] To its discredit, the Cairo Declaration also belied the true extent of the Muslim contribution to the UDHR and other key international instruments, "whether on the part of the Arab states that actively and effectively participated in debates on the substantive elements of human rights standards, or in the ... experts who helped shape international human rights law" (UN Development Program, 2004, p. 75).

Not satisfied with the aspirational content of the Cairo Declaration, the OIC has since moved to solidify the relativist universe of sharia-contingent rights through the drafting of various treaties intended to be binding on state parties. To date, this framework includes a Covenant on the Rights of the Child in Islam (CRCI) (OIC, 2005, June), and plans for an Islamic Charter on Human Rights, a Covenant on the Rights of the Women in Islam, and an Islamic Covenant against Racial Discrimination (OIC Resolution No. 1/37-Leg, 2009, May, para. 17), as well as an International Islamic Court of Justice intended to function as a fourth principal organ in the OIC.[98] Nothing in the CRCI, the only instrument completed to date, indicates a desire on the part of its drafters to safeguard existing international human rights. For example, the CRCI lacks a provision analogous to the one provided in the EU Charter of Fundamental Rights (2007, December 14), which stipulates that:

> Nothing in this Charter shall be interpreted as restricting or adversely affecting human rights and fundamental freedoms as recognised, in their respective fields of application, by Union law and international law and by international agreements to which the Union or all the Member States are party, including the European Convention for the Protection of Human Rights and Fundamental Freedoms, and by the Member States' constitutions (Article 53).

Instead, the CRCI calls on states to "[r]espect the provisions of the Islamic Shari'a, and observe the domestic legislations of the Member States," and further asserts that to achieve the Convention's objectives it is "incumbent to ... [o]bserve non-interference in the internal affairs of any State" (OIC, 2005, June, Articles 3(1) and 3(5)).[99]

CONCLUSION

As the modern framework of international human rights moves into its seventh decade of existence, its dramatic influence continues to be seen in developments such as the International Convention on the Protection of the Rights of All Migrant Workers and Members of Their Families as well as in deeper substantive commitments being adopted by certain states. At the same time, the normative consensus struck in the post-World War II era has been subjected to a revival of relativism that – although couched in the language of rights – threatens not only the content of individual rights but also the underlying premises upon which they are founded. Thus, a prohibition on defamation of religion not only seeks to supplant individual rights in favor of rights for selected religious beliefs but, in the context of the OIC's other efforts, also goes toward propping up a parallel system of norms that challenges the very legitimacy of universality as a cornerstone of the international human rights regime.

The nature of this challenge is made starker when framed as a case study in the migration of anti-constitutional ideas. Choudhry's theory provides a valuable structure for contemplating more fully the international traffic in legal norms and concepts, and also opens up the possibility of assessing the normative content of the actual ideas that are migrating. At the same time, the example of defamation of religion is useful for refining the parameters of Choudhry's model. First, it confirms that migration may occur from the bottom up rather than only in a top-down manner. And second, it demonstrates that migration of anti-constitutional ideas is not a post-9/11 phenomenon restricted to international efforts to stamp out terrorism.

From this vantage point, not only can one trace the journey from domestic blasphemy offenses to the hoped-for international ban on defamation of religion, but importantly, assess and expose the idea's anti-constitutional content as toxic to the existing international constitutional order. This ability to weigh the normative impact of ideas as they migrate and cross boundaries is of particular significance given the increasingly obvious effort to transmogrify the sociological construct of defamation of religion into the legal realm of incitement to religious hatred.

Lastly, by recognizing the migration of constitutional and anti-constitutional ideas, Choudhry's model also provides important space for engagement with Baxi and others. Considering the anti-constitutional implications associated with a ban on defamation of religion against the larger context of the OIC's multipronged challenge to universality, it is difficult to give much credence to the concepts of "plurality consciousness" and "equal discursive dignity." Opening up to revision established international norms simply to have existing rights downgraded seems counter-intuitive at best. At worst, allowing "plurality consciousness" to govern in the context of defamation of religion may generate the perverse result of eliminating plurality in practice by forcing religious minorities, dissenters, and others into silence, to say nothing of the associated chilling effect that would ensue in across a range of disciplines, including the arts, sciences, and academia in general. To be sure, the OIC's explicit denunciation of the universality of human rights as a legitimate basis for scrutinizing states' internal affairs only exacerbates the likelihood of such a perverse outcome.

While the desire of the international community to listen to the lamentation of the millennial losers may be commendable and we can applaud the OIC's efforts to self-confidently assert "non-Western norms" as a testament to the end of colonial control, the listening and applause should not necessarily translate into yielding ground on the long-standing principles of human rights universality and the progression of rights. Ultimately, what matters is not that a proposed constitutional idea originates from a different geographic, cultural, or religious source, but whether its normative effect enriches universal human rights rather than degrades it. With this under-standing, the international community can listen very carefully to the relativist lamentations being mounted by the OIC and others, but must remain vigilant in safeguarding the integrity of universality by carefully scrutinizing the *actual intent and implications* of any effort to modify nearly a century of legal development premised on the idea that all human beings are born free and equal, and are entitled to certain basic rights and freedoms without distinction of any kind.

Using this understanding as a departure point, the challenge of defamation of religion provides those states, scholars, and activists committed to the UDHR's spirit and principles with an opportunity for principled engagement: recognize and reiterate the legitimacy of protection for individuals facing discrimination, deepen the legal framework for accurately identifying genuine incitement to violence and hatred, and address inter and intra-community tensions through cooperation directed at fostering religious understanding through education, exchanges, coalitions, and the rejection of violence, including by those who perceive themselves to be the target of incitement. The umbrella of universal human rights protection is big enough to afford these protections and possibilities without having to undermine the scope and essence of the rights themselves.

NOTES

1. The bluntly titled article even went so far as to place Watson's theory in quotes, as if to lend it less legitimacy.

2. In Legrand's (1997) view: "At best, what can be displaced from one jurisdiction to another is literally, a *meaningless* form of words. To claim more is to claim too much. In any *meaning*-ful sense of the term, 'legal transplants,' therefore, cannot happen" (p. 120).

3. Many of the arguments relating to this debate are summarized in Nelken (2001, pp. 7–54).

4. Legrand (2003) seconds this call for such a break (p. 265).

5. Echoing Nelken's conclusion, James Q. Whitman (2003) acknowledges that even if the term transplant is "at best misleading," "*some* kind of borrowing is surely taking place and we need *some* account of what is going on" (p. 342).

6. The term is borrowed from Claude Levi-Strauss, who reasoned that the bricoleur was "adept at performing a large number of diverse tasks ... [by] mak[ing] do with 'whatever is at hand,' that is to say with a set of tools and materials which is ... heterogeneous because what it contains bears no relation to the current project, or indeed to any particular project, but is the contingent result of all the occasions there have been to renew or enrich the stock" (Tushnet, 1993, p. 1071).

7. As an example, Rosenfeld points to South Africa's express constitutional allowance for judicial consideration of foreign law in interpreting its bill of rights.

8. Oren Gross' contribution to Choudhry's volume addresses the migration of state practices legitimating torture. However, the anti-constitutional ideas in this

context are restricted to "closed circuit" examples – namely French rule in Algeria and British rule in Northern Ireland – with migration occurring within a single overarching "control system" (Gross, 2006, p. 403).

9. Scheppele calls attention in particular to states such as Brunei, Vietnam, and China effectively parlaying Resolution 1373 into anti-constitutional outcomes on the domestic level.

10. In 2004, the UNSC reminded states "that they must ensure that any measures taken to combat terrorism comply with all their obligations under international law, and should adopt such measures in accordance with international law, in particular international human rights, refugee, and humanitarian law" (UNSC, 2004, March 24, Preamble). Similarly, UNSC Resolution 1624 of 2005 expressly stipulated that all member states "ensure that any measures taken to combat terrorism comply with all of their obligations under international law ... in particular international human rights law, refugee law, and humanitarian law" (para. 4).

11. Scheppele identifies the movement of negative constitutional norms in an earlier essay, where she reasons "that there are also negative models lurking around the processes of constitution building that may have even more of an effect than the ones positively chosen." These negative models of constitution drafting are based on drafters intentionally averting from principles that in their view would be "horrifying to adopt" (Scheppele, 2003, pp. 301–303). "Looking an option over and saying 'this won't work here' in a constitutional debate is quite different from saying 'this would be horrifying to adopt.' It is the latter sort of emphatic rejection, a refusal or an aversion," that Scheppele argues carries substantial constitutional weight and embodies her idea of aversive constitutionalism (p. 303).

12. For a longer treatment of this issue in the context of defamation of religion, see Blitt (2010b, pp. 5–13).

13. The Qur'an and the Sunna are silent on the existence of a designated "blasphemy" offense (An-Na'im, 2008, p. 121).

14. The article provides a long list of examples of blasphemy offenses tried in the Muslim world.

15. The last conviction for blasphemy in the United Kingdom occurred in 1979 (*Whitehouse v. Gay News Ltd. and Lemon*, 1979).

16. In Australia, for example, the last successful prosecution for blasphemy occurred in 1871 (*R v. Jones*, 1996).

17. One notable outlier here is Ireland, which recently enacted a law prohibiting anyone from publishing or uttering "blasphemous matter." The law triggered widespread criticism and may be the subject of a future national referendum (Blitt, 2010b, pp. 24–25).

18. Cherif Bassiouni has remarked, "there is no division of church and state [under Islam]; there is no division between matters temporal and religious, and between different aspects of law" (Hannum et al., 1989, p. 433).

19. The study by Stahnke and Blitt classifies 44 predominantly Muslim states based on their constitutional declarations as follows: Ten "Islamic" states, twelve states with Islam declared the official religion, eleven "declared secular" states, and eleven states without any position taken vis-á-vis Islam in the constitutional text. All declared Islamic states also designate Islam the official state religion. Recent

developments in Somalia arguably shift that state from "no declaration" to having Islam as the official religion (Somali Republic, February 2004).

20. Other similar patterns may exist and merit further exploration; this article is focused on the specific issue of blasphemy and defamation of religion.

21. That said, the data supplied in Table 1 indicates that government policy may not necessarily reflect popular support for such measures in every instance.

22. Although state prosecutors sought jail time for the defendants, the court ultimately fined the organizers approximately $5,000 each (Osborn, 2010, July 12).

23. HRW has called upon the appellate court to quash the decision. This is not the first instance where the Russian government has acted to immunize the Russian Orthodox Church from criticism (Blitt, 2010a; Blitt, 2008).

24. The situation in Russia is critical for another reason. It demonstrates with troubling clarity how an offense premised on the ostensibly neutral legal formula of "incitement to religious hatred" can be selectively harnessed to obtain the same net effect as the more controversial concept of "defamation of religion."

25. Consider also Ireland's recently enacted blasphemy law, *supra* note 17. A recent OIC report on Islamophobia extoled the Irish law under a heading entitled "Positive Initiatives and Developments" (Third OIC Observatory Report on Islamophobia, 2010, p. 24).

26. The court's decision to reject an extension of the common law stemmed in part from a 1985 Law Commission conclusion that favored abolition of the offence altogether (*Choudhury v. UK*, 1991, p. 448). The House of Lords Appeal Committee dismissed the applicant's subsequent petition for leave to appeal.

27. The author experienced this firsthand at a recent conference held in Kuala Lumpur sponsored by a prominent consortium of international universities and hosted by a highly regarded center for Islamic theology. During the course of the multiday event an authorized publisher – responsible for printing many well-respected texts on Islamic law – located at the back of the main auditorium had for sale on prominent display copies of the aforementioned texts. The conference theme was "Religion, Law and Governance in Southeast Asia."

28. In the end, the Malaysian government elected to ban all Spielberg films from the country.

29. Major Western news outlets covered the fallout from the speech (*CNN*, 2003, October 16; *USA Today*, 2003, October 16; *BBC News*, 2003, October 17).

30. Mahathir's anti-Semitic and anti-American rants continue to garner press headlines (*Jakarta Globe*, 2010, January 21).

31. For the purpose of these provisions, the term "group" is defined as being distinguished by "race, country of origin, religion, origin, descent, nationality or constitutional condition" (Penal Code of Indonesia, February 1952).

32. Most recently, the U.S. Department of State reported that court proceedings continued in 2010 "against two Muslim converts to Christianity charged with ... inciting hatred against Islam" (U.S. Department of State, 2010).

33. An Istanbul court found Gursel lacked the requisite criminal intent. In Gursel's words, "The offence of blasphemy shouldn't even exist in a secular republic, which is what Turkey considers itself to be" (Lea, 2009, June 26).

34. One year earlier, Turkish prosecutors investigated whether *The God Delusion*, a book penned by Dawkins, attacked religious values. The probe was launched

"after one reader complained that passages in the book were an assault on 'sacred values'" (Associated Press, 2007, November 28).

35. The report also labeled the common law prohibition problematic insofar as it "lacks a mechanism to take account of the proper balance with freedom of expression" (Jahangir, 2008, February 7, p. 21, para. 73).

36. The fact remains that blasphemy laws are often used to target dissenting views from within the predominant faith. For example, most recently in Pakistan a court sentenced a Muslim prayer leader and his son to life in jail for tearing down a poster announcing a Barelvi religious gathering to mark the birthday of the Prophet Muhammad (*BBC News*, 2011, January 12; see also *infra* note 49).

37. Consider also the abysmal effort at balancing competing rights undertaken by the Commission of the European Court of Human Rights in deciding to reject the appeal filed by Denis Lemon, the editor of *Gay News* in the wake of the ruling in the *Whitehouse v. Gay News Ltd. and Lemon* blasphemy case (*X. Ltd. and Y. v. United Kingdom*, 1982 (decision on the admissibility of the application)).

38. Of the 112 individuals with cases pending under Pakistan's blasphemy laws in 2009, 57 were identified as Ahmadis, 47 Muslims, and 8 Christians (U.S. Department of State, 2010).

39. For example, consider the most recent killing with impunity of dozens of Ahmadis in Lahore (Banyan's Notebook, 2010, June 10; *The Economist*, 2010, June 3; see also Human Rights Watch, 2010, June 1).

40. Article 16(3), Constitution of Spain, ratified in 1978 and consolidated to 1992. ("No religion shall have a state character. The public authorities shall take into account the religious beliefs of Spanish society and shall consequently maintain appropriate cooperation relations with the Catholic Church and other confessions.")

41. Spain's penal code (1995) provides eight to twelve months of jail time for publicly offending religious feelings or insulting dogmas, beliefs, rituals, and ceremonies. The same article also protects atheists and nonbelievers against similar ridicule (Art. 525).

42. In February 2000, a radio station in Indonesia broadcasted an interview with a priest who commented that the Prophet Muhammed had been a Christian before becoming a Muslim. This sparked protests and accusations of blasphemy from a local Islamic youth organization, which led to the radio station being "compelled to refrain from broadcasting for a week" and issuing a public apology for the program's content. The police also arrested the priest involved for religious contempt (Amor, 2000, September 8, p. 10, para. 33).

43. Indonesia reiterated its call for deletion of the offensive paragraph on the basis of UNCHR Resolution 1997/125 in a statement made during the substantive session of the Economic and Social Council (Statement by Chairman of the Delegation of Indonesia, 1997, July 23).

44. A search for "Islamist and Arab anti-Semitism" on the Office of the High Commissioner for Human Rights website (http://www.ohchr.org/) returns only one result: UNCHR Resolution 1997/125 demanding that the Special Rapporteur delete his statement that Muslim extremists are using the Qur'an as a source for anti-Semitism. A similar search query from the UN's homepage (http://www.un.org/) retrieves the following result: "Your search – 'Islamist and Arab anti-Semitism' – did not match any documents. No pages were found containing 'Islamist and Arab

anti-Semitism.'" Lastly, the UN's Official Document System "Global Search" feature (http://ods.un.org/) returns 10 results that link to documents from 1997 relating directly to the controversy over the Special Rapporteur's report. The expunging of "Islamist and Arab anti-Semitism" as a legitimate term of reference confirms that in the wake of the OIC's 1997 protest, the UN abandoned any forthright examination of anti-Semitism emanating from "Islamist or Arab sources." The rationale for this decision is premised on an especially glaring sophism in the context of any discussion of anti-Semitism encapsulated in the view expressed by Egypt's UNCHR representative: "The Special Rapporteur should have known that since Arabs themselves were Semites, it was absurd to speak of Islamist and Arab anti-Semitism. [Egypt] wished to protest formally against any such allegation and to express the hope that racial slogans of that type would no longer be use in future ... the very title of the section ... was unacceptable. How could the Special Rapporteur accuse Arabs of anti-Semitism when they were Semites themselves?" (UNCHR, 1997, September 3, paras. 17 and 42). In a similar vein, Syria's Observer to the UNCHR remarked that the very concept of Islamist and Arab anti-Semitism "was most surprising, since Arabs were themselves Semites" (UNCHR, March 21, 1997, para. 59). According to this disingenuous approach, the Arabs are Semites and therefore cannot be responsible for acts of anti-Semitism. What both diplomats fail to appreciate – and a simple dictionary consultation could have clarified – is that in the context of a discussion on anti-Semitism, the intended reference is to "hostility to or prejudice against Jews" (Oxford American Dictionary) specifically, rather than to the technically accurate – though in this context utterly diversionary – understanding that a "Semite" denotes a "member of any of the peoples who speak or spoke a Semitic language, including in particular the Jews and Arabs" (Oxford American Dictionary).

45. For more on the problematic nature of ascribing normative legal value to defamation of religion, see Blitt (2010b, pp. 15–18).

46. For a list of all reports generated on the basis of UN resolutions addressing defamation of religion, see Appendix A. The UNHRC revived a reporting requirement for the Special Rapporteur on Freedom of Religion or Belief in UN Doc. A/HRC/DEC/1/107, June 30, 2006. The subsequent report, prepared jointly with the Special Rapporteur on Racism, was issued as UN Doc. A/HRC/2/3, September 20, 2006.

47. In a separate report to the UNCHR on implementation of the declaration on the elimination of all forms of intolerance and of discrimination based on religion or belief (unrelated to the combating defamation of religions resolution), Amor (February 13, 2001) took the opportunity to reiterate the following reality: "it must be acknowledged that blasphemy or defamation are increasingly used by extremists to censure all legitimate critical debate within religions (Jordan, Egypt, Pakistan) or to bring to heel certain minorities accused of holding erroneous views (Pakistan). Of course, extremism does not and cannot operate in a vacuum, and in fact it frequently receives either active or passive support (in the absence of measures to curb it) from national and foreign State entities" (para. 187).

48. Available at http://www.youtube.com/watch?v=oMOZvbYJMvU, http://www.youtube.com/watch?v=P9yK0u-XH1M&p, and http://www.youtube.com/watch?v=HTYoV-_GlNs.

49. Of note, all of the press accounts concerning these celebrations typically underscored that they did not represent the Palestinian consensus and that the sentiment was more complex.

50. A student from Brazil originally alleged that CNN's footage of Palestinians celebrating the 9/11 attacks dated back to the 1990 Gulf War.

51. In one instance, a high-ranking Palestinian official, Ahmed Abdel Rahman, told the AP bureau chief in Jerusalem that a cameraman's "safety could not be ensured if the footage were released." According to the press account, news organizations "operating in the Palestinian-ruled portions of the West Bank and Gaza" complied with the order (Hockstader, 2001, September 15, p. A42; *The Jerusalem Post*, 2001, September 14, p. 4A).

52. Note that the Diène does not elaborate if the alleged defamation is directed against the state *qua* state, or against the Jewish religion.

53. Van Gogh's film *Submission*, made with Ayaan Hirsi Ali, a Somali-born woman and former member of the Dutch parliament, recounts the story of a Muslim woman forced into an arranged marriage (*BBC News*, 2004, November 2). Muhammed Bouyeri, the Dutch-Moroccan attacker sentenced to life without parole for slashing Van Gogh's throat and shooting him in the middle of the day in Amsterdam, claimed he acted out of religious conviction: "the law compels me to chop off the head of anyone who insults Allah and the prophet" (*BBC News*, 2005, July 26; see also Rovers, 2004, November 24).

54. For a general overview of the affair and its fallout, see Bilefksy (February 11, 2006).

55. But for the decision of *Jyllands-Posten* to run its editorial cartoon competition, one wonders what material Diène would have used to fill his report.

56. For example, Diène makes no mention of evidence that the widespread riots were the product of individual and governmental manipulation rather than spontaneous grassroots outcry (see, e.g., Klausen, 2009; Reuters, 2010, December 29).

57. The assertion of a "general increase" in defamation of religions is made throughout the report without any substantiation (see, e.g., Diène, 2006, February 13, paras. 25, 28, and 33).

58. After several rejections, Bluitgen did find an illustrator (who preferred to remain anonymous) and the book went on to be published in January 2006.

59. The closest cartoon to this depiction is one described by the BBC as portraying "Muhammad with a kind of halo around his head, but it could be a crescent moon, or a pair of devil's horns." Although this interpretive nuance is omitted from Diène's characterization, it remains baffling as to why he felt compelled to fabricate the presence of a grenade – something that simply does not appear in the drawing (Asser, 2010, January 2).

60. The *Jyllands-Posten* editorial cartoons may be viewed at "Muhammed Image Archive" (Available at http://zombietime.com/mohammed_image_archive/jyllands-posten_cartoons/).

61. Between two and four of these images make a link with terrorism, depending on one's subjective perspective.

62. The vote in the UNGA was 111 votes to 54, with 18 abstentions. In the UNHRC, the recorded vote was 24 to 14 with 9 abstentions.

63. For a longer discussion concerning this episode and its relevance for the formulation of customary international law, see Blitt (2010b, Part III(3)).

64. This Charter replaces the previous OIC Charter from February 1974. After the UN, the OIC identifies itself as the world's largest intergovernmental organization (International Center for Not for Profit Law, 2011, "Organization of the Islamic Conference").

65. The thirty-seventh session of the OIC Council of Foreign Ministers (CFM) (May 18–20, 2010) deferred a decision on these rules until its next session. The main dispute over the draft rules is related to OIC member state": OIC member state, namely India. Pakistan's desire to retain language that would prohibit observer status being granted to any state in conflict with an OIC Member State (OIC Resolution No. 1/37, para. 3–4).

66. For example, in 2009 half of the states designated a "Country of Particular Concern" (CPC) by the U.S. Department of State acting under the International Religious Freedom Act (IRFA) were also OIC member states: Iran, Saudi Arabia, Sudan and Uzbekistan (U.S. Department of State, 2009). OIC member states accounted for eight of thirteen states recommended for CPC designation by the bipartisan U.S. Commission on International Religious Freedom (USCIRF, 2011). In addition to those states listed by the U.S. Department of State, USCIRF called for adding Iraq, Nigeria, Pakistan, and Turkmenistan to the CPC list. USCIRF also maintains a "Watch List" of states where ongoing violations of religious freedom exist but do not meet the statutory CPC threshold established under IRFA. Half of states on USCIRF's watch list are OIC member states: Afghanistan, Egypt, Indonesia, Somalia, Tajikistan, and Turkey (USCIRF).

67. This approach is in keeping with the rights extended to dhimmi under historical Muslim rule: Whereas Christians and Jews, as *Ahl al-Kitab*, could attain security of the person and property and freedom to practice their own religion, unbelievers had "no permanent and general sanctity of life or property" (An-Na'im, 1987, pp. 11–12). Donna Arzt (2002) also notes, "Non-Muslims in the *dar al-Islam* were treated differently depending on whether or not they were 'People of the Book,' those whose faith was based, like that of Muslims, on revealed scripture (ahl al-kitab)" (p. 25).

68. These resolutions are particularly egregious insofar as they deflect any responsibility for acts of defamation of religion sanctioned by Muslim states – where, as noted above, such practices occur with regularity and sometimes-deadly results.

69. Arguably, because the proposition is a tenuous one. Consider the more "traditional" though still contemporary view that "Judaism is the first of the three heavenly revealed religions, Christianity being the second and Islam the third and last" (Abdalla, 2001, p. 9).

70. Consider also Egypt's approach to defining religions, whereby its Supreme Court "stipulated that the freedom to have or to adopt any of the *recognized sacred religions* is limited by the condition that public order and morals in the country in which it is adopted must not be jeopardized thereby" (Constitutional Case No. 7, judicial year 2, hearing of March 1, 1975). In other words, no provision is made for the freedom to have or to adopt any religion that is not officially recognized by the state as "sacred" (Arab Republic of Egypt, 2002, April 15, para. 483).

71. These NGOs also note that the "artificial hierarchization of protected religious beliefs" is not in line with Egypt's Constitution, which protects religious freedom and non-discrimination without distinction between 'divine religions' and other beliefs (CIHRS, 2008, August 29, p. 3).

182   ROBERT C. BLITT

72. The UNHRC (2007, April 23) has mandated the ad hoc committee with elaborating, "as a matter of priority and necessity, complementary standards in the form of either a convention or additional protocol(s) to the International Convention on the Elimination of All Forms of Racial Discrimination, filling the existing gaps in the Convention and also providing new normative standards aimed at combating all forms of contemporary racism, including incitement to racial and religious hatred" (para. (a)). The ad hoc committee's curious mandate follows two reports previously prepared by UNHRC-appointed bodies that essentially concluded there were no relevant gaps within the existing international treaty framework addressing intolerance (UNHRC, August 27, 2007; June 15, 2007).

73. The OIC's implicit conclusion here also underscores that the organization equates the effects of defamation of religion with incitement to religious hatred.

74. Algeria recently reported to the UN that under Article 298 of its Criminal Code, any "offence to the Prophet or denigration of Islam and its teachings, by whichever medium, is punishable with three to five years' imprisonment, as well as a fine" (UN Secretary General, 2010, August 9, para. 15). Likewise, Kuwaiti law prescribes imprisonment for defaming the Prophet Muhammad (Hussain, 2000, January 18, para. 134). As noted above, Pakistani law proscribes the death penalty for defaming the Prophet Muhammed.

75. These include Amnesty International; Article 19; the Committee to Protect Journalists; the International Helsinki Federation, and its many national committees; the World Press Freedom Committee; the Norwegian Forum for Freedom of Expression; national chapters of PEN; and Reporters Sans Frontières (Commission on Security and Cooperation in Europe, 2002, January 9). More recently, Article 19 released a special report dedicated to Criminal Defamation and Freedom of Expression (Article 19, December 2005).

76. In the U.S. context, one observer has remarked that "[c]riminal libel law ... is a useless and increasingly unconstitutional remedy for the redress of racial or ethnic group defamation ... Criminal defamation is not recognized in the Model Penal Code or by a leading criminal law treatise. Even though racial and ethnic defamation affect the public weal and not merely individual interests, the criminal law of libel is no longer effective to redress that group wrong" (Polelle, 2003, pp. 257–258).

77. The Special Rapporteur on Freedom of Expression goes on to assert that "criminal defamation laws may not be used to protect abstract or subjective notions or concepts, such as the State, national symbols, national identity, cultures, schools of thought, religions, ideologies or political doctrines. This is consistent with the view ... that international human rights law protects individuals and groups of people, not abstract notions or institutions that are subject to scrutiny, comment or criticism" (La Rue, 2010, April 20, paras. 83–84). This is a long-standing and consistent opinion (Ligabo, 2007, January 2, para. 81 ("The Special Rapporteur strongly recommends to Governments to decriminalize defamation and similar offences. These should be dealt with under civil law."); Hussain, 2000, January 18, para. 52 ("Criminal defamation laws should be repealed in favour of civil laws as the latter are able to provide sufficient protection for reputations.")).

78. See Russian Federation (2009, November 24, para. 24(b)); Italy (2006, April 24, para. 19) ("The State party should ensure that defamation is no longer punishable by imprisonment."); Mexico (2010, May 17, para. 20(d)) ("Take steps to decriminalize

defamation in all states."); The Former Yugoslav Republic of Macedonia (2008, April 17, para. 6) ("welcom[ing] the amendments to the Criminal Code, decriminalizing the offence[] of defamation ... as steps in the right direction towards ensuring freedom of opinion and expression particularly of journalists and publishers.")

79. The correlation between this resolution and the OIC campaign against defamation of religion is unmistakable. Indeed, the government of Pakistan cited the resolution as one of the steps taken "against the countries which published the blasphemous caricatures of Holy Prophet" (Minister for Foreign Affairs Qureshi, 2008, December 18, pp. 21–24, response to question on "steps taken by the Government against the countries which published the blasphemous caricatures of Holy Prophet (PBUH)").

80. The NGO Article 19 (September 23, 2009) expressed concern over the reference to UNHRC Resolution 7/36 insofar as it has "undermined and threatened" protection of the right to freedom of expression under international human rights law and "dilutes and distorts the focus of the mandate of the Special Rapporteur on Freedom of Opinion and Expression" (para. 4).

81. The Association represents more than 18,000 publications across 5 continents.

82. These forms of expression are expressly rejected in the text of the ambassador's letter (Pakistan Ministry of Foreign Affairs, 2006).

83. This shift is supported by Diène, who made an about face in 2008 by reasoning that: "translating religious defamation from a sociological notion into a legal human rights concept, namely incitement to racial and religious hatred," will show "that combating incitement to hatred is not a North-South ideological question but a reality present in a large majority of national legislations in all regions" (Diène, 2008, September 2, para. 45).

84. At most, the experts suggested that the CERD committee "may wish to consider adopting a recommendation stating explicitly the advantages of multi-cultural education in combating religious intolerance" (UNHRC, 2007, August 27, para. 130). The group also endorsed "the importance of multicultural education, including education on the Internet, aimed at promoting understanding, tolerance, peace and friendly relations between communities and nations" as a means of combating defamation rather than any criminal sanctions (para. 149). The expert group specifically solicited views and comments from various stakeholders regarding "the question as to whether there are normative gaps in the existing international legal instruments to combat racism, racial discrimination, xenophobia and related intolerance with regard to ... Religious intolerance and defamation of religious symbols" (Annex, Question I(1)(iv)).

85. In contrast, consider the UK's Racial and Religious Hatred Act 2006. This Act requires showing an actual threat and intent to stir hatred. Moreover, as a means of safeguarding free expression, Article 27J of the Act provides: "Nothing ... shall be read or given effect in a way which prohibits or restricts discussion, criticism or expressions of antipathy, dislike, ridicule, insult or abuse of particular religions or the beliefs or practices of their adherents, or of any other belief system or the beliefs or practices of its adherents, or proselytising or urging adherents of a different religion or belief system to cease practising their religion or belief system."

86. At least in those jurisdictions where an attempt is made to balance freedom of expression with protection against hate speech.

87. The idea for an international communication order revives a concept dating back to the 1970s. In 1980, the International Commission for the Study of Communication Problems, a United Nations Educational, Scientific and Cultural Organization (UNESCO) body, presented a seminal report on the international communication order entitled *Many Voices, One World: Communication and Society Today and Tomorrow*. The report's conclusions – that a new international communication order was necessary to alleviate the dominance of Western states in driving the global news agenda and that greater limitations on freedom of the press might be justifiable – were symptomatic of the problems that ultimately led the United States and United Kingdom to withdraw from UNESCO in 1985. According to the U.S. Department of State, the decision "was based upon our experience that UNESCO has extraneously politicized virtually every subject it deals with [and] has exhibited hostility toward the basic institutions of a free society, especially the free market and the free press" (UN Chronicle, 1984; see also American Society of International Law, January 1984, pp. 218–230; Dutt, 1998).

88. In the same statement, OIC deputy permanent representative to the UN Vahid downplayed the efficacy of education and dialogue without the imposition of additional criminal sanctions. Elsewhere, Masood Khan, Pakistan's UN ambassador, also reminded the UNHRC that the OIC's ultimate objective was nothing less than a "new instrument or convention" addressing defamation (Edwards, 2008, November 24).

89. For example, the parties could not agree on the precise nature of a "gap." The African Group "expressed the view that issues pertaining to implementation could not be considered gaps and that only issues for which no international instrument existed constituted a gap" (Pakistan, 2010, February 17, para. 56).

90. The author eventually found a publisher and the novel has been readily available since late 2008.

91. Random House also chose to ignore this distinction in its decision regarding *The Jewel of Medina*.

92. The picture, a photocopy of an image taken during an unrelated "pig-squealing" competition in France, ultimately was traced back "to a delegation of Danish Muslim leaders who went to the Middle East ... to publicise the cartoons. The visit was organised by Abu Laban, a leading Muslim figure in Denmark" (Reynolds, 2006, February 6).

93. This episode is no longer available for Internet streaming on the official South Park website. See http://www.southparkstudios.com/episodes/103940.

94. In its message to the South Park producers, the website "Revolution Muslim" "included a gruesome picture of [murdered] Theo Van Gogh" and took the trouble of posting "the addresses of Comedy Central's New York office and the California production studio where South Park is made" (Associated Press, 2010, April 23).

95. Although unavailable on the official South Park website, copies of "episode 200" and "episode 201" may still be viewed online at http://vimeo.com/11189168 and http://vimeo.com/11134306. As if to underscore the extent of this informal self-censorship trend, an academic colleague advised the author to forgo publication of

the South Park stills herein. Ultimately, Comedy Central denied the author's request for copyright clearance to republish 11 still images depicting Muhammed and – despite the fact that the U.S. Supreme Court has previously found that denial "of permission to use a work does not weigh against a finding of fair use" (*Campbell v. Acuff-Rose Music, Inc.*, 1994, p. 585 no. 18) – Emerald Group Publishing, the publisher of *Studies in Law, Politics and Society*, refused to include the stills without "clear permission" from Comedy Central.

96. Notably only 8 of the OIC's 57 member states have opted to forgo ratification of the ICCPR: Brunei, Comoros, Malaysia, Oman, Palestine, Qatar, Saudi Arabia, and the United Arab Emirates (UN Treaty Collection, 2011, February 25, ICCPR Ratification Status). Over 100 states have also ratified the ICCPR's optional protocol recognizing the competence of the UN Human Rights Committee to receive and consider human rights complaints filed by individuals directly (UN Treaty Collection, 2011, March 25).

97. Ultimately, Saudi Arabia was the lone abstention among predominantly Muslim UN member states voting on the UDHR. Afghanistan, Egypt, Iran, Iraq, Lebanon, Pakistan, Syria, and Turkey all voted in favor (UN, 1948, § B(2)(C)).

98. The International Islamic Court of Justice was established in Kuwait in 1987 (OIC Resolution No. 12/5-P (IS) adopted by the Fifth Session of the Islamic Summit Conference), but its statute has not entered into force (OIC Charter, 2008, Article 14; see also OIC Resolution No. 1/34-Leg, June 2004).

99. The Covenant references sharia 10 times over 26 articles; it does not make any reference to international law.

REFERENCES

Abdalla, Z. M. (2001). *Islam from a contemporary perspective*. Mansoura: Publishing House for Universities.

American Society of International Law. (1984). United States withdrawal from UNESCO [Electronic version]. *International Legal Materials, 23*(January), 218–230. Retrieved from http://www.jstor.org/stable/20692681.

Amor, A. (1996, January 2). *Report submitted by Mr. Abdelfattah Amor, Special Rapporteur, in accordance with UNCHR Resolution 1995/23* – Addendum visit by the Special Rapporteur to Pakistan (UN Doc. E/CN.4/1996/95/Add.1).

Amor, A. (1996, November 11). *Interim report on the elimination of all forms of religious intolerance relating to a visit to the Sudan, submitted by the Special Rapporteur of the UNCHR, in accordance with UNGA Resolutions 50/183 and 50/197: Sudan* (Addendum 2) (UN Doc. A/51/542/Add.2).

Amor, A. (1997, November 12). *Interim report on the elimination of all forms of religious intolerance, submitted by the Special Rapporteur of the UNCHR in accordance with UNGA Resolution 51/93* (Addendum) (UN Doc. A/52/477/Add.1).

Amor, A. (2000, February 15). *Report submitted by the Special Rapporteur, in accordance with UNCHR Resolution 1999/39, civil and political rights, including religious intolerance* (UN Doc. E/CN.4/2000/65).

Amor, A. (2000, September 8). *Interim report by the Special Rapporteur on the elimination of all forms of intolerance and of discrimination based on religion or belief* (UN Doc. A/55/280).

Amor, A. (2001, February 13). *Report submitted by the Special Rapporteur, in accordance with UNCHR Resolution 2000/33* (UN Doc. E/CN.4/2001/63).

Amor, A. (2001, July 31). *Interim report prepared by the Special Rapporteur of UNCHR on freedom of religion or belief, in accordance with UNGA Resolution 55/97 of 4 December 2000* (UN Doc. A/56/253).

An-Na'im, A. A. (1987). Religious minorities under Islamic law and the limits of cultural relativism. *Human Rights Quarterly, 9*, 1.

An-Na'im, A. A. (2008). *Islam and the secular state: Negotiating the future of Shari'a.* Cambridge: Harvard University Press.

Anti-Defamation League. (2009). *Anti-Semitism in the Egyptian media.* Retrieved from http://www.adl.org/anti_semitism_arab/Egyptian-Media-Report.pdf.

Arab Republic of Egypt. (2002, April 15). *The combined third and fourth periodic reports of Egypt submitted to the UN Human Rights Committee* (UN Doc. CCPR/C/EGY/2001/3).

Arzt, D. E. (1996a). Heroes or heretics: Religious dissidents under Islamic law. *Wisconsin International Law Journal, 14*, 349.

Arzt, D. E. (1996b). Religious human rights in Muslim states of the Middle East and North Africa. *Emory International Law Review, 10*, 139.

Arzt, D. E. (1996c). The treatment of religious dissidents under classical and contemporary Islamic law. In: J. D. van der Vyver & J. Witte (Eds.), *Religious human rights in global perspective: Religious perspectives* (pp. 387–453). The Hague: Kluwer Law International.

Arzt, D. E. (2002). The role of compulsion in Islamic conversion: Jihad, Dhimma and Ridda. *Buffalo Human Rights Law Review, 8*, 15.

Article 19. (2005). Putting expression behind bars: Criminal defamation and freedom of expression. *Article 19*, December. Retrieved from http://www.article19.org/pdfs/conferences/criminal-def-eu-ngo-paper.pdf.

Article 19. (2009). Comment on the draft text of the resolution on freedom of expression proposed by Egypt and the US at the twelfth session of the UN Human Rights Council. *Article 19*, September 23. Retrieved from http://www.article19.org/pdfs/analysis/comment-on-the-draft-text-of-the-resolution-on-freedom-of-expression-propose.pdf.

Asser, M. (2010). What the Muhammad cartoons portray. *BBC News*, January 2. Retrieved from http://news.bbc.co.uk/2/hi/middle_east/4693292.stm.

Associated Press. (2007). Turkey probes Dawkins book. *The Toronto Star*, November 28. Retrieved from http://www.thestar.com/entertainment/article/280649, and reprinted at http://www.guardian.co.uk/books/2007/nov/28/richarddawkins.

Associated Press. (2010). Radical Muslim group warns "South Park" creators. *CBS News*, April 21. Retrieved from http://www.cbsnews.com/stories/2010/04/21/entertainment/main6419829.shtml.

Associated Press. (2010). 'South Park' guys: Comedy Central cut speech due to Muslim warning. *USA Today*, April 23. Retrieved from http://www.usatoday.com/life/television/news/2010-04-22-south-park-censored_N.htm.

Backer, L. C. (2007–2008). God(s) over constitutions: International and religious transnational constitutionalism in the 21st century. *Mississippi College Law Review, 27*, 11.

Banyan's Notebook. (2010). We decide whether you're Muslim or not. *The Economist*, June 10. Retrieved from http://www.economist.com/blogs/banyan/2010/06/state_persecution_ and_pakistans_ahmadi_sect.

Baxi, U. (2003). The colonial heritage. In: P. Legrand & R. Munday (Eds.), *Comparative legal studies: Traditions and transitions* (pp. 46–75). Cambridge: Cambridge University Press.

BBC News. (2002). Egypt airs 'anti-Semitic' series. *BBC News*, November 7. Retrieved from http://news.bbc.co.uk/2/hi/2409591.stm.

BBC News. (2003). Malaysia defends speech on Jews. *BBC News*, October 17. Retrieved from http://news.bbc.co.uk/2/hi/3196234.stm.

BBC News. (2004). Gunman kills Dutch film director. *BBC News*, November 2. Retrieved from http://news.bbc.co.uk/2/hi/europe/3974179.stm.

BBC News. (2005). Van Gogh killer jailed for life. *BBC News*, July 26. Retrieved from http:// news.bbc.co.uk/2/hi/europe/4716909.stm.

BBC News. (2010). Russians convicted and fined over Forbidden Art show. *BBC News*, July 12. Retrieved from http://www.bbc.co.uk/news/10559503.

BBC News. (2011). Life in jail for two Pakistani Muslim blasphemers. *BBC News*, January 12. Retrieved from http://www.bbc.co.uk/news/world-south-asia-12169123.

The Becket Fund. (2009). Malaysia: Legal body faces lawsuit for using word 'Allah.' *The Becket Fund*, March 23. Retrieved from http://becketinternational.wordpress.com/2009/ 03/23/malaysia-legal-body-faces-lawsuit-for-using-word-%E2%80%98allah%E2% 80%99/.

The Becket Fund. (2010). UN efforts to pass a binding international blasphemy law. *The Becket Fund*. Retrieved from http://www.becketfund.org/files/international%20blaspemy% 20memo.pdf.

Ben-Ito, H. (2005). *The lie that wouldn't die: The protocols of the elders of Zion*. London: Vallentine Mitchell.

Bilefsky, D. (2006). Danish cartoon editor on indefinite leave. *New York Times*, February 11. Retrieved from http://www.nytimes.com/2006/02/11/international/europe/11denmark.html.

Blitt, R. C. (2008). How to entrench a de facto state church in Russia: A guide in progress. *Brigham Young University Law Review, 2008*, 707–778.

Blitt, R. C. (2010a). One new president, one new patriarch and a generous disregard for the constitution: A recipe for the continuing decline of secular Russia. *Vanderbilt Journal of Transnational Law, 43*, 1337–1368.

Blitt, R. C. (2010b). Should new bills of rights address emerging international human rights norms? The challenge of "defamation of religion". *Northwestern Journal of International Human Rights, 9*, 1–26.

Butler, D., & Yackley, A. J. (2009). New NATO chief pledges conciliation with Muslims. *Reuters*, April 6. Retrieved from http://www.reuters.com/article/worldNews/ idUSTRE5351GU20090406?sp=true.

Cairo Institute for Human Rights Studies. (2008). *Written statement*, August 29 (UN Doc. A/HRC/9/NGO/33).

Campbell v. Acuff-Rose Music, Inc. (1994). 510 U.S. 569. United States.

Canton, S., Duve, F., & Hussain, A. (2000, February). Statement regarding key issues and challenges in freedom of expression, Agreed by: Santiago Canton, OAS Special Rapporteur on Freedom of Expression, Freimut Duve, OSCE Representative on Freedom of the Media, and Abid Hussain, UN Special Rapporteur on Freedom of

Opinion and Expression. Retrieved from http://www.ifex.org/international/2000/03/07/report_on_key_issues_and_challenges/.

Chairman of the Delegation of Indonesia. (1997, July 23). *Statement by the Chairman of the delegation of Indonesia to the 1997 substantive session of the Economic and Social [Council]* (UN Doc. A/52/256 E/1997/108).

Choudhry, S. (2006a). Migration as a new metaphor in comparative constitutional law. In: S. Choudhry (Ed.), *The migration of constitutional ideas* (pp. 1–35). Cambridge: Cambridge University Press.

Choudhry, S. (Ed.) (2006b). *The migration of constitutional ideas*. Cambridge: Cambridge University Press.

Choudhury v. United Kingdom. (1991). 1 Q.B. 429. United Kingdom.

CNN. (2001a). CNN statement about false claim it used old video. *CNN*, September 20. Retrieved from http://archives.cnn.com/2001/US/09/20/cnn.statement/.

CNN. (2001b). Reuters statement on false claim it used old video. *CNN*, September 20. Retrieved from http://archives.cnn.com/2001/US/09/20/reuters.statement/index.html.

CNN. (2003). Mahathir attack on Jews condemned. *CNN*, October 16. Retrieved from http://www.cnn.com/2003/WORLD/asiapcf/southeast/10/16/oic.mahathir/.

Cohen, P. (2009). Yale press bans images of Muhammad in new book. *New York Times*, August 12. Retrieved from http://www.nytimes.com/2009/08/13/books/13book.html.

Cohn, N. (2005). *Warrant for genocide: The myth of the Jewish world conspiracy and the protocols of the elders of Zion*. London: Serif Publishing.

Commission on Security and Cooperation in Europe. (2002, January 9). Criminal defamation and "Insult" laws: A summary of free speech developments in the Czech Republic. Retrieved from http://csce.gov/index.cfm?Fuseaction=ContentRecords.ViewDetail&ContentRecord_id=20&Region_id=77&Issue_id=0&ContentType=G&CFID=1065519&CFTOKEN=16682030.

Constitution of Spain. (1978). *Constitution of Spain* [Electronic version] ratified in 1978 and consolidated to 1992 [Electronic version]. Retrieved from http://www.senado.es/constitu_i/index.html and http://www.legislationline.org/download/action/download/id/2325/file/Spain_Const_1978_eng.pdf.

Council of Europe. (2010). Blasphemy, insult and hatred: Finding answers in a democratic society. In *Science and Technique in Democracy* (Vol. 47). Strasbourg: Council of Europe Publishing.

Criminal Code of Turkey. (2004, September 26). *Law Nr. 5237*, passed on 26.09.2004 (Official Gazette No. 25611 dated 12.10.2004). Retrieved from http://www.legislationline.org/documents/action/popup/id/6872/preview.

Diène, D. (2003, January 3). *Situation of Muslim and Arab peoples in various parts of the world in the aftermath of the events of 11 September 2001, report by Mr. Doudou Diène, Special Rapporteur on Contemporary Forms of Racism, Racial Discrimination, Xenophobia and Related Intolerance, submitted pursuant to UNCHR Resolution 2002/9* (UN Doc. E/CN.4/2003/23).

Diène, D. (2004, December 13). *Defamation of religions and global efforts to combat racism: Anti-Semitism, Christianophobia and Islamophobia (Addendum)* (UN Doc. E/CN.4/2005/18/Add.4).

Diène, D. (2006, February 13). *Situation of Muslims and Arab peoples in various parts of the world* (UN Doc. E/CN.4/2006/17).

Diène, D. (2007, August 21). *Report of the Special Rapporteur on Contemporary Forms of Racism, Racial Discrimination, Xenophobia and Related Intolerance, Doudou Diène, on the manifestations of defamation of religions and in particular on the serious implications of Islamophobia on the enjoyment of all rights* (UN Doc. A/HRC/6/6).

Diène, D. (2008, September 2). Report of the Special Rapporteur on Contemporary Forms of Racism, Racial Discrimination, Xenophobia and Related Intolerance, Doudou Diène, on the manifestations of defamation of religions and in particular on the serious implications of Islamophobia on the enjoyment of all rights, (UN Doc. A/HRC/9/12).

Dutt, S. (1998). UNESCO: Britain returns to the fold. *New Zealand Int'l Review, 23,* 1.

Gardiner, B. (2001). *World watches in horror as terror unfolds in New York and at Pentagon.* Associated Press Newswires (APRS), September 12, p. A17.

The Economist. (2009). Speech impediments: Anxiety over causing religious offence limits freedom of speech in the West. *The Economist,* February 14. Retrieved from http://www.economist.com/node/13130069.

The Economist. (2010). Into the heartland: Extremists are growing stronger in settled areas of Pakistan. *The Economist,* June 3. Retrieved from http://www.economist.com/node/16281220.

Edwards, S. (2008). UN anti-blasphemy measures have sinister goals, observers say. *Canwest News Service,* November 24. Retrieved from http://www2.canada.com/theprovince/news/story.html?id=9b8e3a6d-795d-440f-a5de-6ff6e78c78d5.

Egyptian Penal Code. (1937). *Law No. 58 of 1937.* Retrieved from http://www.unhcr.org/refworld/docid/3f827fc44.html.

European Union. (2007, December 14). Charter of fundamental rights of the European Union, *Official Journal of the European Union* (2007/C 303/01).

The Former Yugoslav Republic of Macedonia. (2008, April 17). *Concluding observations of the Human Rights Committee: The Former Yugoslav Republic of Macedonia* (UN Doc. CCPR/C/MKD/CO/2). Retrieved from http://www.universalhumanrightsindex.org/documents/825/1318/document/en/pdf/text.pdf.

Galston, M. (1994). Rawlsian dualism and the autonomy of political thought. *Columbia Law Review, 94*(October), 1842.

Gardiner, B. (2001). *World watches in horror as terror unfolds in New York and at Pentagon.* Associated Press Newswires (APRS), September 12, p. A17.

Gelling, P. (2007). Indonesia bans sects it deems blasphemous. *New York Times,* November 16. Retrieved from http://www.nytimes.com/2007/11/16/world/asia/16indo.html.

Gledhill, R. (2008). Dawkins website banned in Turkey. *Times Online,* September 19. Retrieved from http://www.timesonline.co.uk/tol/comment/faith/article4790039.ece.

Glélé-Ahanhanzo, M. (1997, January 16). *Report by Mr. Maurice Glélé-Ahanhanzo, Special Rapporteur on Contemporary Forms of Racism, Racial Discrimination, Xenophobia and Related Intolerance, submitted pursuant to Commission on Human Rights resolution 1996/21*(UN Doc. E/CN.4/1997/71).

Glélé-Ahanhanzo, M. (1997, July 8). *Report by Mr. Maurice Glélé-Ahanhanzo, Special Rapporteur on Contemporary Forms of Racism, Racial Discrimination, Xenophobia and Related Intolerance, submitted pursuant to Commission on Human Rights resolution 1996/21 Corrigendum* (UN Doc. E/CN.4/1997/71/Corr.1).

Goodstein, L. (2001). Falwell: Blame abortionists, feminists and gays. *The Guardian,* September 19. Retrieved from http://www.guardian.co.uk/world/2001/sep/19/september11.usa9. Video available at http://www.youtube.com/watch?v=H-CAcdta_8I. Partial transcript available at http://www.beliefnet.com/Faiths/Christianity/2001/09/You-Helped-This-Happen.aspx.

Gordon, S. (2010). Singer charged over "cooking Christ" spoof. *Sky News*, June 15. Retrieved from http://news.sky.com/skynews/Home/World-News/Spanish-Singer-Javier-Krahe-Charged-With-Blasphemy-Over-Sketch-In-Which-He-Cooks-Christ/Article/2010063156 49553?f=rss.

Gross, O. (2006). "Control systems" and the migration of anomalies. In: S. Choudhry (Ed.), *The migration of constitutional ideas* (pp. 403–430). Cambridge: Cambridge University Press.

Hannum, H., Leary, V., Nanda, V., Bassiouni, M. C., Reisman, W. M., & Shaparis, A. B. (1989, April 5–8). Speech, religious discrimination and blasphemy. The New International Holy Alliance and the Struggle to Appropriate and Censor General Cultural Symbols. American Society of International Law Proceedings (83 ASILPROC 427).

Hassan, R. (2006). Expressions of religiosity and blasphemy in modern societies. In: E.B. Coleman & K. White (Eds.), *Negotiating the sacred: Blasphemy and sacrilege in a multicultural society* (pp. 119–131). Canberra: The Australian National University.

Hockstader, L. (2001). Palestinians suppress coverage of crowds celebrating attacks. *Washington Post*, September 15, p. A42.

Holmes, C. W. (2001). World reaction: Expressions of sorrow, and in rare cases, glee. The *Atlanta Journal-Constitution*, September 12, p. A14.

Human Rights Watch. (2009). 2009 world report. Retrieved from http://www.hrw.org/sites/default/files/reports/wr2009_web.pdf.

Human Rights Watch. (2010, June 1). Pakistan: Massacre of minority Ahmadis. Retrieved from http://www.hrw.org/en/news/2010/05/31/pakistan-massacre-minority-ahmadis.

Human Rights Watch. (2010, July 12). Russia: Reverse judgment against human rights defender. Retrieved from http://www.hrw.org/en/news/2010/07/12/russia-reverse-judgment-against-human-rights-defender.

Hussain, A. (2000, January 18). *Report of the Special Rapporteur on the promotion and protection of the right to freedom of opinion and expression, Mr. Abid Hussain, submitted in accordance with Commission resolution 1999/36* (UN Doc. E/CN.4/2000/63).

Indo-Asian News Service. (2006). Indonesia: Blasphemy case against Adam and Eve photo exhibit. *Indo-Asian News Service*, February 3. Retrieved from http://religion.info/english/articles/article_227.shtml.

International Center for Not-for-Profit Law (2011, January 28). "Organization of the Islamic Conference." Retrieved from http://www.icnl.org/knowledge/ngolawmonitor/pdf/OIC.pdf.

International Pen. (2009). Gürsel trial to continue against prosecutor's advice. *International PEN*, May 11. Retrieved from http://www.internationalpen.org.uk/index.cfm?objectid= 3078B71F-3048-676E-2629E10978C84E33.

ISESCO. (2010, September 9). ISESCO calls on UN to incriminate religious offence. Retrieved from http://www.isesco.org.ma/english/news/news.php?id=1113.

Italy. (2006, April 24). *Concluding observations of the Human Rights Committee: Italy* (UN Doc. CCPR/C/ITA/CO/5). Retrieved from http://www.universalhumanrightsindex.org/documents/825/846/document/en/pdf/text.pdf.

Itzkoff, D. (2010). 'South Park' episode altered after Muslim group's warning. *New York Times*, April 22. Retrieved from http://www.nytimes.com/2010/04/23/arts/television/23park.html.

Jahangir, A. (2007, August 20). *Interim report of the Special Rapporteur on Freedom of Religion or Belief* (UN Doc. A/62/280).

Jahangir, A. (2008, February 7). *Report of the Special Rapporteur on Freedom of Religion or Belief, Asma Jahangir, Mission to the United Kingdom of Great Britain and Northern Ireland* (Addendum) (UN Doc. A/HRC/7/10/Add.3).

Jahangir, A., & Diène, D. (2006, September 20). *A 2006 report to the UNHRC prepared by Special Rapporteurs Asma Jahangir and Doudou Diène* (UN Doc. A/HRC/2/3).

The Jakarta Globe. (2010). If US could create 'Avatar,' it could fake 9/11 attacks: Mahathir. *The Jakarta Globe,* January 21. Retrieved from http://thejakartaglobe.com/home/if-us-could-create-avatar-it-could-fake-911-attacks-mahathir/354031.

The Jerusalem Post. (2001). Foreign Press Association protests PA threats to journalists. *The Jerusalem Post,* September 14, p. 4A.

Jordan. (1999, September 13). *Periodic report by the non-governmental organizations in Jordan on the implementation of the Convention on the Rights of the Child during the period 1993–1998* (Appended to Jordan's periodic report to the Committee on the Rights of the Child) (UN Doc. CRC/C/70/Add.4).

Kamali, M. H. (1997). *Freedom of expression in Islam.* United Kingdom: Islamic Text Society.

Klausen, J. (2009). *The cartoons that shook the world.* New Haven, CT: Yale University Press.

Kommers, D. P. (2002). Comparative constitutional law: Its increasing relevance. In: V. Jackson & M. Tushnet (Eds.), *Defining the field of comparative constitutional law* (pp. 61–70). Westport, CT: Praeger.

Krishnaswami, A. (1960). Study of discrimination in the matter of religious rights and practices, UN Sub-Commission on Prevention of Discrimination and Protection of Minorities. Retrieved from http://www2.ohchr.org/english/issues/religion/docs/Krishnaswami_1960.pdf.

La Rue, F. (2010, April 20). *Report of the Special Rapporteur on the promotion and protection of the right to freedom of opinion and expression, Mr. Frank La Rue* (UN Doc. A/HRC/14/23).

La Rue, F. (2010, June 3). *Statement by the Special Rapporteur on the promotion and protection of the right to freedom of opinion and expression, Frank La Rue, Fourteenth session of the UNHRC, Geneva* [Electronic version]. Retrieved from http://www2.ohchr.org/english/issues/opinion/docs/OralStatement03062010.doc.

Langer, M. (2004). From legal transplants to legal translations: The globalization of plea bargaining and the Americanization thesis in criminal procedure. *Harvard International Law Journal, 45,* 1.

Langlands, E. (2006). The children's author who ignited a worldwide protest. *The Scotsman,* February 8. Retrieved from http://news.scotsman.com/danishcartoonrow/The-childrens-author-who-ignited.2749081.jp.

Lau, J. (2006). Allah und der humor. *Die Welt,* February 1. Retrieved from http://www.zeit.de/2006/06/D_8anemark_neu?page=all. English translation available in Lau, J., *Who's afraid of Muhammad?* at http://www.signandsight.com/features/588.html.

Lea, R. (2009). Turkish novelist cleared of inciting religious hatred. *The Guardian,* June 26. Retrieved from http://www.guardian.co.uk/books/2009/jun/26/turkish-novelist-gursel-religious-hatred.

Legrand, P. (1997). The impossibility of "legal transplants". *Maastricht Journal of European and Comparative Law, 4*(2), 111–124.

Legrand, P. (2003). The same and the different. In: P. Legrand & R. Munday (Eds.), *Comparative legal studies: Traditions and transitions* (pp. 240–311). Cambridge: Cambridge University Press.

Levy, L. W. (1981). *Treason against God*. New York, NY: Schocken Books.

Levy, L. W. (1985). *Emergence of a free press*. Oxford: Oxford University Press.

Ligabo, A. (2007, January 2). *Report of the Special Rapporteur on the promotion and protection of the right to freedom of opinion and expression, Ambeyi Ligabo* (UN Doc. A/HRC/4/27).

Manchester Evening News. (2001). Shook the world-Nation left in a state of shock. *Manchester Evening News*, September 12, p. 17.

Mayer, A. E. (1991). *Islam and human rights: Tradition and politics* (4th ed.). Boulder, CO: Westview Press.

Mayton, W. T. (1982). Toward a theory of first amendment process: Injunctions of speech, subsequent punishment, and the costs of the prior restraint doctrine. *Cornell Law Review*, 67, 245.

McKean, E. (Ed.) (2005). *The new Oxford American dictionary* (2nd ed.). UK: Oxford University Press.

Menski, M. (2006). *Comparative law in a global context* (2nd ed.). Cambridge: Cambridge University Press.

Mexico. (2010, May 17). *Concluding observations of the Human Rights Committee: Mexico* (UN Doc. CCPR/C/MEX/CO/5). Retrieved from http://www.universalhumanrightsindex. org/documents/825/1809/document/en/pdf/text.pdf.

Meyerson, M. I. (2001). The neglected history of the prior restraint doctrine: Rediscovering the link between the first amendment and the separation of powers. *Indiana Law Review*, 34, 295.

Minister for Foreign Affairs Makhdoom Shah Mehmood Qureshi. (2008, December 18). Questions for oral answers and their replies, at a sitting of the National Assembly. Retrieved from http://www.na.gov.pk/questions/session9/thursday181208_9S.pdf.

Moreton, C. (2001, September 16). *America at war-Part Two Tuesday-Minute by minute, hour by hour, the horror unfolds*. The Independent On Sunday (INDOS), September 16.

Muigai, G. (2010, July 12). *Report of the Special Rapporteur on Contemporary Forms of Racism, Racial Discrimination, Xenophobia and Related Intolerance, Githu Muigai, on the manifestations of defamation of religions, and in particular on the ongoing serious implications of Islamophobia, for the enjoyment of all rights by their followers* (UN Doc. A/HRC/15/53).

Nelken, D. (2001). Towards a sociology of legal adaptation. In: D. Nelken & J. Feest (Eds.), *Adapting legal cultures* (pp. 7–54). Oxford: Hart Publishing.

Nelken, D. (2003). Comparatists and transferability. In: P. Legrand & R. Munday (Eds.), *Comparative legal studies: Traditions and transitions* (pp. 437–466). Cambridge: Cambridge University Press.

Nineteenth Islamic Conference of Foreign Ministers. (1990). *The Cairo declaration on human rights in Islam, Cairo*, July 31–August 5 [Electronic version]. Retrieved from http:// www.oic-oci.org/english/article/human.htm.

Organization of the Islamic Conference. (2005, June). *Covenant on the rights of the child in Islam, Adopted by the 32nd Islamic Conference of Foreign Ministers in Sana'a, Republic of Yemen*, (OIC Doc. OIC/9-IGGE/HRI/2004/Rep.Final).

OIC. (2011). "About OIC." Retrieved from http://www.oic-oci.org/page_detail.asp?p_id=52.

OIC. (2006, June). *Draft rules of observer status at the Organization for the Islamic Conference* (OIC Doc. OIC/2-IGGE/2006/OS/REP/FINAL ANNEX 1). In *Reports of the Secretary-General on organic matters submitted to the thirty-third session of the Islamic*

Conference of Foreign Ministers, Baku, Republic of Azerbaijan (OIC Doc. OIC/33-ICFM/2006/ORG/SG.REPs).

OIC. (2008, March 14). Charter of the Organization of the Islamic Conference, at Dakar. Retrieved from http://www.oic-oci.org/is11/english/Charter-en.pdf.

OIC. (2009). Second OIC observatory report on Islamophobia. Thirty-sixth Council of Foreign Ministers, Damascus, Syrian Arab Republic, May 23–25. Retrieved from http://www.oic-oci.org/uploads/file/Islamphobia/Islamophobia_rep_May_23_25_2009 .pdf.

OIC. (2010). Third OIC observatory report on Islamophobia. Thirty-seventh Council of Foreign Ministers, Dushanbe, Republic of Tajikistan, May 18–20. Retrieved from http:// www.oic-oci.org/uploads/file/Islamphobia/2010/en/Islamophobia_rep_May_22_5_2010. pdf.pdf.

OIC Final Communiqué. (2005, December). OIC final communiqué of the Third Extraordinary Session of the Islamic Summit Conference "Meeting the Challenges of the 21st Century, Solidarity in Action," Makkah al Mukarramah, December 7–8, 2005. Retrieved from http://www.oic-oci.org/ex-summit/english/fc-exsumm-en.htm.

OIC Final Communiqué. (2008, May). *OIC final communiqué of the Eleventh Session of the Islamic Summit Conference. Session of the Muslim Ummah in the 21st Century, Dakar, Republic of Senegal*, March 13–14 (OIC Doc. OIC/SUMMIT-11/2008/FC/Final).

OIC Programme. (2005, December). *Ten-year programme of action to meet the challenges facing the Muslim Ummahin in the 21st Century. Third Extraordinary Session of the Islamic Summit Conference, Makkah al Mukarramah*, December 7–8. Retrieved from http:// www.oic-oci.org/ex-summit/english/10-years-plan.htm.

OIC Resolution No. 68/9-P (IS). (2000, November). *Resolution No. 68/9-P (IS) on defamation of Islam. Ninth Session of the Islamic Summit Conference, Session of Peace and Development, Doha, State of Qatar*, November 12–13. Retrieved from http://www.oic-oci.org/english/conf/is/9/9th-is-sum-political_3.htm#68.

OIC Resolution No. 1/34-Leg. (2004, June). *Resolution No. 1/34-Leg on the international Islamic court of justice and cooperation among Islamic states in the judicial field. Thirty-fourth Session of the Islamic Conference of Foreign Ministers, (Session of Peace, Progress and Harmony), Islamabad, Islamic Republic of Pakistan*, June 14–16.

OIC Resolution No. 26/33-DW. (2005, June). *Resolution No. 26/33-DW on eliminating hatred and prejudice against Islam. Thirty-third Session of the Islamic Conference of Foreign Ministers (Session of Harmony of Rights, Freedoms, and Justice), Baku, Republic of Azerbaijan*, June 19–21. Retrieved from http://www.oic-oci.org/baku2006/english/33-icfm-pol-en.htm.

OIC Resolution No. 34/34-Pol. (2007, May). *Resolution No. 34/34-Pol on combating Islamophobia and eliminating hatred and prejudice against Islam. Thirty-fourth Session of the Islamic Conference of Foreign Ministers (Session of Peace, Progress and Harmony), Islamabad, Islamic Republic of Pakistan*, May 15–17 (OIC Doc. OIC/34-ICFM/2007/POL/ R.34).

OIC Resolution No. 11/11-C (IS). (2008, March). *Resolution No. 11/11-C (IS) on the Defamation of religions and discrimination against Muslims. Eleventh Session of the Islamic Summit Conference (Session of the Islamic Ummah in the 21st Century), Dakar, Republic of Senegal*.

OIC Resolution No. 1/35-C. (2008, June). *Resolution No. 1/35-C on combating Islamophobia and eliminating hatred and prejudice against Islam. Thirty-fifth Session of the Council of*

Foreign Ministers (Session of Prosperity and Development), Kampala, Republic of Uganda, June 18–20 (OIC Doc. OIC/35-CFM/2008/C/RES/FINAL).

OIC Resolution No. 2/36-Leg. (2009, May). *Resolution No. 2/36-Leg on follow up and coordination of work on human rights, resolutions on legal affairs. Thirty-sixth Session of the Council of Foreign Ministers (For Enhancing Islamic Solidarity), Damascus, Syrian Arab Republic,* May 23–25 (OIC Doc. OIC/CFM-36/2009/LEG/RES/FINAL).

OIC Resolution No. 34/36-Pol. (2009, May). Resolution No. 34/36-Pol on combating Islamophobia and eliminating hatred and prejudice against Islam, resolutions on political affairs. Thirty-sixth Session of the Council of Foreign Ministers (For Enhancing Islamic Solidarity), Damascus, Syrian Arab Republic, May 23–25 (OIC Doc. OIC/CFM-36/2009/LEG/RES/FINAL).

OIC Resolution No. 1/37-Leg. (2010, May). *Resolution No. 1/37-Leg on follow up and coordination of work on human rights, resolutions on legal affairs. Thirty-seventh Session of the Council of Foreign Ministers (Session of Shared Vision of a More Secure and Prosperous Islamic World), Dushanbe, Republic of Tajikistan,* May 18–20 (OIC Doc. OIC/CFM-37/2010/LEG/RES/FINAL).

OIC Resolution No. 1/37-Org. (2010, May). *Resolution No. 1/37-Org on the rules governing observer status at the Organization of the Islamic Conference.*

OIC Resolution No. 38/37-P. (2010, May). *Resolution No. 38/37-P on combating Islamophobia and eliminating hatred and prejudice against Islam, resolutions on political issues. Adopted by the Council of Foreign Ministers, Session of Shared Vision of a More Secure and Prosperous Islamic World, Dushanbe, Republic of Tajikistan,* May 18–20 (OIC Doc. OIC/CFM-37/2010/POL/RES//FINAL).

Organization of the Islamic Conference. (2005, June). Covenant on the rights of the child in Islam, Adopted by the 32nd Islamic Conference of Foreign Ministers in Sana'a, Republic of Yemen, (OIC Doc. OIC/9-IGGE/HRI/2004/Rep.Final).

Osborn, A. (2010). Museum curators convicted over Mickey Mouse painting. *The Telegraph UK,* July 12. Retrieved from http://www.telegraph.co.uk/news/worldnews/europe/russia/7885474/Museum-curators-convicted-over-Mickey-Mouse-painting.html.

OSCE. (1991, October 4). Document of the Moscow meeting of the Conference on the Human Dimension of the CSCE (Preamble). Retrieved from http://www.osce.org/documents/odihr/1991/10/13995_en.pdf.

OSCE. (2001). *OSCE human dimension commitments: A reference guide* [Electronic version]. Retrieved from http://www.iskran.ru/cd_data/disk2/r3/015.pdf.

OSCE. (2002, December 7). *Charter on preventing and combating terrorism,* para. 7 (MC DOC/1/02) [Electronic version]. Retrieved from http://www.osce.org/item/4162.html.

Pakistan. (2010, February 17). *Pakistan, explanatory letter to ad hoc committee on behalf of OIC* (UN Doc. A/HRC/13/CRP.1) (Annex 1). Retrieved from http://www2.ohchr.org/english/bodies/hrcouncil/docs/13session/A-HRC-13-CRP1.pdf.

Pakistan Ministry of Foreign Affairs. (2006, March 1). Actions taken by the Pakistan Foreign Office following the publication of blasphemous caricatures of the holy prophet (PBUH), press release. Retrieved from http://www.mofa.gov.pk/press_releases/2006/March/PR_77b_06.htm.

Parker, T., & Stone, M. (2006, April 5). *Cartoon wars part I* [Television broadcast]. Retrieved from http://www.southparkstudios.com/episodes/103230.

Parker, T., & Stone, M. (2006, April 12). *Cartoon wars part II* [Television broadcast]. Retrieved from http://www.southparkstudios.com/episodes/103233.

Parker, T., & Stone, M. (2010, April 14). *200* [Television broadcast]. Retrieved from http://www.southparkstudios.com/episodes/267114/.

Parker, T., & Stone, M. (2010, April 21). *201* [Television broadcast]. Retrieved from http://www.southparkstudios.com/episodes/267116.

Penal Code of Pakistan. (1860, October 6). *Ch. XV "Of offenses relating to religion"* [Electronic version]. Retrieved from http://www.punjabpolice.gov.pk/user_files/File/pakistan_penal_code_xlv_of_1860.pdf and http://www.unhcr.org/refworld/docid/485231942.html.

Pink, J. (2003). A post-Quranic religion between apostasy and public order: Egyptian Muftis and courts on the legal status of the Baha'i Faith. *Islamic Law and Society*, *10*, 409–434.

Polelle, M. J. (2003). Racial and ethnic group defamation: A speech-friendly proposal. *Boston College Third World Law Journal*, *23*, 213–258.

Prime Minister Mohamad, M. (2003, October 16). Speech by Prime Minister Mahathir Mohamad of Malaysia to the Tenth Islamic Summit Conference, Putrajaya, Malaysia. Retrieved from http://www.adl.org/anti_semitism/malaysian.asp.

The Random House Publishing Group. (undated). "Medina letter." Retrieved from http://www.randomhouse.com/rhpg/medinaletter.html.

Rennie, D. (2006). Turkey's foreign minister asks the EU for blasphemy laws to protect Islam. *The Telegraph*, March 13. Retrieved from http://www.telegraph.co.uk/news/worldnews/europe/turkey/1512887/Turkeys-foreign-minister-asks-the-EU-for-blasphemy-laws-to-protect-Islam.html.

Reuters. (2009). Turkish blasphemy trial begins against French–Turkish author. *Reuters*, May 26. Retrieved from http://www.rferl.org/content/Turkish_Blasphemy_Trial_Begins_Against_FrenchTurkish_Author/1740260.html.

Reuters. (2010). Syria encouraged anti-cartoon protest: U.S. cables. *Reuters*, December 29.

R v. Jones. (1971). Unreported, Australia. In Butterworths, *Halsbury's Laws of Australia, 23*, 365–695.

Rex v. Gott. (1922). 16 Cr. App. R. 87. United Kingdom.

Reynolds, P. (2006). A clash of rights and responsibilities. *BBC News*, February 6. Retrieved from http://news.bbc.co.uk/2/hi/south_asia/4686536.stm.

Roberts, S. (2010). 'South Park' parody of the Prophet Muhammed is censored following radical Islamists' warning. *N.Y. Daily News*, April 23. Retrieved from http://www.nydailynews.com/entertainment/tv/2010/04/22/2010-04-22_south_park_creators_censor_episode_201_after_warning_over_200th_episodes_prophet.html.

Roth v. U.S. (1957). 354 U.S. 476. United States.

Rosenfeld, M. (2001). Tribute: Constitutional migration and the bounds of comparative analysis. *New York University Annual Survey of American Law*, *58*, 67.

Rovers, R. (2004). The silencing of Theo van Gogh. *Salon*, November 24. Retrieved from http://dir.salon.com/story/news/feature/2004/11/24/vangogh/index.html.

Sawer, P. (2001). Palestinian militants celebrate attack with gunfire; Terror War on US Terrorism USA. The Evening Standard (UK), September 11.

Scheppele, K. L. (2003). Aspirational and aversive constitutionalism: The case for studying cross-constitutional influence through negative models. *International Journal of Constitutional Law*, *1*, 296.

Scheppele, K. L. (2006). The migration of anti-constitutional ideas: The post-9/11 globalization of public law and the international state of emergency. In: S. Choudhry (Ed.), *The migration of constitutional ideas* (pp. 347–373). Cambridge: Cambridge University Press.

Schrag, C. (2003). Malaysia's casual anti-Semitism. *Slate*, October 20. Retrieved from http://www.slate.com/id/2090080.

Shahzad, A. (2010). Internet censorship in Pakistan; Watching Google for blasphemy. *Christian Science Monitor*, June 25. Retrieved from http://www.csmonitor.com/From-the-news-wires/2010/0625/Internet-censorship-in-Pakistan-Watching-Google-for-blasphemy.

Slaughter, A.-M. (2000). Judicial globalization. *Virginia Journal of International Law, 40*, 1103.

Somali Republic. (2004, February). *Transitional federal charter of the Somali Republic* [Electronic version], Retrieved from http://www.iss.co.za/AF/profiles/Somalia/charterfeb04.pdf.

Spain. (1995). *Ley Orgánica 10/1995, de 23 de noviembre, del Código Penal*, November 23 [Organic Law 10/1995 of November 23, Penal Code]. Retrieved from http://noticias.juridicas.com/base_datos/Vacatio/v0-lo10-1995.html.

Stahnke, T. (2010). Pakistan's crackdown on the Internet shows what 'global blasphemy code' could look like. *Huffington Post*, July 12. Retrieved from http://www.huffingtonpost.com/tad-stahnke/pakistans-crackdown-on-th_b_643132.html.

Stahnke, T., & Blitt, R. C. (2005). The religion–state relationship and the right to freedom of religion or belief: A comparative textual analysis of the constitutions of predominantly Muslim countries. *Georgetown Journal of International Law, 36*, 947–1077.

Taylor's Case. (1676). 1 Vent. 293. United Kingdom.

Teubner, G. (1998). Legal irritants: Good faith in British law or how unifying law ends up in new divergences. *Modern Law Review, 61*, 11.

Tocqueville, A. (1990). *Democracy in America* (vol. I). New York, NY: Vintage Books.

Tushnet, M. (1993). The bricoleur at the center [review of the book *The Partial Constitution*]. *University of Chicago Law Review, 60*, 1071–1116.

UK Legislature. (2006). *Racial and religious hatred act 2006* [Electronic version]. Retrieved from http://www.legislation.gov.uk/ukpga/2006/1.

UK Legislature. (2008). *UK criminal justice and immigration act 2008* [Electronic version]. Retrieved from http://www.opsi.gov.uk/acts/acts2008/ukpga_20080004_en_1.

United Nations. (1948). *United Nations yearbook summary*. Retrieved from http://www.udhr.org/history/yearbook.htm.

United Nations. (1995). *Meeting of the Third Committee*, February 3 (UN Doc. A/C.3/49/SR.65).

UN Chronicle. (1984). United States informs UNESCO of intent to withdraw [Electronic version]. *UN Chronicle*, February 1. Retrieved from http://www.highbeam.com/doc/1G1-3117890.html.

UN Commission on Human Rights. (1997, March 21). *Summary record of the 11th meeting* (UN Doc. E/CN.4/1997/SR.11).

UN Commission on Human Rights. (1997, April 18). *Resolution 1997/125: Racism, racial discrimination, xenophobia and related intolerance*.

UN Commission on Human Rights. (1997, April 28). *Summary record of the 70th meeting* (UN Doc. E/CN.4/1997/SR.70).

UN Commission on Human Rights. (1997, September 3). *Summary record of the 68th meeting* (UN Doc. E/CN.4/1997/SR.68).

UN Commission on Human Rights. (1999, April 20). *Defamation of Islam* (UN Doc. E/CN.4/1999/L.40).

UN Commission on Human Rights. (1999, April 28). *Proposed sub-amendments to the amendments to draft resolution E/CN.4/1999/L.40 contained in document E/CN.4/1999/L.90*, April 28 (UN Doc. E/CN.4/1999/L.104).

UN Commission on Human Rights. (1999, April 30). *Resolution 1999/82: Defamation of religions* (UN Doc. E/CN.4/RES/1999/82).

UN Commission on Human Rights. (1999, October 19). *Summary record of the 61st meeting* (UN Doc. E/CN.4/1999/SR.61).

UN Commission on Human Rights. (1999, November 17). *Summary record of the 62nd meeting* (UN Doc. E/CN.4/1999/SR.62).

UN Commission on Human Rights. (2002, April 15). *Resolution 2002/9: Combating defamation of religion* (UN Doc. E/CN.4/RES/2002/9).

UN Commission on Human Rights & UN Human Rights Council. (2000). *Resolutions on defamation of religion*, February 15. Data on file with the author.

UN Development Program. (2004). *Arab human development report 2004: Towards freedom in the Arab world*. United Nations Development Programme, Regional Bureau for Arab States (RBAS), Hashemite Kingdom of Jordan.

UN General Assembly. (1976). *International covenant on civil and political rights*. Retrieved from http://www2.ohchr.org/english/law/pdf/ccpr.pdf.

UN General Assembly. (2007, February 21). *Combating defamation of religions* (UN Doc. A/RES/61/164).

UN Human Rights Committee. (1993, July 30). *General comment no. 22: The right to freedom of thought, conscience and religion, Article 18* (UN Doc. CCPR/C/21/Rev.1/Add.4).

UN Human Rights Committee. (2009, November 24). *Concluding observations of the Human Rights Committee: Russian Federation* (UN Doc. CCPR/C/RUS/CO/6).

UN Human Rights Committee. (2010, October 22). *Draft general comment No. 34* (Upon completion of the first reading by the UN Human Rights Committee) (UN Doc. CCPR/C/GC/34/CRP.4)

UN Human Rights Council. (2006, September 22). *Human Rights Council discusses reports on health, right to food and human rights defenders* (UN Doc. HR/HRC/06/44). Retrieved from http://www.unhchr.ch/huricane/huricane.nsf/view01/16FEF13C726178E8C12571F20028DBEC?opendocument.

UN Human Rights Council. (2007, April 23). *Decision 3/103, Global efforts for the total elimination of racism, racial discrimination, xenophobia and related intolerance and the comprehensive follow-up to the World Conference against Racism, Racial Discrimination, Xenophobia and Related Intolerance and the effective implementation of the Durban Declaration and Programme of Action* (UN Doc. A/HRC/DEC/3/103).

UN Human Rights Council. (2007, April 30). *Combating defamation of religions* (UN Doc. A/HRC/RES/4/9).

UN Human Rights Council. (2007, June 15). *Study of the Committee on the Elimination of Racial Discrimination on possible measures to strengthen implementation through optional recommendations or the update of its monitoring procedures, by the Intergovernmental Working Group on the effective implementation of the Durban Declaration and Programme of Action* (UN Doc. A/HRC/4/WG.3/7).

UN Human Rights Council. (2007, August 27). *Report on the study by the five experts on the content and scope of substantive gaps in the existing international instruments to combat racism, racial discrimination, xenophobia and related intolerance, by the Intergovernmental Working Group on the effective implementation of the Durban Declaration and Programme of Action* (UN Doc. A/HRC/4/WG.3/6).

UN Human Rights Council. (2008, March 28). *Resolution 7/36, Mandate of the Special Rapporteur on the promotion and protection of the right to freedom of opinion and expression* (UN Doc. A/HRC/RES/7/36).

UN Human Rights Council. (2009, August 26). *Outcome referred to in paragraph 2 (d) of the road map on the elaboration of complementary standards, ad hoc committee on the elaboration of complementary standards* (UN Doc. A/HRC/AC.1/2/2).

UN Human Rights Council. (2009, October 12). *Freedom of opinion and expression* (UN Doc. A/HRC/RES/12/16).

UN Human Rights Council. (2010, April 15). *Elaboration of complementary standards to the International Convention on the Elimination of All Forms of Racial Discrimination* (UN Doc. A/HRC/RES/13/18).

UN Security Council. (2001, September 28). *S.C. Res 1373* (UN Doc. S/RES/1373).

UN Security Council. (2003, January 20). *S.C. Res. 1456* (UN Doc. S/RES/1456).

UN Security Council. (2004, March 24). *S.C. Res. 1535* (UN Doc. S/RES/1535).

UN Security Council. (2005, September 14). *S.C. Res. 1624* (UN Doc. S/RES/1624).

UN Secretary General. (2010, August 9). *Combating defamation of religions report of the Secretary-General* (UN Doc. A/65/263).

UN Sub-Commission on Prevention of Discrimination and Protection of Minorities. (1997, December 22). *Summary Record of the 35th Meeting, Aug. 27, 1997* (UN Doc. E/CN.4/Sub.2/1997/SR.35).

UN Treaty Collection. (2011, February 25). ICCPR ratification status. Retrieved from http://treaties.un.org/Pages/ViewDetails.aspx?src=TREATY&mtdsg_no=IV-4&chapter=4&lang=en.

UN Working Group on Minorities. (2004, November). *Report on the sub-regional seminar on minority rights: Cultural diversity and development in South Asia*, Kandy, Sri Lanka, November 21–24, Ms. Asma Jahangir, Mr. M.C.M. Iqbal and Mr. Soli Sorabjee, Co-Chairpersons (UN Doc. E/CN.4/Sub.2/AC.5/2005/WP.6).

U.S. Commission on International Religious Freedom. (2009). *2009 annual report*. Retrieved from http://www.uscirf.gov/images/AR2009/final%20ar2009%20with%20cover.pdf.

U.S. Commission on International Religious Freedom. (2010). *2010 annual report*. Retrieved from http://www.uscirf.gov/images/annual%20report%202010.pdf.

U.S. Commission on International Religious Freedom. (2011). "Countries of particular concern." Retrieved from http://www.uscirf.gov/countries/countries-of-particular-concern.html; "Watch-list countries." Retrieved from http://www.uscirf.gov/countries/watch-list-countries.html.

U.S. Department of State. (2008). *2008 annual report on International religious freedom: Pakistan; Indonesia* [Electronic version]. Retrieved from http://www.state.gov/g/drl/rls/irf.

U.S. Department of State. (2009). *2009 annual report on international religious freedom.* [Electronic version]. Retrieved from http://www.state.gov/g/drl/rls/irf.

U.S. Department of State. (2010). *2010 annual report on international religious freedom: Pakistan; Turkey* [Electronic version]. Retrieved from http://www.state.gov/g/drl/rls/irf.

Vahid, M. A. (2008, October 2). Remarks by Mojtaba Amiri Vahid (Deputy of the Permanent Observer Missions of the OIC to the UN Office in Geneva), Concluding session of the Seminar on Articles 19 and 20, organized by the Office of UNHCR, Geneva. Retrieved from http://www.oic-un.org/document_report/Amiri_15_oct_2008.pdf.

USA Today. (2003). Malaysian PM urges Muslims to unite against 'Jewish domination.' *USA Today*, October 16. Retrieved from http://www.usatoday.com/news/world/2003-10-16-malaysia-summit_x.htm.

Wadlow, R., & Littman, D. (1997). Blasphemy at the United Nations? *Middle East Quarterly, 4.* Retrieved from http://www.meforum.org/379/blasphemy-at-the-united-nations.

Walker, N. (2006). The migration of constitutional ideas and the migration of the constitutional idea: The case of the EU. In: S. Choudhry (Ed.), *The migration of constitutional ideas* (pp. 316–343). Cambridge: Cambridge University Press.

Watson, A. (1993). *Legal transplants: An approach to comparative law* (2nd ed.). Athens: University of Georgia Press.

Whitehouse v. Gay News Ltd. and Lemon. (1979). AC 617. United Kingdom.

Whitman, J. Q. (2003). The neo-romantic turn. In: P. Legrand & R. Munday (Eds.), *Comparative legal studies: Traditions and transitions* (pp. 312–344). Cambridge: Cambridge University Press.

Wisnu, A. (2009). Lia Eden sentenced to prison, again. *The Jakarta Post*, June 3. Retrieved from http://www.thejakartapost.com/news/2009/06/03/lia-eden-sentenced-prison-again.html.

Witte, J., Jr. (2008). Prophets, priests, and kings: John Milton and the reformation of rights and liberties. *Emory Law Journal, 57*, 1527.

World Association of Newspapers. (2008). World's press protests to UN chief over Human Rights Council. *World Association of Newspapers*, April 8. Retrieved from http://www.wan-press.org/article16874.html.

Wright, T., Champion, M., & Efrati, A. (2010, June 26). Pakistan, Turkey target Google, other sites [Electronic version]. *The Wall Street Journal*. Retrieved from http://online.wsj.com/article/NA_WSJ_PUB:SB10001424052748703615104575328712353518780.html#ixzz0wElrpyM2.

X. Ltd. and Y. v. United Kingdom. (1982, May 7). Application 8710/79. European Court of Human Rights.

Yegar, M. (2006). Malaysia: Anti-Semitism without Jews [Electronic version]. *Jewish Political Studies Review, 18*(October), 3–4.

APPENDICES

Appendix A Reports Generated by UN Resolutions Related to Defamation of Religions, by Reporting Mandate

Reporting Mandate	UN Doc No./ Date	Title	Source/Notes
SR FRB[a]	E/CN.4/2000/ 65 February 15, 2000	Civil and political rights, including religious intolerance	CHR Resolution 1999/82[b] *No stand alone reporting required.*
SR CFR[c]	E/CN.4/2003/ 23 January 3, 2003[d]	Situation of Muslim and Arab peoples in various parts of the world in the aftermath of the events of September 11, 2001	CHR Resolution 2002/9 *First request for specific report on situation of Muslim and Arab peoples relating to defamation.*
UNHCHR[e]	E/CN.4/2003/ 17 January 27, 2003	Combating defamation of religions as a means to promote human rights, social harmony, and religious and cultural diversity	CHR Resolution 2002/9 *First request for High Commissioner to report on defamation specifically.*
UNHCHR	E/CN.4/2004/ 16 February 19, 2004	Combating defamation of religions	CHR Resolution 2003/4
SR CFR	E/CN.4/2004/ 19 February 23, 2004	Situation of Muslim and Arab peoples in various parts of the world	CHR Resolution 2003/4

Reporting Mandate	UN Doc No./ Date	Title	Source/Notes
SR CFR	E/CN.4/2005/ 18/Add.4 December 13, 2004	"Defamation of religions and global efforts to combat racism: Anti-Semitism, Christianophobia and Islamophobia"	*Report not mandated by UNCHR. Special Rapporteur Diène unilaterally prepared report because he "considered it necessary, in order to help the Commission to explore" further the question of defamation of religions.*
SR CFR	E/CN.4/2005/ 19 December 23, 2004	Situation of Muslim and Arab peoples in various parts of the world	CHR Resolution 2004/6
UNHCHR	E/CN.4/2005/ 15 February 9, 2005	Combating defamation of religions	CHR Resolution 2004/6
UNHCHR	E/CN.4/2006/ 12 February 6, 2006	Combating defamation of religions	CHR Resolution 2005/3 *Final reporting derived from UNCHR*
SR CFR	E/CN.4/2006/ 17 February 13, 2006	Situation of Muslims and Arab peoples in various parts of the world	CHR Resolution 2005/3 *Final reporting derived from UNCHR.*

Reporting Mandate	UN Doc No./ Date	Title	Source/Notes
UNSG[f]	A/61/325 September 12, 2006	Combating defamation of religions	UNGA Resolution 60/150 *First report mandated by UNGA.*
SR FRB and SR CFR	A/HRC/2/3 September 20, 2006	Report on contemporary forms of racism, racial discrimination, xenophobia, and related intolerance	HRC Decision 1/107 *First time SR FRB and SR CFR prepare joint report.*
UNHCHR	A/HRC/2/6 September 20, 2006	Incitement to racial and religious hatred and the promotion of tolerance	HRC Decision 1/107
SR CFR	A/HRC/4/19 January 12, 2007	Report of the Special Rapporteur on contemporary forms of racism, racial discrimination, xenophobia and related intolerance	HRC Decision 1/102 30 June 2006 *HRC Extension of all mandates, mechanisms,* functions and *responsibilities previously authorized by the UNCHR.*
UNHCHR	A/HRC/4/50 March 1, 2007	Combating defamation of religions	HRC Decision 2/102 6 October 2006 *Extends all reports and studies of mechanisms and mandates previously authorized by the UNCHR.*

Reporting Mandate	UN Doc No./ Date	Title	Source/Notes
SR CFR	A/HRC/6/6 August 21, 2007	Report on the manifestations of defamation of religions and in particular on the serious implications of Islamophobia on the enjoyment of all rights	HRC Resolution 4/9 *First report focusing on manifestations of defamation*
UNSG	A/62/288 August 29, 2007	Combating defamation of religions, including the possible correlation between defamation of religions and the upsurge in incitement	UNGA Resolution 61/164
UNHCHR	A/HRC/6/4 September 4, 2007	Combating defamation of religions	HRC Resolution 4/9
SR CRF	A/HRC/9/12 September 2, 2008	Report on the manifestations of defamation of religions and in particular on the serious implications of Islamophobia on the enjoyment of all rights	HRC Resolution 7/19

Reporting Mandate	UN Doc No./ Date	Title	Source/Notes
UNHCHR	A/HRC/9/25 September 5, 2008	Study compiling existing legislations and jurisprudence concerning defamation of and contempt for religions	HRC Resolution 7/19
UNHCHR	A/HRC/9/7 September 12, 2008	Report on the implementation of HRC Resolution 7/19 ("Combating Defamation of Religions")	HRC Resolution 7/19
UNSG	A/63/365 October 21, 2008	Combating defamation of religions, including the possible correlation between defamation of religions and the upsurge in incitement	UNGA Resolution 62/154
SR CFR	A/HRC/12/ 38 July 1, 2009	Report on the manifestations of defamation of religions, and in particular on the serious implications of Islamophobia, on the enjoyment of all rights by their followers	HRC Resolution 10/22

Reporting Mandate	UN Doc No./ Date	Title	Source/Notes
UNHCHR	A/HRC/12/ 39 July 8, 2009	Report on the implementation of HRC resolution 10/22 ("Combating defamation of religions")	HRC Resolution 10/22
UNSG	A/64/209 July 31, 2009	Combating defamation of religions, including the possible correlation between defamation of religions and the upsurge in incitement	UNGA Resolution 63/171
UNHCHR	A/HRC/13/ 57 January 11, 2010	Report on the implementation of HRC resolution 10/22 ("Combating defamation of religions")	HRC Resolution 10/22
SR CFR	A/HRC/15/ 53 July 12, 2010	Report on all manifestations of defamation of religions, and in particular on the ongoing serious implications of Islamophobia	HRC Resolution 13/16

Reporting Mandate	UN Doc No./ Date	Title	Source/Notes
UNSG	A/65/263 August 9, 2010	Combating defamation of religion, including the correlation between defamation of religions and the intersection of religion and race	UNGA Resolution 64/156
UNSG	TBA	Report on correlation between defamation of religions and the intersection of religion and race, the upsurge in incitement, intolerance, and hatred in many parts of the world and steps taken by states to combat this phenomenon	UNGA Draft Resolution A/C.3/ 65/L.46/Rev.1

[a]Special Rapporteur on Freedom of Religion or Belief. The SR FRB is excluded from reporting requests between 2001 and 2006, at which point the UNCHR is dismantled and replaced with the UNHRC.

[b]The CHR resolution also required that the SR CFR include the issue of defamation in his report for the year 2000.

[c]Special Rapporteur on Contemporary Forms of Racism, Racial Discrimination, Xenophobia, and Related Intolerance.

[d]The gap in reporting between 2000 and 2003 may be partially explained as a consequence of 9/11 and its aftermath.

[e]UN High Commissioner for Human Rights.

[f]UN Secretary General.

Appendix B Reporting Requirements Generated by CHR/HRC and UNGA Resolutions, by Resolution[a]

UN Body/Resolution/Date	Required Reporting
UNCHR E/CN.4/RES/ 1999/82 April 30, 1999	Calls upon the Special Rapporteur on Religious Intolerance and the Special Rapporteur on Racism, Racial Discrimination, Xenophobia, and Related Intolerance to take into account the provisions of the present resolution when reporting to the Commission
UNCHR E/CN.4/RES/ 2000/84 April 26, 2000	Calls upon the Special Rapporteur on Religious Intolerance and the Special Rapporteur on Racism, Racial Discrimination, Xenophobia, and Related Intolerance to take into account the provisions of the present resolution when reporting to the Commission
	Invites the UN Secretary-General of the World Conference [Against Racism] ... to present [governmental views on combating racism] to the World Conference
UNCHR E/CN.4/RES/ 2001/4 April 18, 2001	Requests the High Commissioner to report to the Commission at its 58th session on the implementation of the present resolution
UNCHR E/CN.4/RES/ 2002/9 April 15, 2002	Requests the High Commissioner to report to the Commission at its 59th session on the implementation of the present resolution
	Requests the Special Rapporteur on Contemporary Forms of Racism, Racial Discrimination, Xenophobia, and Related Intolerance to examine the situation of Muslim and Arab peoples

UN Body/Resolution/Date	Required Reporting
	in various parts of the world with special reference to physical assaults and attacks against their places of worship, cultural centers, businesses, and properties in the aftermath of the events of September 11, 2001
UNCHR E/CN.4/RES/ 2003/4 April 14, 2003	Requests the High Commissioner to report to the Commission at its 60th session on the implementation of the present resolution Requests the Special Rapporteur on Contemporary Forms of Racism, Racial Discrimination, Xenophobia, and Related Intolerance to examine the situation of Muslim and Arab peoples
UNCHR E/CN.4/RES/ 2004/6 April 13, 2004	Requests the Special Rapporteur on Contemporary Forms of Racism, Racial Discrimination, Xenophobia, and Related Intolerance to examine the situation of Muslim and Arab peoples Requests the High Commissioner to report to the Commission at its 61st session on the implementation of the present resolution
UNCHR E/CN.4/RES/ 2005/3 April 12, 2005	Special Rapporteur on Contemporary Forms of Racism, Racial Discrimination, Xenophobia, and Related Intolerance to continue to examine the situation of Muslims and Arab peoples Requests the High Commissioner to report to the Commission at its 62nd session on the implementation of the present resolution
UNGA A/RES/60/150 January 20, 2006	Requests the UN Secretary-General to submit a report on the implementation of the present resolution

UN Body/Resolution/Date	Required Reporting
UNHRC A/HRC/DEC/1/ 107 June 30, 2006	Special Rapporteur on Freedom of Religion or Belief and the Special Rapporteur on Contemporary Forms of Racism, to report on increasing trend of defamation of religions, incitement to racial and religious hatred, and its recent manifestations
	United Nations High Commissioner for Human Rights report on increasing trend of defamation of religions, incitement to racial and religious hatred, and its recent manifestations
UNGA A/RES/61/164 February 21, 2007	Requests the UN Secretary-General to submit a report on the implementation of the present resolution, including on the possible correlation between defamation of religions and the upsurge in incitement
UNHRC A/HRC/RES/4/9 March 30, 2007	Invites the Special Rapporteur on Contemporary Forms of Racism, Racial Discrimination, Xenophobia, and Related Intolerance to report on all manifestations of defamation of religions and in particular on the serious implications of Islamophobia
	Requests the High Commissioner for Human Rights to report to the Human Rights Council on the implementation of this resolution at its sixth session
UNGA A/RES/62/154 March 6, 2008	Requests the UN Secretary-General to submit a report on the implementation of the present resolution, including on the possible correlation between defamation of religions and the upsurge in incitement

UN Body/Resolution/Date	Required Reporting
UNHRC A/HRC/RES/7/ 19 March 27, 2008	Invites the Special Rapporteur on Contemporary Forms of Racism, Racial Discrimination, Xenophobia, and Related Intolerance to continue to report on all manifestations of defamation of religions, and in particular on the serious implications of Islamophobia Requests the High Commissioner for Human Rights to report on the implementation of the present resolution Requests High Commissioner for Human Rights to submit a study compiling relevant existing legislations and jurisprudence concerning defamation of and contempt for religions
UNGA A/RES/63/171 March 24, 2009	Requests the Secretary-General to submit a report on the implementation of the present resolution, including on the possible correlation between defamation of religions and the upsurge in incitement
UNHRC A/HRC/RES/10/ 22 March 26, 2009	Requests the Special Rapporteur on Contemporary Forms of Racism, Racial Discrimination, Xenophobia, and Related Intolerance to report on all manifestations of defamation of religions, and in particular on the serious implications of Islamophobia Requests the High Commissioner for Human Rights to report to the Council at its 12th session on the implementation of the present resolution, including on the possible correlation between defamation of religions and the upsurge in incitement, intolerance, and hatred in many parts of the world.

UN Body/Resolution/Date	Required Reporting
UNGA A/RES/64/156 March 8, 2010	Requests the UN Secretary-General to submit a report on the implementation of the present resolution, including the correlation between defamation of religions and the intersection of religion and race
UNHRC A/HRC/RES/13/ 16 March 25, 2010	Requests the Special Rapporteur on Contemporary Forms of Racism, Racial Discrimination, Xenophobia, and Related Intolerance to report on all manifestations of defamation of religions, and in particular on the ongoing serious implications of Islamophobia
UNGA A/C.3/65/L.46/ Rev.1 November 19, 2010	Combating defamation of religions (Morocco: revised draft resolution)

[a]This table is limited to written reports requested through UNCHR/HRC/UNGA resolutions. It therefore excludes various workshops and other dialogues addressing defamation of religions. For example, the "Expert Seminar on Defamation of Religions and the Global Combat against Racism: Anti-Semitism, Christianophobia, Islamophobia" held in Barcelona November 11–14, 2004, is omitted.

THE STATE ACTION DOCTRINE IN INTERNATIONAL LAW

Laura A. Dickinson

ABSTRACT

Because international human rights and humanitarian law traditionally binds only state action, courts must reconceive the state so that nominally nonstate activity, such as the acts of private military contractors, fits within this legal framework. I summarize state action cases under U.S. constitutional law and the nascent jurisprudence in U.S. courts involving the application of international law norms to government contractors. I also consider holding nonstate actors accountable for violations of international law norms through ordinary U.S. domestic law tort suits. Yet, even in this context delineating the public/private divide is a core part of the analysis.

In an era of increasing privatization, those applying international legal norms must confront the changing nature of state action. In the nineteenth and much of the twentieth centuries, public international law, including international human rights law and humanitarian law (also called the law of armed conflict), concerned itself primarily with relations between and among states. To be sure, nonstate entities such as the Catholic Church played key roles in the emergence of a transnational law that predated the modern state. And in the last century, international human rights treaties provided that

Special Issue: Human Rights: New Possibilities/New Problems
Studies in Law, Politics, and Society, Volume 56, 213–232
Copyright © 2011 by Emerald Group Publishing Limited
All rights of reproduction in any form reserved
ISSN: 1059-4337/doi:10.1108/S1059-4337(2011)0000056009

individuals, and not just states, could hold rights under international law. Yet these rights were in the main rights against *state* misconduct in the case of negative rights, and rights to *state* action in the provision of services in the case of positive rights (also known as economic, social, and cultural rights). Similarly, in the arena of humanitarian law, the obligations such as those found in the Geneva conventions were conceptualized primarily as limits on *government* armed forces.

In the last 30 years, however, we have witnessed tremendous changes to the international arena. Nonstate insurgent forces and guerrilla movements are fighting wars as much as states. Terrorists who may not be associated with any one state launch attacks that may be more deadly than those launched by official governments. Multinational corporations do business around the world and in many cases are larger than states. Nongovernmental organizations are championing causes and delivering aid abroad. And, perhaps most significantly, governments, international organizations, corporations, and nonprofit institutions are increasingly hiring private military and security contractors to fight wars, keep peace, and protect assets and personnel. These various nonstate actors inevitably are involved in the ongoing definition of rules that regulate conduct in areas as diverse as environmental protection, global health, education, and conduct of armed conflict. Moreover, individuals associated with these nominally nonstate entities may sometimes act in ways that might violate fundamental international law principles. Private security contractors, for example, have fired on civilians apparently without observing the limitations on the use of force that soldiers are normally expected to respect. Terrorists have wreaked havoc and destruction without any regard for human life. And some corporations have reportedly hired thugs to brutalize their workforces.

But where is the state in all this activity? This is a crucial legal question because, as noted above, international legal norms traditionally bind only state action. Thus, in applying such norms, courts need to determine how best to conceive of state action so as to bring at least some of this nominally nonstate activity within the ambit of international human rights and humanitarian law.

Interestingly, U.S. constitutional law has long grappled with precisely this question. Most constitutional commandments have been deemed to proscribe only the conduct of governmental actors. For example, the Fourteenth Amendment provides that "No *state* shall...." As a result, the Supreme Court has often refused to apply these constitutional provisions to so-called "private" action. Yet, as many critics have noted, it is often difficult to determine when private action is so entangled with the government that such action should be deemed governmental for purposes of the constitution. And indeed it may be impossible to draw a coherent dividing line between the two.

Because U.S. constitutional law has such a well-established state action jurisprudence, it may be particularly useful to see how U.S. courts conceive of state action in the context of applying international law norms to nominally private actors. For example, is the inquiry precisely the same? Or is activity that is deemed nonstate for domestic law purposes deemed state for international purposes? Significantly, though the jurisprudence is still developing, U.S. courts appear to be taking a broader view of what counts as state action in the international law context than they do when applying U.S. constitutional norms. Thus, we may be seeing a re-examination of the very definition of the state in an era of foreign affairs privatization. And ultimately the jurisprudence in international cases may come to affect the domestic doctrine. Or, we may see the international state action line start to resemble the domestic one. But whatever the future developments, it is crucial to study the evolution of this new jurisprudence because such study allows us to see courts redefining the state itself, to address the new privatized reality. Moreover, it is in the delineation of public and private action that our conceptions of both the state and the laws of war will increasingly be played out.

This essay begins to surface these issues by briefly summarizing the state action debate in U.S. constitutional law and the nascent jurisprudence in U.S. courts involving the application of international human rights and humanitarian law norms to government contractors. In addition, I also consider an alternative route to holding nonstate actors accountable for violations of international law norms: ordinary U.S. domestic law tort suits that do not appear to require state action at all. Yet, even in this context, there must always be a determination regarding whether the contractors are sufficiently intertwined with the state that governmental sovereign immunity should immunize the contractors from suit. Thus, we see that sometimes a finding of state action is necessary to bring a substantive cause of action, but other times a finding of state action may mean that private contractors can invoke immunities from suit that were intended only for governmental actors. Such immunities, though slightly different in definition, are likely also to be relevant in tort suits brought outside the United States as well. Accordingly, delineating the public/private divide is a core part of all conceivable suits seeking vindication of international norms, whether criminal or civil.

THE STATE ACTION DOCTRINE IN U.S. CONSTITUTIONAL LAW

As noted above, the U.S. Supreme Court has traditionally interpreted most constitutional commands to apply only against governmental acts and actors. By most accounts, this conception derives from a case in which the court struck down the Civil Rights Act of 1875, ruling that Congress lacked the authority to prohibit race discrimination in public accommodations, such as railroads, inns, theaters, and places of public amusement (The Civil Rights Cases, 1883). According to the court, Congress could only use its Fourteenth Amendment enforcement power to stop state governments, but not private actors, from discriminating on the basis of race. Likewise, the court ruled in *United States v. Harris* that Congress could not punish nonstate actors for conspiring to deny equal protection of the laws enacted by the state.

This seemingly clear dividing line between state and nonstate action has bedeviled the court in practical application for over a century. And though an exhaustive analysis of state action cases is beyond the scope of this essay, two basic analytical frameworks can be identified. First, courts ask whether the private party is performing a "public function" – that is, whether the private party is sufficiently "state-like" to be treated as the state for purposes of applying constitutional guarantees. Second, courts examine the points of contact between the government and the private party to assess whether there is a sufficient nexus between the two to justify imposing constitutional restraints on the private actor – as, for example, when the government jointly participates in or compels the private actor's conduct.

With regard to both inquiries, the paradigmatic state action case has involved racial discrimination by nominally private entities. For example, in *Evans v. Newton*, the Supreme Court invalidated the exclusion of blacks from a private park, in large part because of the park's public character:

> The service rendered even by a private park of this character is municipal in nature. It is open to every white person, there being no selective element other than race. Golf clubs, social centers, luncheon clubs, schools such as Tuskegee was at least in origin, and other like organizations in the private sector are often racially oriented. A park, on the other hand, is more like a fire department or police department that traditionally serves the community. Mass recreation through the use of parks is plainly in the public domain, and state courts that aid private parties to perform that public function on a segregated basis implicate the State in conduct proscribed by the Fourteenth Amendment.

Other cases also have used a public function rationale to hold private actors liable for constitutional violations.

Turning to the second state action rationale – focusing on the entanglement between government and private actor – the most aggressive use of the state action doctrine has also involved private racial discrimination. In *Shelley v. Kraemer*, the Supreme Court ruled that the Equal Protection Clause precluded a court from enforcing a private, racially restrictive covenant. In so doing, the court determined that, although the covenant itself was entered into by private actors who were not subject to the commands of the Fourteenth Amendment, the fact that courts would be asked to *enforce* the covenant constituted sufficient state action to trigger constitutional scrutiny. *Shelley*, therefore, appears to block judicial enforcement of any private agreement that would be unconstitutional.

Since the time *Shelley* was issued, however, courts and commentators have backed away from its sweeping ramifications. This is because, under *Shelley*'s reasoning, any private contract that is enforced by a police officer or court would be transformed into state action (Tribe, 1988, p. 1697). Although generations of legal realists and critical legal studies scholars have articulated similarly broad conceptions of state action (Berman, 2000, pp. 1279–1281), courts have largely resisted *Shelley* and have limited its holding only to the context of racially restrictive covenants. Indeed, even in cases implicating the First Amendment, "with virtually no exceptions, courts have concluded that the judicial enforcement of private agreements inhibiting speech does not trigger constitutional review, despite the fact that identical legislative limitations on speech would have" (Rosen, 2004). Thus, it is not clear how robust *Shelley* still is.

Nevertheless, the conceptual difficulties posed by *Shelley* make it clear just how difficult it is to differentiate public from private action. Indeed, those who criticize the distinction between public and private in constitutional adjudication argue that the state action doctrine is not just difficult to delineate but is fundamentally incoherent, because the state always plays a major role, implicitly or explicitly, in any legal relationship. This is true for at least five reasons.

First, all private actions take place against a background of laws. These laws embody state decisions to either permit or proscribe behavior. For example, legally permitted actions are permitted solely because the state has made a decision not to prohibit those actions. If such actions ultimately cause harm, it is therefore difficult to say the state has played no role.

Second, individual choices are strongly influenced by the context of state-created law. For example, a governmental zoning scheme may well be the motivating force behind an ostensibly private decision about private property. Similarly, scholars have demonstrated that the seemingly private behavior within a family is in fact heavily influenced by laws governing marriage, divorce, custody, property, and education. As Frances Olsen (1985, p. 837) has observed,

Both laissez faire and nonintervention in the family are false ideals. As long as a state exists and enforces any laws at all, it makes political choices. The state cannot be neutral or remain uninvolved, nor would anyone want the state to do so. The staunchest supporters of laissez faire always insisted that the state protect their property interests and that courts enforce contracts and adjudicate torts. They took this state action for granted and chose not to consider such protection a form of state intervention. Yet the so-called "free market" does not function except for such laws; the free market could not exist independently of the state. The enforcement of property, tort, and contract law requires constant political choices that may benefit one economic actor, usually at the expense of another. As Robert Hale pointed out more than a half century ago, these legal decisions "are bound to affect the distribution of income and the direction of economic activities." Any choice the courts make will affect the market, and there is seldom any meaningful way to label one choice intervention and the other laissez faire. When the state enforces any of these laws it must make political decisions that affect society.

Third, the state plays a role in defining what even counts as a legally cognizable injury. Our property regime would permit me as a property owner to exclude a trespasser who wishes to put wallpaper over my windows, thus obstructing my view of a beautiful vista. Yet that same property regime likely would not permit me to prevent my neighbor from adding three floors to her house, causing the very same obstruction to the very same view. Thus, "[t]here is no clear distinction between a state invasion of property interests and its inevitable role in defining those interests" (Kay, 1993, p. 335).

Fourth, even the definition of what constitutes a legally cognizable person is dependent on law. For example, the state has chosen to treat a corporation like a person. The state has also implicitly conferred standing on human beings, but not on trees (Stone, 1973). And, of course, as anyone with knowledge of the history of slavery in this country knows, the legal definition of a human being is subject to change over time based on state decisions.

Finally, scholars have pointed out that the idea of a public sphere is itself a cultural construction, and that what an individual views as "public" will be a projection of his or her own values and assumptions. Accordingly, the public sphere will inevitably tend to reflect the perspective of more dominant groups within society (Minow, 1987). Or, one can flip the argument around, and similarly view the idea of a "private" sphere as a cultural construction. Because one's private choices are always made through values, language, and beliefs inherited from and influenced by the culture at large, the state will always play a constitutive role in the shaping of such choices (Lacey, 1988; Taylor, 1985; Unger, 1975; Winter, 1992). Thus, the "conceptual categories in which we define what is an injury, who has caused it, and who has suffered from it are public artifacts" (Kay, 1993, p. 337). Moreover, the distinction between public and private itself rests on cultural constructions that tend to reflect dominant players in society. Accordingly, the very determination of what is public and what is private is inevitably public.

Yet, although the state action doctrine has repeatedly been described as fundamentally incoherent and although multiple articles have predicted its demise (e.g., Black, 1966; Silard, 1966; Williams, 1963), it continues to play an important role in policing boundaries between public and private behavior. Indeed, the state action doctrine has grown ever more significant, as domestic governments have privatized traditionally governmental functions, such as prisons. In *Richardson v. McKnight*, for example, the Supreme Court distinguished private prison guards from state actors in denying governmental immunities to the private guards. Likewise, in *Correctional Services Corporation v. Malesko*, the court again distinguished public and private in ruling that a suit seeking to directly vindicate a constitutional right may not be brought by individuals against private corporations operating prisons under color of federal law, even though such actions may be brought against federal prison guards.

It is unclear how much guidance these cases offer for courts attempting to grapple with private actors overseas in the application of international legal norms, rather than constitutional ones. Although, as discussed below, many international legal norms do contain a form of state action requirement, there is no intrinsic reason to use the same test as for U.S. constitutional cases. Indeed, cases applying international law to nominally private actors may ultimately come to inform domestic state action cases, as judges work through their intuitions about the increasingly important role of private actors on the war-time battlefield. The next section of this essay addresses the emerging U.S. lower court jurisprudence in this ever more important area of law.

THE STATE ACTION DOCTRINE AND INTERNATIONAL LEGAL NORMS

International Humanitarian Law (the Law of Armed Conflict)

International humanitarian law, also known as the law of armed conflict, restricts a broad range of actors from committing atrocities on the battlefield, though the precise reach of this body of law over particular actors – such as private military and security companies and their employees – is unsettled.

The most significant humanitarian law treaty regime – the four Geneva conventions negotiated shortly after World War II and the two additional protocols – outlaws certain categories of extreme abuse, such as torture, executions, and other "grave breaches" without requiring a particular link to the state (see Geneva Conventions I–IV and Protocols I–II). In addition, although, as we shall see, application of some legal regimes varies depending on whether individuals are classified as governmental employees or nonstate actors, key provisions of international humanitarian law apply regardless of classification. Specifically, Common Article 3, a provision identical in each treaty, criminalizes these acts, whether committed in international or in internal armed conflict, and provides that "all parties to the conflict" are bound to refrain from such acts. The provision thus clearly applies to nonstate actors, which is not surprising given that the drafters of the provision constructed it with nonstate guerrilla movements in mind (Junod, 1983). Moreover, Additional Protocol II explicitly applies to armed conflicts that "take place in the territory of a High Contracting Party between its armed forces and dissident armed forces *or other organized armed groups* which, under responsible command, exercise such control over a part of its territory as to enable them to carry out sustained and concerted military operations and to implement this Protocol." Accordingly, nonstate actors during internal armed conflict are clearly governed by this protocol.

Courts have also held that nonstate actors may be held criminally and civilly accountable for committing war crimes. For example, in the proceedings at Nuremberg following World War II, the tribunal convicted several corporate managers for such crimes, including the makers of the Xyklon B gas that the Nazis used for mass killings (*United States v. Flick*, 1952; *United States v. Krupp*, 1950; *United States v. Krauch*, 1952). The International Criminal Tribunal for the former Yugoslavia has stated in dicta that there is no "state action" requirement for war crimes, including torture, even though international human rights law defines torture as actions committed only by "official" actors (*Prosecutor v. Kunarac*, 2001, 2002). And in a civil suit brought against self-proclaimed Bosnian–Serb leader Radovan Karadzic in U.S. court under the Alien Tort Statute (ATS) (which permits aliens to sue in U.S. federal courts for alleged violations of international law), the court allowed a war crimes claim (among others) to proceed without requiring plaintiffs to show that Karadzic was a state actor, concluding that "private persons may be found liable under the Alien Tort Act for acts of genocide, war crimes, and other violations of international humanitarian law" (*Kadic v. Karadzic*, 1995). Likewise, in a case against Blackwater and several affiliated firms, a U.S. district court has made clear that corporations can be held liable for war crimes without a showing of state action (In re XE Services Alien Tort Litigation, 2009). That case has since settled.

Two other crimes that stand at the intersection of international humanitarian and human rights law – genocide and crimes against humanity – even more explicitly apply to nonstate actors. The Genocide Convention provides that "persons committing genocide … shall be punished, *whether they are constitutionally responsible rulers, public officials or private individuals.*" Likewise, the statute of the International Criminal Court designates certain acts as crimes against humanity so long as they are committed as part of a "widespread or systematic attack directed against any civilian population, with knowledge of the attack." This provision therefore contains no state action requirement. Moreover, the statute elsewhere defines "attack" as a series of acts "pursuant to or in furtherance of a State *or organizational policy*" (Rome Statute, 1998). Accordingly, so long as nonstate actors are following some type of organizational policy, international law would prohibit them from committing a crime against humanity.

International humanitarian law thus exerts some control over private actors, at least as a formal matter. Moreover, even if a particular crime were interpreted not to apply to nonstate actors directly, such actors might still face criminal liability if they were deemed sufficiently intertwined with the state so as to be considered governmental actors. On the other hand, it is less clear whether international humanitarian law could be used against the corporate entity as a whole, as opposed to individual employees (Vázquez, 2005).

International Human Rights Law

International human rights law also constrains nonstate actors, though its effective reach in this context is perhaps more unsettled than that of international humanitarian law. This is because much of international human rights law contains state action requirements that ostensibly limit liability for abuses to state actors. For example, although the Torture Convention broadly defines torture as "intentionally inflicted" acts of "severe pain or suffering" for the purpose of obtaining information from, punishing, intimidating, or discriminating against the victim or third person, such acts must be "inflicted by or at the instigation of or with the consent or acquiescence of a public official or other person acting in an official capacity." Similarly, many of the rights defined in the International Covenant on Civil and Political Rights (ICCPR) – such as the right to be free from summary execution and to be imprisoned without charges – are generally conceived as rights only against misconduct by official governmental actors.

To be sure, *states themselves* may sometimes be deemed responsible for abuses committed by nonstate actors, if those actors are sufficiently linked to the state. The ICCPR, for example, imposes obligations on states not only to "respect" but also to "ensure" the protection of human rights. Regional human rights treaties contain similar terms, which tribunals have interpreted to hold states liable for the actions of death squads and armed militias that are not technically state actors (e.g., Velasquez Rodriguez Case, 1988). Likewise, courts and tribunals have at times held states liable for the actions of companies that were effectively controlled by those states. The United Nations' recent Draft Articles on Responsibility of States for Internationally Wrongful Acts aim to make these principles clear, asserting that the "conduct of any State organ shall be considered an act of that State under international law," and that a person's conduct shall be attributed to the state if he or she is acting on the state's instructions or under the state's direction (Paust, 2002).

At the same time, courts and tribunals have permitted cases to proceed against nonstate actors. Some have done so on the ground that, as with international humanitarian law, violations of certain international human rights, such as torture, do not require a nexus to state action (e.g., *Bowoto v. Chevron Corp.*, 2008; In re XE Services Alien Tort Litigation, 2009). But even courts that do not go that far have used various theories that link those actors to the state, such as conspiracy or aiding and abetting (e.g., *Doe I. v. Unocal*, 2002). And at least one federal circuit, in considering violations of international law brought under the ATS, appears to construe the state action requirements in international human rights law in a broader way than it would in considering claims of domestic constitutional rights that also have a state action requirement. The discrepancy is particularly striking because, although the court purports to use the U.S. constitutional test for measuring state action in the international law context, it seems to be applying that test in a way that is more likely to result in a finding of state action.

For example, in *Abdullahi v. Pfizer* Nigerian citizens brought an ATS suit against the pharmaceutical company Pfizer for using a new antibiotic drug Trovan to treat Nigerian children suffering from meningitis and other diseases. They alleged that Pfizer was essentially using Nigerian children (many of whom died) as subjects to test the drug's effectiveness, and that these actions violated various provisions of the ICCPR. The U.S. Court of Appeals for the Second Circuit determined that plaintiffs had made sufficient allegations of state action. The court applied the test from domestic constitutional jurisprudence that private activity can become actionable misconduct when "there is such a 'close nexus between the State and the challenged action' that seemingly private behavior 'may be fairly treated as that of the State itself.'" It further found that a nexus may exist "where a private actor has operated as willful participant in joint activity with the State or its agents." The court then reasoned that such a nexus existed (assuming the complaint's allegations were true) because the Nigerian government allegedly sent a letter to the Food and Drug Administration requesting that the agency authorize Trovan's export, arranged for Pfizer's accommodation in a Nigerian hospital, backdated an approval letter to the U.S. government, and silenced Nigerian physicians critical of the test. This relatively limited degree of government involvement would arguably fall short of state action in a domestic constitutional case applying the very same test. Indeed, in contrast to *Abdullahi*, the U.S. Supreme Court has held, in *American Manufacturers Mutual Insurance Co. v. Sullivan*, that the government entity must actually participate in the "specific conduct" in question for state action to be found for purposes of U.S. constitutional adjudication. Knowledge of the activities and background assistance of the sort deemed sufficient in *Abdullahi* therefore appears to be insufficient to support a finding of state action in the domestic context.

Likewise, the Second Circuit permitted ATS claims to proceed against Shell Oil Co. and individual defendant employees of Shell (*Wiwa v. Royal Dutch Petroleum Co.*, 2002). The plaintiffs, members of Nigeria's Ogoni ethnic group, alleged that Shell had instigated and supported a Nigerian government campaign of repression against the Ogoni people, who were protesting Shell's activities in Nigeria. Plaintiffs' complaint contained allegations of numerous international human rights violations, including torture, cruel, inhuman, and degrading treatment, summary arrest and arbitrary detention, and interference with the right of peaceful protest, all of which the district court concluded were claims that required a showing of state action. Unlike in *Abdullahi*, the involvement of the Nigerian government was not in question, as the complaint alleged that Nigerian officials had directly tortured, attacked, and killed plaintiffs. Rather, the issue was whether Shell and its employees were sufficiently involved in the Nigerian government's actions. Applying the state action test from U.S. constitutional law, the district court explicitly rejected an interpretation of *Sullivan* that would have required actual corporate knowledge of, or participation in, each instance of abuse. Again, the Second Circuit permitted the case to go forward using an expansive interpretation of state action.

Nevertheless, the substantive scope of the ATS itself is uncertain, and some courts have taken a narrower view of the state action doctrine as applied to international law claims. In 2004, in *Sosa v. Alvarez-Machain*, the U.S. Supreme Court limited the types of international law violations that may be subject to suit under the ATS. The court denied a claim of arbitrary arrest, concluding that the statute conferred jurisdiction on the federal courts to consider only a "modest" number of international law violations: those violations of the "present day law of nations" which "rest on a norm of international character accepted by the civilized world and defined with a specificity comparable to the features of the eighteenth century paradigms we have recognized." The court reasoned that an alleged arbitrary arrest and detention of one day did not satisfy this standard.

In the wake of *Sosa*, one district court dismissed torture claims against private contractors on the ground that the scope of the ATS only applies to "official" torture, and the U.S. Court of Appeals for the D.C. Circuit affirmed that decision (*Ibrahim v. Titan Corp.*, 2007). The plaintiffs had brought suit against government contractor interrogators and translators at the Abu Ghraib prison in Iraq, who allegedly tortured and abused detainees there. Moreover, in a bizarre sort of Catch-22, the court ruled that, if the plaintiffs *could* show that the contractors were sufficiently tied to the state so as to render the actions "official," the ATS claims would again be barred because then the suit would be tantamount to suing the government itself, thereby violating sovereign immunity. This decision fit in with a narrow approach to the ATS generally in the D.C. Circuit, as well as a relatively restrictive view of the state action doctrine in international law. Several decades earlier, the court had rejected international law claims, brought under the ATS, against the Palestine Liberation Organization for its alleged role in a terrorist bombing. While the judges of the panel rejected the suit on various grounds, Judge Edwards noted that claims against nonstate actors were not commonly accepted under international law, and therefore could not form the basis for claims under the ATS (*Tel-Oren v. Libyan Arab Republic*, 1984).

The D.C. Circuit's reasoning will undoubtedly be tested in the future. As discussed above, numerous tribunals have now held that multiple types of international law violations, from war crimes, to crimes against humanity, to genocide, bar not only governmental but also nongovernmental actors from misconduct. Where the international law violation prohibits governmental abuse, as in the case of torture, actors affiliated with the government may be brought within the prohibition's reach. And there is no reason to believe that, at the moment an action is sufficiently linked to the state that it constitutes an international law violation, sovereign immunity would necessarily apply. That is, the ATS state action inquiry and the sovereign immunity determination need not be tied together in the way the D.C. Circuit suggested in the Abu Ghraib case. Indeed, just because a contractor is sufficiently linked to the government to overcome state action requirements does not automatically transform the suit into one against the government itself. In contrast with the D.C. Circuit, the Second and Eleventh Circuits, along with several district courts, have interpreted the ATS more broadly and permitted it to be used in suits against nonstate actors in a variety of contexts. However, even if other courts ultimately followed the D.C. Circuit's reasoning in this respect, it would not, in any event, bar claims based on other international law provisions, domestic statutes, or common law torts that do not require state action.

Likewise, though the Second Circuit has recently precluded ATS suits against corporations, that ruling has no bearing on the ability to bring suits against *individuals* working for such corporations, and of course it would not prevent suits in non-ATS cases (*Kiobel v. Royal Dutch Petroleum*, 2010). Indeed, the court was explicit on the matter, stating that "nothing in this opinion limits or forecloses suits under the ATS against the individual perpetrators of violations of customary international law – including the employees, managers, officers, and directors of a corporation – as well as anyone who purposefully aids and abets a violation of customary international law. Nor does anything in this opinion limit or foreclose criminal, administrative, or civil actions against any corporation under a body of law other than customary international law – for example, the domestic laws of any State." Thus, we should expect to see continued suits against corporate actors under the ATS and other provisions of international or domestic law.

VINDICATING INTERNATIONAL LAW THROUGH DOMESTIC TORT SUITS

One way of trying to bypass the state action requirement altogether is to bring domestic tort claims against the individuals or entities who have committed abuses. For example, assault or battery in the law of many countries would cover the same conduct that would give rise to a torture claim. In many suits brought under the ATS in the United States, plaintiffs assert state law tort claims under a theory of supplemental jurisdiction. But such claims might also be asserted directly through forms of transnational tort litigation, and some scholars view domestic private tort claims as a principal means of protecting the same values embedded in international public law (Scott, 2001). Common law or statutory torts such as assault require no "state action" showing, and arguably address the same underlying conduct that could give rise to a human rights claim such as torture. Some might contend that the failure to bring international law expressly into the litigation could retard the development of such international norms. Yet, whether framed as violations of international or domestic law, the underlying harm is the same. Moreover, to the extent that international legal norms are vindicated in suits brought based on domestic law, such actions could be seen as part of the process whereby these international norms are inculcated into domestic legal systems (Koh, 1998).

Tort suits against individual contractors and contract firms may take a number of different forms. First, foreign victims of contractor activities may file suit, assuming domestic law provides them standing. Second, we may see suits brought by contractor employees against their employers. For example, one still-pending wrongful death action against Blackwater arises from the murder and mutilation of four of its employees in Fallujah, Iraq (In re Blackwater Security Consulting, LLC, 2006), and another alleges that Halliburton knowingly used one convoy as a decoy for a second, resulting in the deaths of at least 6 drivers, and injuries to 11 others (*Lane v. Halliburton*, 2008). Third, domestic actors harmed by private contractors abroad may seek redress, as in the variety of actions that have been brought by U.S. military personnel killed or injured in accidents involving airplanes and trucks operated by contractors.

For these cases, at least in the United States, there is a preliminary obstacle in the political question doctrine, which has been deployed by courts sporadically over the years to dismiss cases deemed to be best resolved in the political arena by the other two branches of government. Yet, although courts have in fact dismissed suits against contractors on this ground, it may well be an inappropriate use of the political question idea. After all, the doctrine is only meant to exclude from judicial review "those controversies which revolve around policy choices and value determinations constitutionally committed for resolution to the halls of Congress or the confines of the Executive Branch" (*Japan Whaling Ass'n. v. Am. Cetacean Soc'y*, 1986). As one court held in refusing to dismiss a case against a contractor on political question grounds, "Controversies stemming from war are not automatically deemed political questions merely because militaristic activities are within the province of the Executive. ... Tort suits are within the province of the judiciary, and that conclusion is not automatically negated simply because the claim arises in a military context, or because it bears tangentially on the powers of the executive and legislative branches" (*McMahon v. Presidential Airways, Inc.*, 2006, pp. 1320–1321). Thus, the political question doctrine seems to be a dubious rationale for dismissing tort suits against contractors.

Assuming a plaintiff can get past the political question issue, a form of state action inquiry rears its head again as courts determine whether a variety of doctrines that provide immunity from suit for governmental actors should also apply to private contractors. Ironically, whereas earlier we encountered situations where plaintiffs needed to show state action in order to pursue substantive international law claims, here it is defendant contractors attempting to don the mantle of the state in order to take advantage of governmental immunities. On this score, at least some governmental immunities have been deemed not to apply to private actors. For example, as noted previously, the U.S. Supreme Court, in *Richardson v. McKnight*, has refused to extend to private prison guards certain individual governmental immunities from suit.

Nevertheless, contractors have attempted to block entire claims from proceeding by invoking federal sovereign immunity, requiring courts to again try to distinguish public from private action. The Federal Tort Claims Act seeks to balance the need of government employees to do their work without fear of litigation against the rights of individuals to seek compensation when government actions injure them. Accordingly, the Act allows plaintiffs to sue the government, but only when government employees are negligent and when a private person would be liable under similar circumstances. In *Boyle v. United Technologies Corp.*, this immunity was extended to government contractors. However, *Boyle* involved a products liability claim (not a claim regarding a services contract) and also limited the defense to circumstances in which the government set the design specifications with reasonable precision, leaving little discretion to the contractor. Accordingly, at least one court has concluded that the defense does not apply to international human rights claims at all (In re Agent Orange Prod. Liab. Litig., 2005). And even for domestic claims arising from tort and contract, an argument could be made that *Boyle* only reaches procurement contractors supplying weapons and other materials, not contractors who provide services, particularly where the contractor exercises a wide degree of discretion.

To give a sense of how courts applying *Boyle* need to draw lines between governmental and nongovernmental action, consider a federal district court in the District of Columbia that allowed a case to proceed against contract interrogators implicated in the abuses at Abu Ghraib prison, but not against the Abu Ghraib contract translators. The court reasoned that the plaintiffs' ability to sue depended on the degree to which the contractors were integrated into the military command structure: whether the military had direct command and exclusive operational control. Because there was undisputed evidence that the military had incorporated contract translators within its chain of command, and the contractors essentially stood in the shoes of government actors, the court dismissed the suit against them. But because there was at least some evidence that the contract interrogators took orders from managers within their company, and not solely from government officials, the court determined that the case against them could proceed (*Ibrahim v. Titan Corp.*, 2007).

This seems to be a reasonable basis for determining potential tort immunity for contractors, and it may gain traction. However, the U.S. Court of Appeals for the D.C. Circuit has, at least for the moment, adopted a broader test that would give far more sweeping immunity to contractors. The appellate court concluded that the key test was not whether the military had exclusive control over the contractors but rather whether "during wartime, … a private service contractor is integrated into combatant activities over which the military retains command authority." Thus, the court articulated a surprisingly broad definition that would immunize contractors whenever the military has overall command authority for a conflict (seemingly regardless of whether the military has control over the particular contractors being sued). Ultimately, the court concluded that because both the contract interrogators and the translators were integrated into combat activities at least to some degree, the federal immunity preempted any claims under state (or foreign) law against either group of contractors. According to the majority, allowing such claims to proceed would improperly interfere with the military's conduct of war, and would set perverse incentives because contractors would "obviously be deterred from reporting abuse to military authorities if such reporting alone is taken to be evidence of retained operational control" (*Saleh v. Titan Corp.*, 2009).

Yet, as the dissent observed, the reach of the Federal Tort Claims Act immunity provisions to contractors should be narrow, as the statute does not explicitly apply to contractors at all but rather is designed to safeguard *governmental* immunities. Here, the military did not dispute that the contractors fell outside the chain of command, as numerous contractual provisions, DOD regulations, and military rules made clear. Moreover, the U.S. government did not authorize, and indeed expressly prohibited, the abuse in question. Finally, the concern about interference in the military's conduct of war seems unwarranted. After all, courts could wait to hear suits until after hostilities concluded or could simply apply normal privileges and rules to prohibit gathering or presenting evidence in such a way that would harm national security.

Thus, unless the D.C. Circuit's rule is broadly adopted, civil suits remain a possible avenue for vindicating the values embedded in international human rights and humanitarian law. Other circuits may take a more expansive approach to tort liability, and Congress could also step in to define a role for tort litigation against military and security contractors. Accordingly, tort claims against private military and security contractors have proceeded in the United States primarily as domestic claims – and the central issue for litigation is the question of how *Richardson* and *Boyle* will ultimately apply to private security contractors acting abroad. In addition, as I have discussed elsewhere, another possibility is a suit to enforce the contractual terms under which the private firms operate (Dickinson, 2006, 2011). Currently, only the government itself or specific classes of contractors can bring such claims, but Congress could act to expand the possibility of third-party-beneficiary suits. In any event, when the government privatizes military functions, individuals seeking redress may sometimes have more avenues to pursue legal accountability than when the government performs military functions directly, because the scope of immunities may be narrower for such private actors.

CONCLUSION

There is much still to be resolved here, as courts are obliged to confront suits against private actors alleged to have committed abuses abroad. And if domestic constitutional cases are any indication, the ongoing delineation of public and private with regard to such suits may never be fully satisfactory or even coherent. Yet, the stakes are high. In an era of foreign affairs privatization it is essential that private actors somehow be held accountable for violations of international and domestic law. Accordingly, though seemingly technical, the state action doctrine is likely to be the terrain on which many of the key international human rights issues of the coming decades will be fought. Indeed, as governments extend their power by outsourcing their core, the intertwining of public and private grows ever more complicated. And when courts consider both the substantive scope of legal norms with regard to private actors and the circumstances under which private actors can invoke governmental immunities, they are inevitably defining the very future of international human rights and humanitarian law. We must closely attend, therefore, to law's continued evolution in response to our increasingly privatized world.

REFERENCES

Abdullahi v. Pfizer, Inc., 562 F.3d 163 (2d Cir. 2009).

American Manufacturers Mutual Insurance Co. v. Sullivan, 526 U.S. 40, 50–55 (1999).

Berman, P. S. (2000). Cyberspace and the state action debate: The cultural value of applying constitutional norms to "private" regulation. *University of Colorado Law Review, 71,* 1263.

Black, C. L. (1966). Foreword: "State action," equal protection, and California's Proposition 14. *Harvard Law Review, 81,* p. 69.

Bowoto v. Chevron Corp., 557 F. Supp. 2d 1080, 1095 (N.D. Cal. 2008).

Boyle v. United Techs. Corp., 487 U.S. 500 (1988).

Civil Rights Cases, 109 U.S. 3 (1883).

Convention for the Amelioration of the Condition of the Wounded and Sick in Armed Forces in the Field, Aug. 12, 1949, 6 U.S.T. 3114, 75 U.N.T.S. 31 (entered into force Oct. 21, 1950, for the United States Feb. 2, 1956) [Geneva Convention I].

Convention for the Amelioration of the Condition of the Wounded, Sick, and Shipwrecked Members of Armed Forces at Sea, Aug. 12, 1949, 6 U.S.T. 3217, 75 U.N.T.S. 85 (entered into force Oct. 21, 1950, for the United States Feb. 2, 1956) [Geneva Convention II].

Convention Relative to the Treatment of Prisoners of War, Aug. 12, 1949, 6 U.S.T. 3316, 75 U.N.T.S. 135 (entered into force Oct. 21, 1950, for the United States Feb. 2, 1956) [Geneva Convention III].

Convention Relative to the Protection of Civilian Persons in Time of War, Aug. 12, 1949, 6 U.S.T. 3516, 75 U.N.T.S. 287 (entered into force Oct. 21, 1950, for the United States Feb. 2, 1956) [Geneva Convention IV].

Convention on the Prevention and Punishment of the Crime of Genocide art. 4, Dec. 9, 1948, 102 Stat. 3045, 78 U.N.T.S. 277 (entered into force Jan. 12, 1951, for the United States Feb. 23, 1989) [Genocide Convention].

Convention Against Torture and Other Cruel, Inhuman or Degrading Treatment or Punishment art. 1, Dec. 10, 1984, S. Treaty Doc. No. 100-20 (1988), 1465 U.N.T.S. 85, 113–14. Retrieved from http://www2.ohchr.org/english/law/cat.htm [Torture Convention].

Correctional Services Corporation v. Malesko, 534 U.S. 61 (2001).

Dickinson, L. A. (2006). Public Law values in a privatized world. *Yale Journal of International Law, 31,* 383.

Dickinson, L. A. (2011). *Outsourcing war and peace: Protecting public values in a world of privatized foreign affairs.* New Haven: Yale University Press.

Doe I v. Unocal Corp., 395 F.3d 932, 936 (9th Cir. 2002).

Evans v. Newton, 382 U.S. 296 (1966).

Federal Tort Claims Act, 28 U.S.C. 1346(b).

Ibrahim v. Titan Corp., 556 F. Supp. 2d 1 (D.D.C. 2007).

In re Agent Orange Prod. Liab. Litig., 373 F. Supp. 7 (E.D.N.Y. 2005).

In re Blackwater Security Consulting, LLC, 460 F.3d 576 (4th Cir. 2006).

In re XE Services Alien Tort Litigation, 665 F. Supp. 2d 569 (E.D. Va. 2009).

International Covenant on Civil and Political Rights arts. 7, 9, Dec. 16, 1966, 999 U.N.T.S. 171 (1966). Retrieved from http://www1.umn.edu/humanrts/instree/b3ccpr.htm [ICCPR].

Japan Whaling Ass'n. v. Am. Cetacean Soc'y, 478 U.S. 221, 230 (1986).

Junod, S. (1983). Additional Protocol II: History and scope. *American University Law Review, 33*, 29.

Kadic v. Karadzic, 70 F.3d 232, 239–40, 243 (2d Cir. 1995).

Kay, R. S. (1993). The state action doctrine, the public–private distinction, and the independence of constitutional law. *Constitutional Comment, 10*, 329.

Kiobel v. Royal Dutch Petroleum, 621 F.3rd 111 (2010).

Koh, H. H. (1998). Bringing international law home. *Houston Law Review, 35*, p. 623.

Lacey, N. (1988). *State punishment: Political principles and community values*. London: Routledge Press.

Lane v. Halliburton, 529 F. 3d 548 (5th Cir. 2008).

McMahon v. Presidential Airways, Inc., 460 F. Supp. 2d 1315 (M.D. Fla. 2006).

Minow, M. (1987). The Supreme Court, 1986 term – Foreword: Justice engendered. *Harvard Law Review, 101*, 10.

Olsen, F. E. (1985). The myth of state intervention in the family. *University of Michigan Law Review, 18*, 835.

Paust, J. J. (2002). Human rights responsibilities of private corporations. *Vanderbilt Journal of Transnational Law, 35*, 801.

Prosecutor v. Kunarac, Case No. IT-96-23-T & IT-96–23/1-T, Judgment, 496 (Feb. 22, 2001). Retrieved from http://www.unhcr.org/cgi-bin/texis/vtx/refworld/rwmain?docid=3ae6b7560 [Kunarac Trial Judgment].

Prosecutor v. Kunarac, IT-96-23 & IT-96-23/1-A, Appellate Judgment, 148 (June 12, 2002). Retrieved from http://www.unhcr.org/cgi-bin/texis/vtx/refworld/rwmain?docid=3debaafe4 [Kunarac Appellate Judgment].

Protocol Additional to the Geneva Conventions of 12 August 1949a, and Relating to the Protection of Victims of International Armed Conflicts, June 8, 1977, 1125 U.N.T.S. 3 [Protocol I].

Protocol Additional to the Geneva Conventions of 12 August 1949b, Relating to the Protection of Victims of Non-International Armed Conflicts, June 8, 1977, 1125 U.N.T.S. 609 [Protocol II].

Richardson v. McKnight, 521 U.S. 399 (1997).

Rome Statute of the International Criminal Court art. 7, July 17, 1998, 2187 U.N.T.S. 90.

Rosen, M. D. (2004). Exporting the constitution. *Emory Law Journal, 53*, 171.

Saleh v. Titan Corp., 580 F.3d 1 (C.A.D.C., 2009).

Scott, C., (Ed.) (2001). *Torture as tort: Comparative perspectives on the development of transnational human rights litigation*. Oxford: Hart Publishing.

Shelley v. Kraemer, 334 U.S. 1 (1948).

Silard, J. (1966). A constitutional forecast: Demise of "state action" limit on equal protection guarantee. *Columbia Law Review, 66*, 855.

Sosa v. Alvarez-Machain, 542 U.S. 692 (2004).

Stone, C. D. (1973). Should trees have standing? – Toward legal rights for natural objects. *Southern California Law Review, 45*, 450.

Taylor, C. (1985). *Philosophy and the human sciences*. Cambridge: Cambridge University Press.
Tel-Oren v. Libyan Arab Republic, 726 F.2d 774 (1984).
Tribe, L. H. (2d ed. 1988). *American Constitutional Law*. St. Paul, Minnesota: Foundation Press.
United States v. Krauch, 7 Trials of War Criminals Before the Nuremberg Military Tribunals Under Control Council Law No. 10 (1952).
United States v. Flick, 6 Trials of War Criminals Before the Nuremberg Military Tribunals Under Control Council Law No. 10 (1952).
United States v. Harris, 106 U.S. 629 (1883).
United States v. Krupp, 9 Trials of War Criminals Before the Nuremberg Military Tribunals Under Control Council Law No. 10 (1950).
Unger, R. M. (1975). *Knowledge and politics*.
Vázquez, C. M. (2005). Direct vs. indirect obligations of corporations under international law. *Columbia Journal of Transnational Law*, *43*, 927.
Velasquez Rodriguez Case, 1988 Inter-Am. Ct. H.R. (ser. C) No. 4 (July 29, 1988).
Winter, S. L. (1992). The meaning of "under color of" law. *Michigan Law Review*, *91*, 323.
Williams, J. S. (1963). The twilight of state action. *Texas Law Review*, *41*, 437.
Wiwa v. Royal Dutch Petroleum Co., No. 96 CIV-8386, 2002 WL 319887, at *3–4 (S.D.N.Y. Feb. 28, 2002), affirmed in relevant part, 226 F.3d 88 (2d Cir. 2009).